Action, Action, Action

THE SUNY SERIES
HORIZONS OF CINEMA
MURRAY POMERANCE | EDITOR

RECENT TITLES

Lindsay Coleman and Roberto Schaefer, editors, *The Cinematographer's Voice*

Fareed Ben-Youssef, *No Jurisdiction*

Nolwenn Mingant, *Hollywood Films in North Africa and the Middle East*

†Charles Warren, edited by William Rothman and Joshua Schulze, *Writ on Water*

Jason Sperb, *The Hard Sell of Paradise*

William Rothman, *The Holiday in His Eye*

Brendan Hennessey, *Luchino Visconti and the Alchemy of Adaptation*

Alexander Sergeant, *Encountering the Impossible*

Erica Stein, *Seeing Symphonically*

George Toles, *Curtains of Light*

Neil Badmington, *Perpetual Movement*

Merrill Schleier, editor, *Race and the Suburbs in American Film*

Matthew Leggatt, editor, *Was It Yesterday?*

Homer B. Pettey, editor, *Mind Reeling*

Alexia Kannas, *Giallo!*

Bill Krohn, *Letters from Hollywood*

Alex Clayton, *Funny How?*

Niels Niessen, *Miraculous Realism*

Burke Hilsabeck, *The Slapstick Camera*

Michael Hammond, *The Great War in Hollywood Memory, 1918–1939*

A complete listing of books in this series can be found online at www.sunypress.edu

Action, Action, Action
The Early Cinema of Raoul Walsh

Tom Conley

Cover: The travelers descend a vertiginous cliffside in *The Big Trail* (1930).

Published by State University of New York Press, Albany

© 2022 State University of New York

All rights reserved

Printed in the United States of America

No part of this book may be used or reproduced in any manner whatsoever without written permission. No part of this book may be stored in a retrieval system or transmitted in any form or by any means including electronic, electrostatic, magnetic tape, mechanical, photocopying, recording, or otherwise without the prior permission in writing of the publisher.

For information, contact State University of New York Press, Albany, NY
www.sunypress.edu

Library of Congress Cataloging-in-Publication Data

Name: Conley, Tom, author.
Title: Action, action, action : the early cinema of Raoul Walsh / Tom Conley.
Description: Albany : State University of New York, [2022] | Series: SUNY series, horizons of cinema | Includes bibliographical references and index.
Identifiers: LCCN 2022003293 (print) | LCCN 2022003294 (ebook) | ISBN 9781438488851 (hardcover : alk. paper) | ISBN 9781438488875 (ebook) | ISBN 9781438488868 (pbk. : alk. paper)
Subjects: LCSH: Walsh, Raoul, 1887–1980—Criticism and interpretation. | Motion pictures—History—20th century. | Motion picture producers and directors—United States—Biography.
Classification: LCC PN1998.3.W35 C66 2022 (print) | LCC PN1998.3.W35 (ebook) | DDC 791.4302/33092—dc23/eng/20220304
LC record available at https://lccn.loc.gov/2022003293
LC ebook record available at https://lccn.loc.gov/2022003294

10 9 8 7 6 5 4 3 2 1

Contents

List of Illustrations		vii
Preface and Acknowledgments		xi
1	On the Lower East Side: *Regeneration*	1
2	A Monkey Talks to *Sadie Thompson*	27
3	Eyes and Cockeyes: *The Cock-Eyed World*	55
4	From Sadie to Mamie: *The Revolt of Mamie Stover*	85
5	Big Trees, Tall Men: *The Big Trail*	111
6	Me, My Gal, My Brother: *Me and My Gal*	137
7	The Good, The Bad, *The Bowery*	165
Conclusion: What Became of *The Wrath of the Just?*		189
Notes		203
Bibliography		235
Index		245

Illustrations

1.1	A beginning: Owen orphaned.	8
1.2	A coffin in a hearse: the filmmakers shown in their film.	8
1.3	Orphaned Owen and the broom that sweeps clean.	10
1.4	The Bowery market: Maggie and Owen go shopping.	12
1.5	Local color on the Bowery.	13
1.6	Owen looks at his past and future.	15
1.7	The SHAM of the *Shamrock Queen*.	16
1.8	Owen and Skinny in a tussle.	22
1.9	Owen writes that he owes nothing to Skinny.	22
1.10	Skinny, his eyepatch removed, behind him the sign of his demise.	24
1.11	Marie sees a thug's eye behind a knothole at the entry to the gang's den.	25
2.1	*Sadie Thompson*, first title card.	33
2.2	Second title card.	34
2.3	List of dramatis personae.	34
2.4	Idle Marines at the port of Pago Pago.	37
2.5	Long shot of the boat arriving in Pago Pago.	38
2.6	The captain orders the crew to moor the boat to the dock.	42

2.7	A crewmember ties the boat to the dock, following the captain's orders.	43
2.8	Portrait of the director as a grown baby: O'Hara/Walsh in the photo album.	46
2.9	Sadie, abject, under Davidson's spell, ruminates in bed.	49
2.10	A native finds Davidson's corpse in his fishing net.	51
2.11	Photo-op of Swanson and Walsh on the set of *Sadie Thompson*.	52
3.1	A photo op: the players and eye-patched director of *The Cock-Eyed World*. From left: Victor McLaglen, Lili Damita, Edmund Lowe, and Raoul Walsh.	56
3.2	*The Cock-Eyed World*, title card and front credit.	58
3.3	An accusative index finger points at Harry Quirt.	61
3.4	Quirt's eye sliced by a knife in the tavern and bordello in Vladivostok.	64
3.5	Her right eye sliced by a shadow, a maid watches a magic trick Quirt performs on Olga.	65
3.6	Fanny readies to jump into the pool at Coney Island.	69
3.7	Flagg receives orders to command a "dangerous mission."	71
3.8	Flagg and a sergeant discuss their expedition to the tropics.	75
3.9	Mariana bids adieu to the marines.	81
3.10	End credit of *The Cock-Eyed World*.	81
4.1	*The Revolt of Mamie Stover*, front credit.	87
4.2	Mamie and Jim embrace in front of two portholes.	92
4.3	Jim looks at Pearl Harbor from deck of his villa.	100
4.4	Mamie sees a future in the pandemonium of the bombing of Pearl Harbor.	100
4.5	Spectators behold the devastation of Honolulu.	101
4.6	Mamie becomes a reproducible image.	103

4.7	Holding a newspaper, oblivious to the headline, Mamie bargains with Bertha.	104
4.8	Soldiers ogle a pin-up photograph of Mamie.	105
5.1	*The Big Trail*, title card.	116
5.2	An epic takes shape: title credits in dissolve.	117
5.3	Voyagers prepare for travel: the first shot of the film.	121
5.4	A painting of sorts: caring little about who sees them, the westward women comb their hair.	124
5.5	Wearing a bowler hat, a child watches the movement of the wagons (and the movie).	126
5.6	While Native Americans beat drums in preparation for battle, in the center, an elder contemplates the fate of his people.	127
5.7	Frightened, Ruth stands to the left and right of two noble Native Americans.	128
5.8	A dog remains at the grave of its master as the wagon train departs.	129
5.9	Holding to ropes, the travelers descend a vertiginous cliffside.	130
5.10	Brett and Flack on either side of the monumental trunk of a fallen sequoia.	134
5.11	Brett meets Ruth in the great forest of sequoias.	135
6.1	Proud of his uniform, Danny opens the film when he dons his officer's visored cap.	143
6.2	Frank (Frank Moran) gobbles a banana.	145
6.3	Amidst laborers in the background, the old man leaves the dog he will drown before Officer Dolan intervenes.	146
6.4	A plate of lobsters in the foreground the interior of Ed's Chowder House.	148
6.5	In front of a porthole, Helen smiles to conquer.	150

6.6	Danny proposes to Helen over a doughnut jar.	152
6.7	A bill, its copy, and a message: an imprint of the film.	156
6.8	In a local haberdashery, a bald salesman comments on the hat Danny will soon purchase.	158
6.9	Wearing Danny's bowler hat, Helen adjusts the volume of a radio playing upbeat jazz.	159
6.10	Ending the film, Pop winks at the viewer.	161
7.1	Connors and Brodie are off to war.	168
7.2	The *Police Gazette* that masks its reader (Chuck Connors) and displays John L. Sullivan (for whom George Walsh will have a cameo).	172
7.3	And its reader, Chuck Connors, while getting his shoes shined.	173
7.4	Connors (Beery) sipping his beer.	174
7.5	John L. Sullivan (George Walsh) exits the boxing palace.	178
7.6	A body plummets from the Brooklyn Bridge.	180
7.7	Connors squints at the mural in Brodie's new saloon.	185
C.1	The emblem of the Pinkerton Agency, circa 1850.	195

Preface and Acknowledgments

A CHILDHOOD MEMORY finds me in 1948, in the darkness of a movie theater, adjacent to the town square in Guilford, Connecticut, then a village of fifteen hundred residents. Walter, my father, had taken me to a Saturday matinee. Sitting on the upright edge of the erect seat cushion, turning left and right to catch sight of the screen between the gigantic heads and shoulders of adults in the row in front of us, I watch the movie as best I can. After the program is over, we walk back home to the little saltbox (the Nathan Bradley House, built in 1665) at 72 State Street (my father tells me, formerly known as Crooked Lane). Walter extends a microphone toward my face. A Dictaphone starts to whir. He asks me what I had seen. I reply: it was dark, but flashes of light and noise were so scary that (he reminded me) I had to hide behind the seat in front of me. The Dictaphone still whirling, he tells me we had just seen *Objective, Burma!*

Memory unspools further. In the early 1950s, in an apartment in New York, fiddling with Walter's cache of 16 mm films in yellow Kodak boxes, finding a couple of movies from Blackhawk Films, then threading a Keystone Projector aimed at a white wall, I look at a home movie he shot and edited in 1942. It includes a long take of the same Guilford movie theater in winter, its marquee announcing *They Died with Their Boots On*. It was the moment when that loathsome, despicable thug, Wisconsin Senator Joseph McCarthy, was ridding the nation of its great actors and movie directors. I recall my father taking me to back rooms of movie clubs and venues where he and members of the Theodore Huff Film Society ran prints of blacklisted or hard-to-get films. Having recently seen a German copy of *Shoulder Arms*, I am in tears when he announces that the House Un-American Activities Committee has ordered Charlie Chaplin to leave the country. Soon after, we see *The Kid* in the lower depths of the MOMA, with the piano accompaniment of Arthur Kleiner. And after that, in the same space one Saturday morning, *Intolerance*. During the great battle in the Babylon sequence, he whispers in my ear, "Now watch out for the warrior who gets beheaded!"). When we view *The 39 Steps*, he warns me, "Mr. Memory is not to be trusted." The great films and great directors, he insists relentlessly, belong to the silent tradition. At home, in the evening, mellow after a drink, stressing each of the name's five syllables as if from a pulpit, he's standing erect as he intones in admiration, *Da-vid Wark Grif-fith*!! And he adds, pronouncing the forename to sound like the howl of a wolf in moonlight, "and the genius of . . . *Raoooooul Walsh*!"

Flash forward: in East Sandwich (Massachusetts), late in his life, a resident house custodian at the Riverview School (an institution serving underachieving adolescents), in his free time he rekindles his passion for silent cinema. He subscribes to *The Silent Picture*, a modest British journal under the aegis of Anthony Slide and Paul O'Dell. Impassioned correspondent, hunting and pecking on the keys of a Royal typewriter, he jots off a letter to Slide, making known his love of Brothers George and Raoul Walsh. Slide invites him to assemble a bio-filmography of Raoul's work.

Impressed by what he sees, Slide invites Walter to do a sequel on the cinema of George Walsh, great silent actor and rival of Douglas Fairbanks, someone for whom the advent of the talkie had meant consignment to oblivion. Lo and behold, he writes to George, living in California, who replies by return mail, including in his correspondence copious packets of memorabilia. By then, having learned of Walter's passion, the MOMA invites him to take part in the Walsh retrospective scheduled for early 1974. He meets Raoul and George. His life is complete, and more so, in rejoicing over of the demise of ignominious Richard Nixon and soon after, receiving word that his bio-filmography will be included in the *acta* of a colloquium on Walsh in Edinburgh.[3]

On August 4, 1974, during a visit to his quarters in East Sandwich, Walter, David (our son, then six years old, and not long ago, his father boasts, leader of the team that won an Oscar for the visual effects of Ang Lee's *Life of Pi*), and I drive to Pawtucket to see its Red Sox square off against the Rochester Orioles. Sitting in the grandstand along the third-base line, watching Freddie Lynn in centerfield and Jim Rice in right, we speak about the retrospective and Walter's two articles. Almost in concert: "Why don't we write a book on Raoul Walsh?" He would scout for materials while I write (as best as I possibly could, given that

I was under the sway of structural analysis) "theoretically" inspired readings, which he would revise for a general public. Excited, in a wave of inspiration, I return with David to Minneapolis. On the thirteenth, at 7:30 p.m., the phone rings. Steve, my elder brother (a painter), tersely announces: "Walter is dead." Late in the morning of the fourteenth, dumbfounded, I fly to Boston where Steve and I meet and drive to East Sandwich to help our mother, Hazel, clean up and pack away Walter's books and belongings. A graphic artist and portrait painter who cared little about cinema, Hazel recounts how it happened: they had gone to Hanover, New Hampshire, to visit a long-standing friend, an author of pulp western novels penned under the pseudonym of Peter Field.[1] Staying in a local motel, they meet with the novelist for a drink and a light meal. At happy hour the two men share a cocktail. Hazel leaves the room to buy sandwiches at a deli across the street. As the novelist reported: raising his glass, looking skyward, Walter tries to remember the name of a silent actress for whom he had boundless affection. (I think it was Blanche Sweet because he had mentioned her name often and was happy to have seen her at the MOMA retrospective.) Suddenly, glassy eyed, he falls over. Hazel returns, drops her sandwiches, and arches over the body to administer CPR. Too late. She calls the state troopers who soon arrive and dispatch the corpse to the Massachusetts border. The police take over and deliver the cadaver to Boston. At the morgue they discover (unbeknownst to us) that Walter had prepared for his end by donating his body to Harvard's Medical School. When the shock wears away, our sister-in-law, Ellen Alexander Conley (a novelist), is quick to remark that Walter is the first in the family to go to Harvard.

Carried too long, difficult to write and release, what follows, I hope, will meet Walter's expectations. Since 1974 Walsh studies have become an industry. The extensive filmography (404–46) and selected bibliography (465–70) buttressing Marilyn Ann Moss's superb *Raoul Walsh: The True Adventures of Hollywood's Legendary Director* (2011) affirms that the literature surrounding his name is no less stupendous than the 160-plus films he wrote, directed, and edited, including those in which he acted, served as a consultant, or had been a script doctor. Extending from 1912 to 1964, given to many genres and situations, the oeuvre defies holistic interpretation. In the spirit of Walter's love of Walsh and his attraction to directors who found a style and signature in silent cinema, for this monograph, what is slated to be the first panel of a diptych, I have chosen to study features close to either side of 1928, all of which are eminently available in DVD or via streaming.

The study builds on the hypothesis that certain films acquire a signature status in what they do with a play of binocular and monocular vision, and in turn with framing and composition. The conviction is that both before and after Walsh's traumatic enucleation in 1929—a jackrabbit, dazed by the headlights of the vehicle in which the director was being driven from the on-location shooting to a lodging near Bryce Canyon, jumped and smashed the windshield, throwing a shard of glass into his right eye—the *ocular* character of the films becomes an enduring autographic trait.[2] Rehearsed in *They Drive by Night, High Sierra, White Heat*, and other features, the event pertains as much to cinema as to the director himself. And in line with what Bertrand Tavernier in admiration called the taste the Lumière Brothers and Walsh share for *diagonal* perspective, the analysis cues on how obliquities and matter proper to cinema tend to overtake the narratives in which they figure.[3] Although Walsh adamantly contended that cinema is about telling stories, and in line with Aristotle's *Poetics* (without referring to the philosopher), he suggested that it deals less with psychology than pure *action*. It happens, nonetheless, that his films invite spectators to consider their visual styles and their angularities: in short, their graphic and visual mettle. And no less, perhaps at the cost of annoying and fastidiously protracted shot-by-shot study, it seeks to dwell on aesthetic and political contradictions and contrarieties that make the features current, pertinent, and timely for study.

I begin with a first masterpiece, *Regeneration* (1915), a feature of almost seventy-three minutes. With its relentless action, fraught with extraordinary tension in crosscut or oppositional montage, *Regeneration* juxtaposes binocular and monocular vision. Set on Manhattan's Lower East Side, a *locus amoenus* to which Walsh returns eighteen years later in *The Bowery*, it stands in strong contrast to the feature I have chosen to bookend this monograph. In working through *Sadie Thompson* (1928), the second chapter briefly alludes to or jumps over many silent films, some lost or in fragments, others only available for viewing in archives, such as *Blue Blood and Red*, in the George Eastman House in Rochester, and *The Wanderer*, accessible in the UCLA archive.[4] Films in the public domain, available via YouTube, in disrepair or fuzzy focus, include *The Lucky Lady* (1926); *The Monkey Talks* (1927), *The Loves of Carmen* (1927), *The Man Who Came Back* (1931), *The Yellow Ticket* (1933), and others.[5] The third chapter presupposes that *The Revolt of Mamie Stover* (1956), a cult film at the time when Laura Mulvey's landmark study of the male gaze applied Lacan's concept of castration to cinema, can be taken as a remake in the rhetoric of post-1945 or Cold War Hollywood cinema. The monograph is obliged to skip over *What Price Glory?* (1926), a film whose tracking shots and unsparing battle scenes inspired Stanley Kubrick's *Paths of Glory* (1962), to sort through a sequel, *The Cock-Eyed World*, one of Walsh's "turkeys," a long feature, rife with creative contradiction, that says much about the ideology of authority and (as if appealing to the military complex) makes a plea for the deployment of air power in the colonies under American jurisdiction. From there I proceed to sound films, like the well-named *Cock-Eyed World*, shot in a quasi-silent mode, that betray the anomalies of the Great Depression, the moment in which they are filmed. A failed blockbuster that is no less a masterpiece, *The Big Trail*, a 70-mm epic of travel across western America, is studied for what it does with the silent tradition in its depiction of movement, in line with what theorists have noted, that turns *places* into *spaces*.[6] Ending in the sequoia forest of northern California, it becomes the setting for *Wild Girl* (1932), a film, alas, whose only mastered copy is in the MOMA, which by choice I have set aside in the hopes that fresh copies will be made available. Hence the work goes to *Me and My Gal* (1932), a feature in which George Walsh, the great star and muscle man of the silent era, plays an important role. But not only for fraternal reasons: the film carries in its editing the sense of *action* that clearly, in sly references to Walsh in their films, directors Martin Scorsese and Steven Spielberg have embraced.

Anchored in textual explication, the method and manner of reading seek to draw attention somewhat less to narrative continuity or plotline than to contradiction and to contrariety between what is seen and what is heard. The mode of interpretation owes much, as noted above, to Jacques Rancière's concept of the "film fable," of cinema as a visual medium (in either fiction or documentary) whose optical character works both with and against its narrative.[7] But much is also owed to my former colleague and mentor at the University of Paris-VIII (then located at Vincennes and not yet Saint-Denis), Marie-Claire Ropars-Wuilleumier, who understood cinema as a "divided text" that "writes" the space it portrays, hence a force field whose graphic register is at odds or tends to interfere with its narrative. Her uniquely Derridean analyses are close in style and manner to what Rancière later specifies as "deviations of film," forces of attraction and repulsion that *cinema*, a composite medium, exerts on what it portrays.[8]

Many have stood by the project, nudging it forward, with encouragement, at times with gentle castigation ("Tom, please, let's go, get off the pot"), and always in good faith: Rolf Belgum, former student, sculptor, and filmmaker, for whom *White Heat* is a point of reference and inspiration; Haden Guest, head of the Harvard Film Archive, who graciously agreed, with David Pendleton (who has sadly passed away since), to co-curate and run a quasi-complete (and immensely successful) retrospective in 2013, for which I wrote the program notes that match the title of this project;[9] Ron and Gai Russo, who have stood by the work for over three decades; Toni d'Angela, whose support and whose *Raoul Walsh: O'dell'avventura singolare* (2008) continue to lead the way; Louis Kaplan, specialist in photography and former student whose writing remains a model and who has told me that my oedipal relation with the topic is overbearing; Clayton Mattos, projectionist at the Harvard Film Archive who knows good cinema when he sees it, and with whom *millésimes* of Minervois and Menetou-Salon have been shared; Marc Cérisuelo, accomplished specialist of great directors on both sides of the Atlantic, whose knowledge and passion for cinema are boundless and with whom it has been a joy to confer in a long-past pre-COVID age when we were at the EHESS in Paris; Elisabeth Bronfen, who allowed me to dilate about *Objective, Burma!* at the English seminar she held at the University of Zürich; Clara Rowland, upon invitation to lead seminars on Walsh and preface viewings at the University of Lisbon and the Cinemateca, along with her colleagues, students, and friends, including film critic Mario Jorge Torres, José Bertolo, and Jeff Childs; wonderful and wondrous colleagues, Ross McElwee and Robb Moss, who have insisted that the autobiographical background, sketched above, be included in this study. Truncated by COVID-19, under the title of the "Berlin Prize," a residential fellowship the American Academy of Berlin graciously (or by clerical error) awarded in the spring of 2020, offered time to take up the project and, along the way, find counsel and friendship in members of a cohort that included genial filmmaker Kevin Everson. By every measure it is Murray Pomerance, with whom I have had the pleasure of collaborating since the beginning of the century, who has been dearly, patiently, and unstintingly supportive from beginning to end. And above all else, Verena Conley, to whom this book is dedicated, has put up with viewings from the days in the 1970s when we toted 16 mm prints of films and Bell & Howell projectors to and from classes at the University of Minnesota and home, for study and for the pleasure of our two children and neighbors to watch on our weekday "movie nights." My hope is that by virtue of the encouragement of so many, and with her by my side, a sequel will soon appear.

East Sandwich, MA
January/June 2021

1

On the Lower East Side

Regeneration (1915)

REGENERATION IS BASED ON Owen Kildare's *My Mamie Rose, an Autobiography and a Parable of Self-Redemption*. Published in 1903, quickly witnessing lucrative sales, his account found a sympathetic and enthusiastic public.[1] Set in the early twentieth century, the memoir is a somewhat picaresque confession and story of the early life and hard times of a person born on the Bowery, thanks to a woman's care and love, who mends his ways and becomes a noted journalist. Orphaned in infancy, Kildare lives with foster parents who welcome him into their household. A strapping figure in his youth and in his early twenties, a feared pugilist, he makes his living as a bouncer in taverns in his neighborhood. He briefly travels to France and Algeria before returning to the slums where his prestige remains unquestioned. Two-thirds of the way into the memoir, he recalls how, on a street one warm afternoon in the month of June, "'Skinny' McCarthy, one of my intimate pals . . . who belonged to the class of meanest grifters" (200), wanted to display his prowess to his hooligan friends. Catching sight of an attractive female who was passing by, Skinny accosts her to make a show of his gumption. First enthused, then confused, at the sight of Skinny's actions, Owen suddenly sees himself and his cronies being seen by the woman in her desperation. "Before my facial muscles had time to sharpen themselves into a brutish laugh the girl wheeled around, looked at McCarthy, at me, at all of us and, quite distinctly could I read there the sentence: 'And you are MEN!'" (202).

The episode is a turning point in the first-person narrative. Then an illiterate, thuggish wastrel, Owen intuitively *reads* on her face the words we *see* on the printed page—especially the majuscules and exclamation point. His impression of her reaction conveys what he believes is a female's anger and resentment at being a pawn in a "man's world." In a rush of empathy and pity (Kildare's prose exuding disavowed self-interest and "manliness"), Owen strikes Skinny with a blow to his ear, flattening his ally and friend. "The doors of my old life creakingly began to turn on their rusty hinges and slowly started to close themselves entirely" (204). Thus begins a regeneration. He soon learns that the woman's name is Marie Deering and that she is a schoolteacher. He submits to her charm, calling her "Mamie" as if she were a maternal object, and eagerly subscribes to her lessons in reading and writing. Through her encouragement he discovers his innate talents as a writer. And through her impetus and his own labors in learning how to write, he and Mamie fall in love and decide to marry. Early in 1900, a month before their nuptials, Mamie catches pneumonia and dies. Acknowledging that she changed his life in helping him discover his innate gifts and to look forward in life, he attributes his success at the *New York Sunday News* to her example. Yet, when all is said and done, when Mamie degenerates, Owen regenerates. The hero's success comes with the demise of the female who cared for him.

Yet on that day in June, when her facial gesture told Owen that she abhorred how men treated women, Mamie expressed anger and frustration that mark many of the females in Raoul Walsh's early cinema, in at least three films, *The Lucky Lady* (1926), *Sadie Thompson* (1927), *The Yellow Ticket* (1933), and much later, perhaps tellingly, in the story of another "Mamie," in *The Revolt of Mamie Stover* (1956). From this perspective *Regeneration* (1915) qualifies as a precocious feature and template for other films under Walsh's direction. While Kildare's best-seller of times past is confined to the vaults of university libraries, were it not for cinephiles or a team of archivists and restorers at the Museum of Modern Art, *Regeneration* (1915) might have had a similar fate. Although the feature is initially based on *My Mamie Rose*, we quickly discover that in taking leave of Kildare's self-aggrandizing autobiography, the feature centers less on the hero's resurrection than on unresolved conflict and, best of all, on cinema as such: in other words, on what the film is doing as a moving pictorial and graphic medium. First shown on September 15, 1915, *Regeneration* reminds us of the virtues both of the silent style and of the first traits of its director's signature. Its editing is uniquely open ended, and its montage is relentlessly fast paced and crosscut. On initial viewing it resembles parts of *The Birth of a Nation* (first shown on March 15, 1915)—notably, the sequence in which Walsh, playing John Wilkes Booth, assassinates Lincoln—while anticipating *Intolerance* that would premiere the following year.

The composition of almost seventy-two minutes draws attention to how the images invite viewers to see the film at once from within and outside of the narrative frame. Its photographic virtue suggests that the film is as much about its ocular and lenticular character as the tale it tells. Shot outdoors, on location in lower Manhattan, and indoors in claustrophobic settings of tenements, gangsters' dens, a dance hall and a settlement house while shifting incessantly from one closed area to another, the film is a study of conflict and social hierarchies at war with one another in ever-confined and confining spaces. In practically every one of its more than nine-hundred shots, a multifaceted visual composition stresses unyielding contradiction. Setting the tempo of what follows, by virtue of rapid-fire crosscutting, the first hundred shots of the film take up 8:12 minutes (each averaging 4.9 seconds). Of oppressive stasis and immobility, the world depicted in this feature—the world of Walsh and his Irish forebears—is riddled with action. Crosscutting is rife. We witness an art that builds visual and psychic tensions on the time-held traditions of fraternal rivalry or enemy brothers; focuses on a copresence of shallow and great depth of field; presents a condition where *war* and violence sustain the economy of life; shows how conflict, a total social fact, is punctuated only intermittently in the breath we take during infrequent but vital moments of peace and calm.

The Narrative

As if inspired not only by Kildare's memoir but also Jacob Riis *(How the Other Half Lives* and *The Battle with the Slum)*, Dickens *(Oliver Twist)*, Chaplin *(Caught in a Cabaret* [1914], a one-reeler about members of an idle class who go slumming), or Griffith *(The Musketeers of Pig Alley* [1912]), *Regeneration* mixes melodrama and cinema verité. The film tells of labors of social reform and, albeit less obviously, what it means to make a documentary fiction. The feature is composed of four panels: (1) the first depicts Owen (John McCann) age ten, following the death of his mother, orphaned and alone in a squalid apartment. Alone, left on his own, from the window of a cluttered flat he watches a hearse carry off the casket containing his mother's corpse. Maggie Conway (Maggie Weston), a matronly and robust neighbor living in a flat across the stairway, invites him to move into her household, a pigsty under the rule of husband Jim Conway (James Marcus), an abusive, obese, and drunken husband. Ever at odds with Jim, Owen eventually takes to the streets where he becomes a ragamuffin (1:00–09:31). (2) The second, albeit brief, establishes the world of war in which Owen has grown up. Now, age seventeen, a svelte adolescent and an icebreaker who works on the docks of the New York harbor, Owen (played by H. McCoy), works with a diminutive hunchback, a youth (unnamed and unattributed in the film) who is taunted by a young hooligan (William Sheer) and his friends. Defending the boy, witnessed by local color worthy of caricature (no doubt residents of the Bowery), Owen confronts, tussles, and pummels the thug (who happens to be Skinny—although he is not yet identified by an eyepatch—an attribute that will become one of Walsh's emblems). Coming to the boy's defense, two Irish locals and an old man (afflicted with a grotesquely deformed nose, shown in close-up) witness the scene and applaud the winner of the fight (09:52–11:20).

We discover in next panel (3), seven years later (11:20–1:04:48), that the hunchback has become Owen's faithful friend, and the hooligan, now wearing an eyepatch, is a comrade in crime named "Skinny." Enter Marie Deering (Anna Q. Nilsson), an idle maiden of upper Manhattan and her erstwhile brother, Ames Deering (Carl Harbaugh), a newly elected district attorney vowing to wipe out crime. Marie takes interest in "how the other half lives" while Ames, at the very least to be faithful to his calling, wishes to get a better sense of immigrant life and squalor in the nether regions. They dare to journey to the Bowery where they visit Grogan's, a rough-and-tumble tavern and dance hall (an establishment of the same name that will play a role eighteen years later in *The Bowery*). Indolent, Owen (now played by Rockcliffe Fellowes) happens to be sitting at a table in the company of the gang members. Inexplicably, he begins to contemplate his past and present life when peering into a mug of beer. Looking into the schooner, in a protracted dissolve he sees himself in his childhood licking an ice cream cone.[2] Raising his eyes, he glimpses Marie, Ames, and their company, whom his brutish friends suddenly rattle and intimidate. Attracted to Marie, he successfully escorts the frightened group to a limousine that awaits them outside to safety near where a boyish, Ivy League–like social worker wearing tortoise shell glasses preaches reform.

Marie is moved by the quality of life she has witnessed. Following her brother's will to reform the city, she establishes a settlement house that as the story unfolds will become the counterpart to the gang's den. There follows a celebrated sequence of the settlement's annual outing on the New York harbor (24:08–32:17): Marie shepherds her flock of indigents to board the *Shamrock Queen*, a pleasure craft hired for an afternoon of sightseeing. She coaxes Owen and his cronies—and even beckons the spectator (25:22)—to come along to enjoy an afternoon of dancing and dining. During the excursion, sitting apart from the community, Skinny flicks a cigarette butt onto a pile of frayed rope. Soon ignited, it sets the boat aflame. In the pandemonium men and women jump from the upper decks into the waters while Owen and Marie, gathering the children in their arms and lifting them into lifeboats, become the heroes of the day.

Marie brings Owen into her orbit. Upon her command, putting his fists to good use, he rescues a baby from an abusive household (32:18–41:58) and, unbeknownst to himself, feels an affection for forlorn infants and children.[3] Marie convinces Owen to devote his energies to the settlement house where, along with other homeless ne'er-do-wells, she teaches him how to read and write (44:32–46:13). In Owen's absence, Skinny, now the appointed leader of the gang, confronts and knifes a police inspector who had knocked at the door of the gang's den. Fleeing in panic, Skinny seeks sanctuary in the settlement house where Owen reluctantly offers him a place to hide. A plainclothesman arrives, finds no one, but insists that Owen is in collusion with the gang. Distraught, torn between devotion to Owen and her zealous brother's wish that she be rid of him, Marie despairs. Distraught over losing her sympathy, Owen confesses to a priest. Inspired, now having learned how to write, he scripts a note telling Skinny to get lost. His long-standing pal, the hunchback, delivers it to the gang (46:14–56:47).

The narrative hastens: upon reading the message, crazed, Skinny and his thugs thrash and knock the boy unconscious, kick and shove him under the stairwell leading to the entry. Anguished, Marie runs to the gangster's den in search of Owen. Peering through a hole in the door to the entry, Skinny recognizes her and welcomes her into their lair. The hunchback recovers his senses, glimpses Marie, furtively crawls into a sewer main, emerges from under a manhole cover, and dashes off to inform Owen and the police of the fate awaiting Marie at the hands of Skinny and his gang. Meanwhile, back at the den, Skinny lures Marie into a room where he molests her before she breaks free and locks herself in a closet. Owen enters the lair, confronting and fighting the gang in the basement while, simultaneously, the hunchback informs the police and leads two carloads of officers who drive to the scene at breakneck speed. In the melee on the lower floor, Owen lays waste to his opponents. The police arrive, club the criminals (and even suffer a loss when one of the gang members shoots an officer clambering into the den). Above, Skinny hacks at the door of the closet in which Marie hides in anguish. Owen arrives, smashes his way into the room, confronts Skinny (wielding a gun), who escapes from a window from where he fires a shot that strikes Marie. Owen opens the closet door then discovers and rescues Marie, tousled, who wilts in his arms. Skinny climbs a fire escape while below, and inside the lair the police put an end to the battle with the gang of thugs. Owen lovingly carries Marie away (56:47–1:04:48).

(4) The final panel, "The Journey Homeward" (1:04:49–1:11:33), sets Marie's death in counterpoint with Owen's pursuit of Skinny. While inside, the heroine expires in bed amidst the company of Ames, the hunchback, and Owen (who kisses her goodbye), in another compartment Skinny packs his effects together. Removing his eyepatch (that will be one of the director's emblems) and changing his clothes, he sets about to escape unnoticed. Owen hustles to the rooftop of the settlement where, finding and looking through a skylight, he witnesses Skinny preparing his getaway. He jumps down, confronts, and tussles with his adversary whom he begins to strangle before a memory-image of Marie (inserted at the upper right corner of the frame) compels him not to commit murder. Skinny escapes Owen's clutches, exits from a window giving onto a fire escape, and takes hold of a clothesline to inch his way to an adjacent tenement.[4] Below, the hunchback looks skyward, spots Skinny, pulls a revolver from a pocket of his jacket with his left hand, aims, and fires. Amidst a swirl of trash and debris, Skinny crashes onto the pavement. The film ends at Marie's grave where Owen and the hunchback gather to grieve. Of a style at a light year's distance from the text of *My Mamie Rose*, returning to Kildare's memoir, a long and teary intertitle (lasting thirty-three seconds, 1:11:10–33) reads,

> She lies here, this girl o'mine,
> but her soul, the noblest and purest
> thing I ever knew, lives on in me.
> It was she, my Mamie Rose, who
> taught me that within was a
> mind and a God-given heart. She
> made of my life a changed thing
> and never can it be the same again!

The Film within the Film

The beginning betrays some initial traits of a signature style. The front credits include five title cards, three of which mention the director and the last leading into the narrative that lays stress on adaptation and alteration of its source: (1) "William Fox presents R. A. Walsh's Drama *Regeneration*" (00:02–14); (2) "Copyright William Fox" (00:15–18); (3) "Direction by R.A. Walsh" (00:19–26); (4) "Adapted from Owen Kildare's 'My Mamie Rose,' by R. A. Walsh and Carl Harbaugh. Photography by Georges Benoit" (00:26–40). And the lead-in: (5) "Owen's mother, passing gratefully on to another and, we believe, happier world, leaves ten-year-old Owen to fight his way as best he can in this. Owen——John McCann" (00:42–59). The four credits that follow are decorated with a headpiece composed of a lozenge containing the initials WF that stand in front of a banderole composed of what seems to be a strip of 35 mm filmstock with which the name of the director (the abbreviations suggesting a "raw" and truculent Walsh) is front and center.

The first shot (1:00–04) (1) fades in to an iris portrait of child Owen, solitary, sitting alone adjacent to a table in a cluttered room, his bare legs crossed, staring accusingly at the viewer (fig. 1.1). A pot, an empty coffee cup, and a plate on the edge of a table draw our eyes toward a broken window. A calico cat climbs out of a box and onto an empty and ragged armchair adjacent to a window opening onto a fire escape where a tattered curtain flutters in the breeze. On the wall in the background hangs a cheap print of what seems to be a haloed Virgin Mary (01: 01–05). An abrupt cut—nothing indicates how or why—to the next take (2) (01:06–07) is clearly not from Owen's point of view. We note an undertaker pushing a wicker coffin into the rear of a horse-drawn hearse, its righthand panel open while in the foreground, seen from behind, a boy's head (to the left) and those of two girls (to the right), their hair scruffy and tousled, look upon the scene from the viewer's vantage point (fig. 1.2). Cut (3) to Owen in his apartment above the street, in iris, now in medium close-up, who continues to stare but seems to bemoan—he scratches the back of his head—the condition of the world (01:07–10). The film shifts abruptly (4) back to the hearse (01:10–12). Pressing and sealing the right rear door with his hands, the driver calls attention to the mirrorlike sheen of the side of the vehicle. In the shot of barely two seconds, he passes across the vehicle, exiting right, revealing the diagonal position of the hearse. Reflected on the right panel we discern a person wearing a white shirt, seated, who cranks a camera on a tripod while to his left stands a person wearing a white hat, sporting a necktie, who

Figure 1.1. A beginning: Owen orphaned (1:00).

Figure 1.2. A coffin in a hearse: the filmmakers shown in their film (1:11).

seems to be looking at the action as it unfolds. Could it be the director? Could the man at the camera be Georges Benoit? Whoever they are, the moving reflections count among the crew, shown here and elsewhere on windows or reflective surfaces.

The beginning indicates that *the film is being made.*[5] The next shot (5) cuts back to a close-up of Owen in iris, who turns his head to the right (00:01:13–15), as if responding to a sound cue off-frame. In the next shot (6), recouping the medium take that established the setting, Owen walks to the window in the background (00:01:15–21). From there, in chiaroscuro, in close-up in three-quarter view (7), perplexed, lost in thought, Owen looks upon what can only be the event just seen (01:21:22). In the loose (and, for viewers in 1915, it can be assumed, weakened) deixis the removal of the coffin, including the brief display of the film as it is being made, could be part of Owen's "indirect subjectivity," in other words, his vision of the coffin being driven off *before* he actually sees the traumatic separation from the upper window.[6] His can only be a *mental image* before the next shot (8), a cavalier view of the horse drawing the hearse away (01:23–26), locates his point of view overhead: which is confirmed by the following shot (9) that portrays him looking downward (01:26–28) as a tear rolls down his left cheek. After an uncommonly long take of nine seconds, what would qualify as a "affect-image," in a sudden return to the composition (10) of the first shot of the film, turning away from the window in the background, Owen wipes his nose, pivots, and walks back into the space while the cat crawls about the armchair (01:28–37).[7]

Owen's movement brings two objects into view: the back of the empty chair on which he had been sitting is now shown broken in half; in the background an old broom leans against the armchair. The boy's tear in the preceding shot becomes a motif and point of affective reflection, a sign not only of emotion (and motion) but also of the lenticular character of what will follow. Adjacent to Owen, who looks out of the window in the background, in the frame of the iris, the broken chair he has just vacated has the trappings of a still-life that includes, on the left, the edge of the table on which an empty plate and coffee cup are placed; to the right, behind the chair, leaning on the arm of a mangy armchair, a broom; and on the floor, leaning into the shot, an empty shopping basket (fig. 1.3). The broom is destined to become an object of iconic charge when the neighbor, Maggie Conway all of a sudden enters the apartment, grabs the handle, and sweeps Owen into her squalid flat across the hall.[8] The action is shown soon after the second intertitle (01:38–48), which identifies the Conway family "across the landing." Rotund, robust, in tatters, Maggie is introduced (11) scrubbing laundry (01:49–52) on a

Figure 1.3. Orphaned Owen and the broom that sweeps clean (1:29).

washboard in a basin while her obese husband, Jim, bedraggled, sitting at a table in the foreground and suddenly shown in close-up, gulps (13) beer from a pail, then wipes his mouth with his forearm (01:53–56). Cut (14) to a close-up of Maggie, in turn, who wipes her hands and then her brow (02:00–01). Her gesture is contrary to her husband's: she works and sweats while he drinks and drools. Cut (15) to a half-iris shot of Owen (02:01–04) in his apartment where he puts a harmonica to his mouth and breathes into it, the sound cue prompting Maggie's decision to take the orphan into her custody.

Fifteen shots in less than fifty-one seconds: the average take of three-plus seconds becomes the mean for the film comprising about nine hundred shots over almost seventy-two-plus minutes, whose breakneck rapidity stands in glaring contrast to the social immobility and depravity of the community of tenements. In this sequence and what immediately follows, rapid crosscutting underscores the presence of the apparatus or the technical "condition of possibility" of what we are seeing. In this moment and others, brief as they may be, the film indicates that it is being made in medias res, going as it goes, and that its process is becoming a strand of the narrative it tells, notably when Owen moves from his family's apartment into the Conway's. In between the stairwell and landing, an antechamber or intermediate area becomes the site of conflict. A window in the background looks onto the face of another tenement, implying that we are within an infinite labyrinth of slum. Playing on the landing, an unsupervised baby and child witness Jim, in a drunken stupor, struggling up the staircase. Losing his footing, almost crushing the infant (3:48:40–4:05), the obese figure makes his way into the flat where he fights with Owen. Using extreme crosscutting from one confining space to another, the sequence is patterned according to the enclosed (and socially immobile) area Riis and Kildare had described in their assessments of the Bowery. Paradoxically elliptical yet executed in terse composition, however much its legacy tells us the feature is born of Griffith in his Biograph years, the montage seems to anticipate much of the action and relentless movement that marks the director's later work.

Inside and Out

Divided into compartments, closets, rooms, dens, and lairs, dark areas *inside* are complemented, in documentary fashion, by infrequent takes of areas of a confined world *outside*, bathed in the light of day. In one of several sequences that could be called cinema verité (before it indicates that Maggie and young Owen are shopping), the camera records a busy marketplace on the Lower East Side (05:44–47) (fig. 1.4). In the foreground to the right, fussing over her hair and oblivious to the camera, a young girl attracts the viewer's attention before Maggie and Owen emerge from the crowd, turn right, and exit the frame. Implying that the setting is of greater interest than the couple, the shot holds briefly to witness the girl's defensive reaction when a young man approaches her.[9] The film cuts to a diagonal view of a tavern from whose swinging doors exit the inebriated Jim and his drinking companion (05:47–51). The frame is split in two. On the left the two men make their way into the light, and to the right, the bay window of the saloon displays its wares (the emblem of V. Loewer's Lager and two posters), and on its glass a world at large is registered in reflection. A vehicle passes while, immobile, two blindered horses on another pane, astonishingly and fleetingly, are set between them as they exit (05:50). The camera (its lens directly facing the scene), its tripod, and the operator filming the scene are faintly visible.

Figure 1.4. The Bowery market: Maggie and Owen go shopping (5:46).

Here and elsewhere a mirage of the apparatus *in* the film would be an accident or mishap unless, in strong likelihood, the film establishes a quasi-documentary character that invites us to look at the settings and the actions on which they are staged as an ongoing production of physical and social space.[10] In daylight, and in the passage of less than seven seconds, the crosscutting stresses the female and the child at work in contrast to the "men," slime of the earth, who waste themselves in drink and disorder.

The film further compartmentalizes its action. From the outside (05:51–06:06), in a long take of fifteen seconds, Maggie and Owen return home. The shot begins in front of the stoop at the entry of the brownstone whose tawdry interior has been a site of conflict. Bathed in bright light, the stairs and iron balustrade stand in contrast to a dark doorway, a boarded window (left) and its open complement (right) behind which, *inside*, the backside of a seated person in a white shirt indicates that they have no interest in what is happening *outside*. The shot records, first, two barefoot urchins exiting through the door, one with a (ubiquitous) broom in hand while Maggie and Owen trundle up the stairs and *into* the dark area. She shoos the kids away before pushing two, three, then four and five boys out of the dark space. Cut to the drunkards, in a complementary setting, exiting the tavern, then entering the brownstone (6:06–6:13) without interference, where more domestic violence ensues.[11] Jim tosses Owen out of the apartment and into the flight of stairs. He flees *outside* into daylight (08:50–09:02 and 09:06–11) in a sequence crosscut with shots of the wastrels (09:11–14) *inside* the apartment. Barefoot, in full daylight, he finds a place to curl up and sleep on a metal grate under the storefront of a bakery. In the implicit narrative the new life that inaugurates the next panel, also outdoors, could be a dream and a series of caricatures, even a memory-cloud, much like the local color the film discovers and records as the narrative unwinds. In one of the finest shots in the tradition of "realism" or depiction of "local color" on the Bowery, smoking a stogie, a grotesque spectator (whom Walsh or Benoit might have found while filming the sequence) enjoys either the making of the scene we are witnessing or the chaos of the world in which he lives (fig. 1.5).

Figure 1.5. Local color on the Bowery (21:49).

In the first panel, like a child or reflector in a novel of Henry James (as in *What Maisie Knew*—but who could not say), Owen looks on a world he cannot understand or assimilate into language. In the second, in his adolescence (and now better equipped), he observes the milieu in which he is embroiled. Placed outdoors (10:00–11:19), by the dockyards of New York, in another flair for cinema verité the camera stresses the closure of the open space and an unchanging condition of male conflict and violence. Now seventeen, Owen (H. McCoy) confronts but is hard put to discern an order of things other than what the intertitle states: "Where the prizes of existence go to who has the most daring in defying the law" (09:52). Here, in the third panel, the camera is angled to show how Owen, who first saw the world through a glass darkly, has gained perspective on his milieu and condition. What appears to be one of the most carefully staged shots, a virtual flashback *within* a shot (42:21–28, amidst the most damaged parts of the film), we witness Owen looking intesnsely at a window of an apartment on the ground floor of a brownstone tenement building. Behind a pane of glass, cared for by a nurse, peering out from the dark interior, two infants mirror the gaze he casts upon their world. Owen's sightline follows a diagonal axis, from the lower right corner of the frame to the window, on the upper left. When he raises his arm to offer an gift to the babies who catch sight of him, from our angle his gesture indicates an innate empathy and nascent generosity (fig. 1.6). Emphasizing the angle from which the shot is taken, in tendering a stick of candy to the baby on the other side of the glass, Owen's affection for children blueprints his rescue of the youngsters from the burning deck of the Shamrock Queen (31:53–32:20) and immediately afterward, of the baby from the crib in the Flaherty household (32:04–37:00). The composition leads us to believe that in his attraction Owen intuits how "the child is the father of man." In the window before his eyes is he reminded of a former, even preconscious life but also, in accord with his life story, a continuum of conflict and social contradiction in the difference of the three stages—childhood, adolescence, adulthood—in his life that the film is given to depict? What he beholds inside is a past present, a space where, thanks to cinema, chronological time is flattened, while the outside world, rife with conflict, is momentarily bracketed or kept at bay.[12]

The implications of the shot and what it does as *cinema* owe to the air and atmosphere of the best remembered sequence, begun earlier in the same panel with the intertitle announcing, "The treat of the season/ The settlement's annual outing" (24:37), the episode staging the confla-

Figure 1.6. Owen looks at his past and future (16:57).

gration aboard the *Shamrock Queen* during the settlement's annual outing (24:40–32:10). In what begins as theater-in-a-theater, indigents under Marie's wing are led onto the craft, inside, as if entering a movie show or an "attraction." Standing near the gangplank, spotting the hoodlums at the dockside, Marie faces the camera in close-up, beckoning everyone, viewers and thugs alike, to come aboard. Cut to Owen, smoking a cigarette, and his villainous friends; then cut back to the crowd that continues to board the boat and then to Skinny and his four cronies who are playing craps; back to Marie and company where the last of the guests cross the gangplank; cut to Skinny and his cohort. Succumbing to her charm, the members of the gang leave the dock where they have been loitering, revealing in the background a shard of writing, "SH," the first two letters of the *Shamrock Queen*. After the thugs make their way to the gangplank, the camera holds on what for a second (at the most) becomes another still-life of an unremitting milieu. Everyone is aboard while some dockhands tend to the mooring. Holding for an instant, a last shot (26:29) from the pier displays the area of the dock. A stark wooden frame of two tiers of logs is bolted to the corner of a dock, a chain stretches across a row of planks, and a piece of the dock enters the frame diagonally, set in counterpoint to paper detritus on the ground. On the other side, a sizable cast-iron pylon looms in the foreground, an attribute of the ropes and chains of a stevedore's world, while the upper story of the hull displays a panel now spelling SHAM. The setting displays on the pier in the foreground an imposingly erect mooring pole and in the background the bulkhead of the dock adjacent to the boat, which displays a ventilating stack and over its gunnels a shard of its Irish name. SHAM (fig. 1.7) calls into question the veracity of film as such, much like it had when the apparatus was shown reflected on the hearse in the opening sequence. Now, at dockside, the montage draws attention to how it is socially and spatially constructed.

Better known among historians, the shots recording the pyre and escape from the *Shamrock Queen* also oscillate between staging and verité. Walsh recalls how, after getting background takes of the Bowery and more at Fort Lee, New Jersey,

Figure 1.7. The SHAM of the *Shamrock Queen* (26:38).

[I] wanted to get the river scenes, where the big action would be—an excursion on the Hudson for the mission's indigent members. The script called for the boat to catch on fire. After renting an excursion boat with an upper deck, I went to Hell's Kitchen and hunted through the dives until I found a pair of typical hooligans. I managed to get through their heads that I needed a hundred or so men and about fifty women for passengers. (1974, 116)

He could not find enough females, "and time and money and sunlight were wasting. I found the answer: *some men would have to act as women*" (1974, 116; emphasis added). When by megaphone he ordered the extras to jump from the ship, "the women jumped, their skirts ballooned up and I was sure that some of them were not wearing anything underneath" (117). In reviewing the dailies he noted that "[a]t least a dozen of the females were as naked as jaybirds under their long dresses" (119), adding that he had a negative doctor "put pants on twenty of the females in every one of those frames" (120).[13] In the remastered print (in red tint), those who jump from the craft are in pants and, for all exhaustive purposes, would seem to be male, and those wearing dresses in the director's recollection are pure fantasy. The mythic memory of the sequence tells more about sexual *indifference* and, perhaps from what is found in the memoir of 1974, a shoot that turned out to be a publicity stunt for New Yorkers before it was completed, even if Walsh said that it was "[f]or that era . . . a good picture," a mix of action and "solid corn" with a tearjerker ending (119). But also, and to its credit, in its mix of record and fiction the episode calls into question suspension of disbelief, implicitly theorizing its force of attraction.

Scenes of Writing

In "Freud et la scène d'écriture" (Freud and the scene of writing), a famous essay on the psychoanalyst's "Notes on the Mystic Writing Pad," Jacques Derrida studies how primal events cannot be separated from the psychic and technical machineries of representation—in other words, from the character, movement, and staging of their writing. So also in the writing scenes in *Regeneration*. Given that *My Mamie Rose* is a story about an orphan, later a challenged youth who learns how to manage pencil and paper, Walsh's film doubles its hero's sentimental and professional education through a montage of *visual* writing, calling attention to how it can be both seen and read. Front credits and writing in the montage excepted (newspaper headlines, personal letters, pages from a diary, a scribbled note), the film includes forty-one intertitles over a duration of almost seventy-two minutes. Eight minutes of the film are seen to be read. Where the text is ample, holding for a long duration, the intertitles suggest that viewers—perhaps, like the personages, hardly literate or learning to read through movies—need time to decipher the words. Thus the juncture between the first and second panels: a refugee from his adoptive household, Owen, barefoot, takes to the street (8:51–9:03, crosscut with a fight between Jim and Maggie, 9:03–05), where he stops to look longingly at cakes on display behind the front window of a bakery (9:06–09, crosscut with the fight, 9:10–9:14), where his reflection is visible. He finds a grate beneath the window, curls up and, in an iris that closes, he goes to sleep (9:16–32). An intertitle follows, the text so consuming that the Fox logo and decoration are elided to make space for the writing that mediates dreams of the passage of time:

> And then years pass and Owen
> still lives in a world where
> might is right—and where the prizes
> of existence go to the man
> who has the most daring in
> defying the law, and the quickest
> fist in defending his own rights.
> Owen, at seventeen——H. McCoy. (9:32–59/27 seconds)

Between the sleeping boy in the first panel and the shot placing the young Owen among a group of ice breakers that begins the second panel, the intertitle of long duration implies that the past could have been a nightmare (in glaring daylight), or that what will become of him (child Owen's dream) is unremittingly real. In the time it requires to be read, the intertitle conveys the burden of Owen's growth into the world.

Only minutes later, a card (with Fox logo and decoration) announces the third panel:

> Owen's twenty-fifth year
> finds him a leader of the
> gang, by virtue of a
> complete assortment of the

> virtues the gangsters most
> admire.
> Owen, at twenty-five
> —Rockcliffe Fellowes. (11:18–11:40/22 seconds)

The sequence begins in the outdoor setting, ostensibly by the East River, not far from the Bowery, where young Owen (H. McCoy) has pinned the young tough (Skinny in his first appearance, unnamed, *without* an eye patch). In the last shot (11:15–17) one of the spectators, cigar in jowl and wearing a bowler hat—a promotor or boxing agent—congratulates Owen. In concert with the many pugilistic sequences in Walsh's cinema, as if anticipating the fistfights in *The Bowery* (1933) and *Gentleman Jim* (1942), he negotiates with the strapping Owen, arms on hips, who stares at the camera.[14] The scene fades quickly to the intertitle, after which, in conjunction with its words, a widening iris displays a "portrait" of the future hero, wearing a cap, smoking a cigarette, staring suspiciously at whatever might stand before him. We glimpse on a mirror of the tavern behind him—a vague face of a cameraman and the roof of a passing vehicle. Owen draws on a cigarette and exhales a waft of smoke that blows in the atmosphere (11:41–47) before the next intertitle presents "Skinny, one of the gang.—William Sheer" (11:48–55), also in medium close-up, in front of a Lion's Brew logo. He dons a cap (11:56–12:02) before an establishing shot locates the pair sitting with the hunchback and another crony. They enter the tavern (12:02–04)—Skinny is shown mirrored on the swinging door (1:07)—where they accost a client who has put his money on the bar. Owen gesticulates, grabs him by the arm:

> "Buy the drinks!" (12:32–35)

In the frenzied alternation of spaces inside and outside, cut to another intertitle announcing and portraying the district attorney, "like all proverbial new brooms . . . [who] resolves to sweep the city clean" (12:40–48): taking up thirty-seven of the first eighty-two seconds of the second panel, the serial disposition of the intertitles goes hand in hand with the frenetic shifts to the world of the gang—the tavern, Grogan's dance hall—and that of the well-healed Deering household. From the beginning, images of writing work on or infuse the visual matter, presaging what will become the "writing lesson" in the narrative. Like other captions in the montage, the signboard by the stoop of the "Settlement House" heralds the space where the sight of alphabetical characters—ABCs, the hunchback tracing ciphers on a blackboard, Marie seated in front of books, journals on a desk (32:46–50; 32:53–57, 33:03–08; 33:14–16, 44:26–28, etc.)—takes command over the episode that had Owen, bereft of adequate words, using might to bring order to the Flaherty household.

The sequence that portrays Owen learning to write could be a template for a classical *scène d'écriture*, the staging of an act of writing stressing that, insofar as it is an "optical machine," for literate and illiterate viewers alike, an unspoken aim of the film is to trace graphic marks in moving images.[15] Freud could not have done better: an inkling of the writing lesson is given when Owen, having left the gang's lair in favor of the settlement house, thinks about purchasing a bouquet from an old lady, outdoors, who sits on a stoop (44:05–11). The shot is crosscut with a scene where, standing and turning around, Deering confronts Marie, at her desk, who is busy writing (44:11–18); cut back to Owen, in medium close-up, who makes his purchase (44:19–24); then to Deering, who closes an open book on the desk when Marie implores him to bear with her (44:25–29). An intertitle (without the Fox logo) supplies the words he had just uttered: "Give up this life, Marie. What is its attraction? Won't you come back to the world where you belong?" (44:29–43, thirteen seconds being accorded for its reading!) while, his arm extended, she clasps his hand in her palms (44:43–44). Cut to Owen, now in a medium shot in a wide iris, rhyming with the previous shot, who has just extended his arm to pay the old lady who smiles before he exits the frame (left), revealing a crudely written signboard in the background that begs to be read, leaving an effect of coequal heat and frigidity:

"584 Tom Ice Coal Wood."

A writing table occupies the space Owen evacuates, implying that, given the gift of the bouquet (flowers being the figure of fine speech), his body is about to be ciphered (44:44–50). Back to Deering and Marie where the attorney, turning about and pacing, expresses frustration over his sister's stubborn commitment to her mission (44:50–57). In a diagonal close-up on the doorway Owen enters, looks around, and is upset (44:58–5:02) when what he sees is the scene being shown: Marie, rustling papers, in intimate dialogue with her brother (45:03–06). A primal scene stirs when he sees himself as an excluded figure at the instant his eyes (it is inferred) fix entirely on Marie. When Deering enters the background of the scene, he is now the excluded other who looks jealously at Marie when Owen, smiling, offers her the bouquet.

In a shot of almost twenty seconds, set in perfect spatial triangulation, Deering fiddles anxiously with his cane (his writing instrument) and exits (left), in what seems to be jealous anger while Owen, offering Marie his bouquet (his writing instrument) before he sits with her, when she will offer him her pen (her writing instrument) (45:10–39). Cut to diagonal take on Deering who approaches a vacant chair and desk adjacent to a blackboard—a hieroglyph—riddled with ciphers. He looks at what follows with unresolved anger: won over, Owen looks in admiration at Marie, in the guise of a schoolteacher (for a child, both a mother and an erotic object) who holds his right hand affectionately while training him to trace characters on a sheet of paper (45:43–50—eighteen seconds). Simultaneously, outside, Skinny encounters and knifes a policeman (with his writing instrument). He runs off and seeks Owen's protection while Deering, as if reviewing the screenplay, reads Marie's diary. In an iris, *contrary to the action*, Marie's words, written in cursive (comprising a hidden intertitle of long duration) and in a shot assuming his point of view, we read words that augur well: "Aug 24. Owen is getting along splendidly. He has left his former associates forever and is heart and soul in his new position" (50.00–50.18). Deering is reading Marie's private diary at the moment a detective enters another room in the settlement where Owen *pretends* to be reading a magazine. Skinny sneaks off and returns to the thieves' lair.

After confession and soul searching, scribbling a note to Skinny, Owen enacts a second *scène d'écriture* in what might be a "becoming-space of time." Eleven minutes pass between Owen's initial writing lesson and his careful scripting of the note that tells his former ally to get lost. Running off, his hunchback friend on his heels, he passes a woman seated on the stoop of a brownstone. Shrouded in black, she holds a baby—the father of man—in her arms. He approaches a doorway (55:59) to a tenement where, after looking at the woman and child (seen in a cutaway shot in closeup), in an iris-shot, he searches his pockets for a pencil and paper (56:10–14). In extreme close-up, his gigantic hands (and dirty fingernails) filling the frame (56:14–44) in one of the longest shots of the film, he writes, slowly and surely, a note that the hunchback will deliver to Skinny (fig. 1.9):

We are even now
Keep out of my way
Beat it—get me
    Owen.

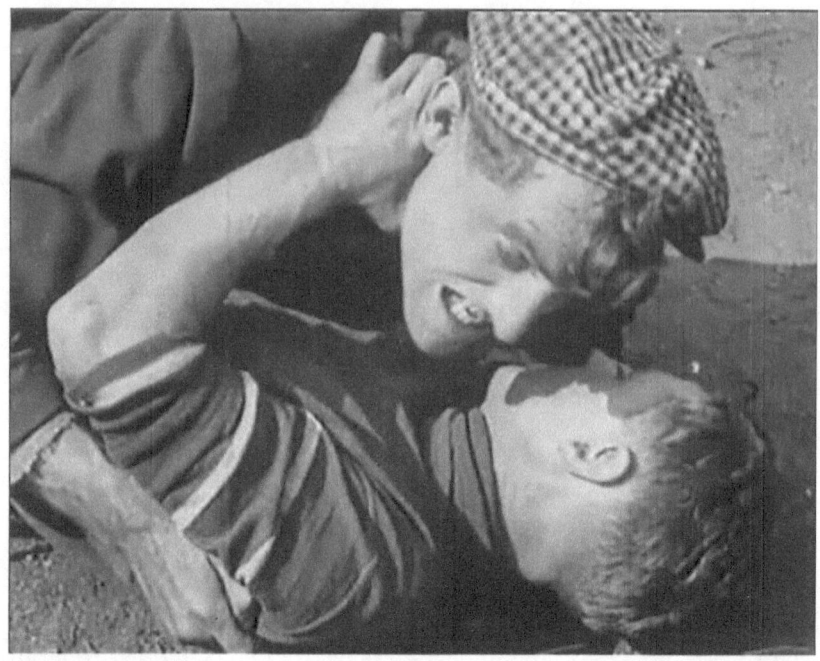

Figure 1.8. Owen and Skinny in a tussle (10:49).

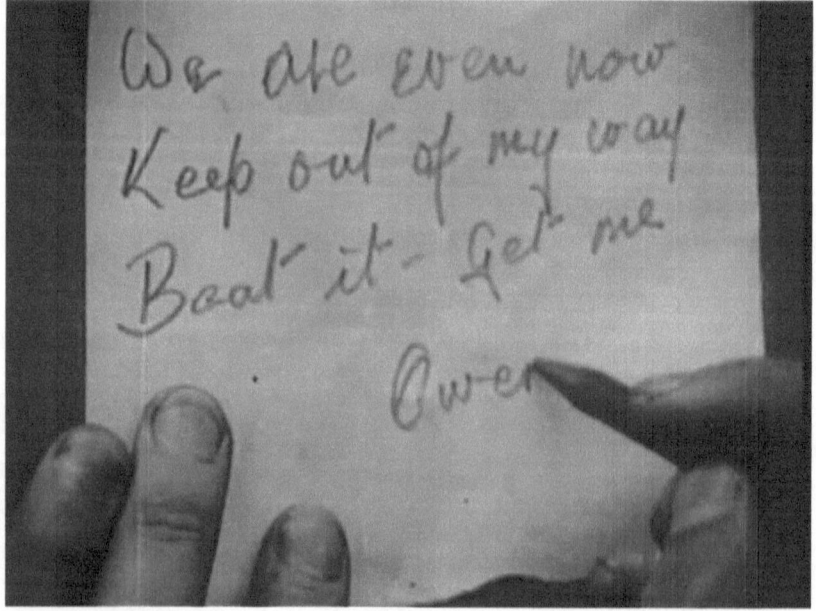

Figure 1.9. Owen writes that he owes nothing to Skinny (56:41).

The message spells out what philosophers have called a "libidinal economy" where writing mediates unconscious (and often murderous) proclivities.[16] As we recall, in the second panel of the film Owen and Skinny (unidentified and not wearing an eyepatch) were portrayed as a couple that for a moment embrace when in combat (fig. 1.9). At the beginning of the third they are partners in crime before Owen begins to mend his ways and when, finally, he becomes an enemy brother, even an alter ego. Read doubly, the message confirms that Owen and Skinny are of the same order, *even now*. The two being coequals, one in the underworld and the other above, their debts have been paid. *Even now* carries the echo of Owen whose name is doubled in the signature. Because of the thirty seconds taken in the writing of the message, in *becoming* an intertitle, the words elicit reflection on the film in general: as *discourse* how do they *figure* in the moving images? Does this message open the film onto an unconscious that, at the same time (1915) in his essays on war and death, Freud was theorizing?[17] If it does, especially in its extreme close-up, it bears on how and why the film brings ocular forms into its narrative and photographer Georges Benoit's visual compositions. From the beginning, iterated time and again in the intertitles, "Owen" becomes a hieroglyph, something other or more than a proper name—a visual sign that marks where reading and seeing are one and the same and where the field of the image is both flat and of extreme depth.

Ocular and Monocular

Skinny first appears without an eyepatch (10:06–08). Sitting by a dock with two cronies, he calls and taunts Owen's hunchback friend. At the end, in two dramatic iris shots (1:04:15–16), having shot Marie, he desperately climbs out of a window (1:04–15–16) and climbs the ladder of a fire escape (1:04:26–28) during a ruckus between the gang and the police in the basement and, on an upper floor, Owen embracing Marie. In the final segment, "The Journey Homeward," Owen and friends pay respects to Marie while Skinny prepares to leave. Changing clothes in the attic of the settlement house, as if it were a valuable identity card, he removes his eyepatch (see fig. 1.10), then wraps and puts it in his traveling bag (1:06:01–02). We realize that the patch has been a visual shifter, a sign indicating not only that the character is devious, or that Owen sees the world in its depth of field while Skinny does not, but now the patch becomes an emblem of the film as a whole. It is a "cache" or sign indicating that "seeing is concealing" or being blind to what is evident, in

Figure 1.10. Skinny, his eyepatch removed, behind him the sign of his demise (1:07:51).

other words, "selecting and keeping from sight part of what is visible," the "visible and the non-visible [being] bound, inseparable, co-dependent."[18]

However conventional it may be in the lexicon of silent cinema, in *Regeneration* the iris, what elsewhere is called a circular mask, becomes a partial cache or even a lure that invites us to see and to read the moving images in different ways.[19] Everywhere in the film, from the first shot that locates child Owen, orphaned in his flat, who goes to a window to watch the hearse take his mother away, the iris suggests that we are looking at the film through an aperture. And later, too, when Marie gazes upon an eye peering through a hole in a doorway (fig. 1.11). Hardly confined to portraits or close-ups of faces, to scenes in the dance hall and so on, deployed so often that it becomes invisible, the iris functions as a "perspectival object," inviting what analysts (using the vocabulary of cinema) call *projective identification*: when used in accord with establishing shots certain objects are in focus, while others are outside of a given field of view. The analogy of the iris or mask to the viewfinder of the camera is cause for reflection on how the apparatus or the mechanical cause of

Figure 1.11. Marie sees a thug's eye behind a knothole at the entry to the gang's den (57:44).

the film is shown within it, thus becoming an agent that both pulls us into a narrative and draws us away, to repeat, forcibly eliciting a critical relation with what is being shown.[20]

An Iris for an Iris

In the final minutes the iris sums up what the camera and the editing have been doing to establish and drive the narrative forward. Skinny has inadvertently shot Marie, who had been hiding in a closet. Owen finds her and takes her into his arms. When in his embrace, she begins to expire (and not as she had in Kildare's memoir). Delivered to a bed, in supine pose, she soon dies. Grieving her death, now in ire, Owen turns away (1:06:30) and exits (to the right) into the settlement schoolroom, seemingly hearing Skinny or intuiting his presence. He is followed by the faithful hunchback who packs a revolver into his jacket. Skinny, now fully dressed, stands next to a wall (1:07:19–21). Suddenly, on a rooftop before a maze of tenements, Owen emerges from behind a brick chimney, approaches a skylight (1:07:31–36), then (in medium close-up) peers through a broken pane (1:07–36–38). Denoting Owen's point of view, a tightly circumscribed iris (1:07:39–42) centers on Skinny, now seen from above, who continues to pack his bags. The accelerated montage (for which the finale of *Intolerance* is the usual trademark) cuts between Skinny, below; Owen, on the roof; the hunchback, in the street, who summons the police.[21] As if it were a totem of Skinny who seeks a way to escape, an iris-shot (1:10:04–07) displays a rat emerging from a hole in a wall (itself a partial mask), in bold contrast with the immediate close up of Owen's hands holding a handkerchief embroidered with a monogrammed M (1:10:09–11), cipher and memory-figure of Marie. The next emphatic iris records Skinny, inside, having just crawled through a window in the dark interior of a row of stairs, exiting outside into broad daylight, climbing over an iron balustrade, grasping a clothesline and inching his way across the cityscape of tenements (1:10:18–26). As if it were a telescopic gunsight, the iris sets Skinny in its invisible crosshairs. The final and only iris-in frames Owen and his friend at the grave before the final intertitle records Owen's (and not author Owen Kildare's) last words.

Until seen and read in conjunction with the "apparatus" and with a play of monocular and binocular perspectives, irises seem to go without saying. They pass before our eyes as a "convention" common to silent film, be it the first shot that focuses on the orphaned child in his tawdry milieu, the portraits of Skinny sporting his eyepatch, or any of the many scenes in which characters peer through knotholes in fences or peepholes in doors (fig. 1.11). The commonplace becomes part and parcel not only of the film in its production and process but also (and somewhat uncannily) in the trait of a director, fourteen years later, whose enucleation will be tied to the ways his films are conceived, read, and seen. How *Regeneration* foresees or foretells a defining event in the director's career remains a telling enigma. And in the terse and tight editing, in the relentless crosscutting—in sum, its unyielding action—the feature displays and concretizes a sense of style and composition that will be modified and attenuated in the director's work over the next forty-nine years. At the cost of repetition in the paragraphs above (symptom of an impassioned relation with the film), and of leaving aside numerous films directed in the years 1915 to 1927, it suffices to jump forward to a late feature in the silent phase to see how and why.

2

A Monkey Talks to *Sadie Thompson*

In November of 1926 New Yorkers saw a sound-edited version of *What Price Glory?* Based on a Broadway play by Maxwell Anderson, shot on the heels of King Vidor's masterful *Big Parade* (1925), the feature was destined to become the first panel of a trilogy featuring top sergeant Flagg (Victor McLaglen) and his rival in rank, a trickster named Harry Quirt (Edmund Lowe), who form an odd couple of sorts (enemy brothers in love with each other), fighting heroically in the trenches and battling over Charmaine (Dolores del Rio), the attractive hostess of an inn behind the lines. Accompanied by an experimental soundtrack punctuated with noise and shards of voice—loud, brash, and raunchy for lipreaders—the war movie was a hit at the box office (Moss 2011, 98). Clearly designed not to have a conclusion, the film called for sequels that would be *The Cock-Eyed World* (1929) and *Women of All Nations* (1931).

Simians and Simulation

Yet it might have had a prequel: three months after its premiere, Walsh had completed *The Monkey Talks*, based on *Le Singe qui parle* (1924), a play dramatist René Fauchois (author of *Boudu Saved from Drowning*, from which Jean Renoir derived his eponymous classic of 1932), staged ostensibly to address (and, perhaps, to alleviate) the disillusionment and trauma haunting survivors of 1914–1918. Despite the horrible condition of the copy available on YouTube, eerie and unsettling, *The Monkey Talks* merits juxtaposition with *Sadie Thompson* (1928), a landmark feature in the careers of Walsh and Gloria Swanson. Both films are about monstrous or evil designs and murder. Both lay stress on the hypnotic effects of attraction, and both deal with repression of speech in a medium, their scenarios seem to imply (like *What Price Glory?*), yet to be engineered with sound. In *Raoul Walsh* (2020), in a first chapter on the director's "stumbling poetics" ("La poética del traspié"), Carlos Losilla remarks that like so many films to follow, *The Monkey Talks* deals with the play of things visible and invisible. "[O]ne of the strangest films Walsh ever directed," close in spirit with *The Devil's Circus* (d. Benjamin Christenson, 1926) or more famously, Todd Browning's *Freaks* (1932), the silent feature of sixty-two minutes asks us how it feels to live when we are *unable to speak*.[1] And, in view of its own economy, as Maisie (Jane Winton), one of the evil characters claims in a scenario of revenge, what matters most in the greater economy of things—hence cinema—is that *money talks*.

The first reel is so damaged that the narrative seems to begin in the second.[2] From the perspective of *What Price Glory?*, *The Monkey Talks* builds on Walsh's films set in World War I or its aftermath.[3] Don Alvarado (Sam Wicke), a veteran aviator who is soon to inherit a fortune, has a passion for Maisie (Jane Winton), a member of a traveling circus. Smitten by his means and status, she keeps him in tow, but when his father, livid over Alvrado's cross-class attraction, disinherits him, she turns toward Bergerin the Magnificent (Malcolm Waite), the troupe's lion tamer.[4] Disconsolate, sitting in a café with diminutive François Faho (Jacques Lerner), a comrade aviator and an acrobat, Armand seeks a new life. Mata (August Tollaire), the manager of a traveling circus, and Lorenzo (Raymond Hitchcock), one of its performers, are convinced enough to hire him. Riddled with debts, the circus is forced to shut down. With the police hot on their heels, the three "musketeers" (as they call themselves), reduced to their underwear, take refuge in a forest where they have hidden their winter clothing in a valise they had suspended from a tree. Shimmying up the rope to retrieve the troupe's effects, little Faho displays simian talents, inspiring them to create an act featuring a talking monkey. Soon after, with stunningly beautiful tightrope performer Olivette (Olive Borden) on board, they craft a show that quickly becomes the rage of Paris. Realizing that Faho the monkey (who goes by the name of Jocko) has fallen in love with Olivette (his own love object), Armand declares to his diminutive friend (implicitly referring to silent cinema), "I will not speak while she cannot see you as a man." Unknowingly hired by Mata to fill out the program with a lion-taming act, Maisie and Bergerin enter the scene. Mata voids the contract he had tendered when the musketeers apprise him of Maisie's intentions. Jilted and enervated, hellbent on destroying the act, Maisie encourages Bergerin to replace Jocko with a real monkey who rapes Olivette before Jocko escapes from his cage in time to free the lion from an adjacent cage. The beast ravages Bergerin and (implicitly) devours Maisie in her dressing room. Jocko escapes on the rooftops of Paris, but the police eventually shoot him. Wounded, he has strength enough to return to the stage to perform the act in which he rides a bicycle in a circle before he expires in Olivette's embrace.

Enter Sadie Thompson

The Monkey Talks includes close-ups of Fano's face in costume: staring accusingly at the camera, angrily, as if he were behind invisible bars, he seems to ask us why he is masked and gagged and why he deserves the sorry condition to which he has been consigned. Summoning the simian condition of both the narrative and the industry producing its effects, the shots prompt us to wonder why, as if in a zoo, we are looking at the film. No wonder, perhaps, that it goes unmentioned in *Each Man in His Time*, for reason of its beastly underside and what it implies about the impact of the Great War and the imminent onslaught of the Depression. Not so, however, with what in his recollections Walsh reports about *Sadie Thompson*, in which we are invited to behold and enjoy unabashed beauty that wins the day. The inverse of the forbidding, moody, and depressive *Monkey Talks*, appearing on its heels, *Sadie Thompson* is percussive, boisterous, and in the end a testament to women's cinema. Counting among the last silent films Walsh directed before adapting to the talkie, it displays the swaggering director in his last days before losing his right eye while filming *In Old Arizona* (1929), in which he had been cast as the Cisco Kid.

Exploiting the talents of two established stars (Gloria Swanson and Lionel Barrymore, one of his close friends), Walsh wrote a version of the script that included a leading role for which he was the model. Actor and codirector, Walsh had before him a consummate supporting cast (including Will Stanton and James Marcus, who had been the infamous Conway of *Regeneration*), an accomplished set designer (William Cameron Menzies), and three seasoned directors of photography (George Barnes, Robert Kurrle, and Oliver Marsh). Responding to trends of the moment, *Sadie Thompson* brings to the screen a freewheeling adaptation of W. Somerset Maugham's 1921 well-known novella, "Miss Thompson." First published in *The Smart Set*, soon retitled under the name of *Rain*, the story was fashioned into a Broadway play that witnessed considerable success. Along with *The Moon and Sixpence*, the British author's trenchant critique of colonial control under the cloak of Christian piety (including what today is called compulsory heterosexuality), the gist of the story suggests that in view of the Hays Code it would be tricky to put on screen. And, after what Walsh had done to defy censure and censorship in other films of the 1920s, tricky it was. Fox Studios, for whom he had directed twenty-three films since *Regeneration*, backed off. Walsh wrote a script and, as history would have it, asked Swanson to encourage Maugham to write another story about the same character. Producers at United Artists found the ideal character for its title role in Swanson, a seductive and seasoned actress of mettle, beauty, and swagger. But what about "Handsome O'Hara," Sadie's lover, who was central to the stage play on Broadway? Swanson, who codirected the feature, "told Walsh he should play Handsome" (Moss 2011, 103). He reputedly "blushed" at the thought, especially since his last screen appearance had been thirteen years before, in 1915, as John Wilkes Booth in *The Birth of a Nation*. Given his role as an unabashed and clear-sighted sergeant of Irish character, under Walsh's command *Sadie Thompson* emerges from correlative features portraying the lives and times of soldiers in the First World War and after (Moss 2011, 1:01–04).[5] By a short stretch of the imagination, parts of *Sadie* seem paradigmatic of *The Naked and the Dead* (1958), *Marines, Let's Go* (1961), and, above all and even intimately (as noted in chapter 4), *The Revolt of Mamie Stover* (1956), a late feature that today holds a high place in studies of cinema and feminism.

The Story

Maugham's "Miss Thompson" begins on a boat en route to Apia that moors in the harbor of Pago Pago. A measles epidemic requires the crew and passengers to disembark and remain in isolation for ten days. Two couples, the Macphails (the husband, from whose point of view the narrative is told, is a veteran of the World War I) and the Davidsons (the husband a missionary hellbent on converting natives to Christianity and his wife, in unstinting admiration of her husband's person and project) have been unaware of Miss Thompson, a solitary traveler and also disembarking, who is obliged to share lodging with them in Trader Horn's rickety hotel. In a room adjacent to a dining area where the couples sit at the table to get acquainted, Miss Thompson gathers some sailors around a Victrola. Flirting and cavorting with the men, she enlivens the atmosphere. Din and joyous noise enrage Davidson. Beside himself, the missionary orders the music and revelry to stop. Suddenly recalling that Miss Thompson had boarded the ship at Honolulu, he surmises she had been a denizen of the city's red-light district, whereupon, with due diligence, he orders her to be shipped to a "penitentiary" in San Francisco where she must "repent" to save her soul. Afraid and distraught, Miss Thompson, whom Davidson (unbeknownst to himself) now calls "Sadie," finally yields to his commands. Crazed with desire, obsessed by the relentless pounding of rain, for three days he holds her in a hypnotic spell. On a morning when the sky finally clears some natives discover Davidson's body, its throat severed, lying on a beach. After learning of what appears to have been Davidson's suicide, and after a brief moment of remorse, Sadie comes to her senses. Famously, and in the tenor of a committed feminist, her last words ring in her company's ears: "You men! You filthy, dirty pigs! You're all the same, all of you. Pigs! Pigs!" As Maugham wrote them, the last words of the tale shift to the point of view of the implicit narrator: "Dr Macphail grasped. He understood."[6]

At its outset, unlike the first sentences of Maugham's short story, *Sadie Thompson* begins *not* from the point of view of the ship approaching the harbor but amidst Marines (residents of the "barracks" in Walsh's war movies), in listless isolation in the South Seas, billeted to occupy an outpost under American possession. Comprising a chorus of sorts, the soldiers thirst after white men and white women (the intertitles suggest that either sex will do), objects of reverie and fantasy, until Sadie's arrival.[7] Told from a neutral, even indeterminate standpoint that sets Macphail in the background, the film juxtaposes the missionary's power to hypnotize (a power not unrelated to cinema) with farce and healthy obscenity that punctuate the War Trilogy.[8] From the get-go an implicit, almost proto-Brechtian aesthetic deploys comedy to mock the prurience of missionary righteousness. Herein a political issue that in his memoir Walsh had made oblique allusion to: Why are the Marines on Pago Pago? What are the soldiers really doing? Present in the film (and hardly in the tale), they beg us to wonder who or what authority told them to "occupy" the territory and why they must shoulder what Kipling infamously called "the white man's burden."[9] Unlike the tale, the montage begs us to wonder exactly where and how the film conveys Maugham's scathing critique of missionary Christianity. The narrative offers no clues, although it clearly correlates the missionary's hypnotic powers with those of silent cinema and its stars—especially Swanson—in their time of "glory." Conveyed in a lascivious stare Davidson (Lionel Barrymore) casts upon the heroine, it is countered by the bright eyes of the mediator-hero, Tim (Handsome) O'Hara (Walsh, director of the film within the film), a corrective force, who sees the world as it is.[10]

Contradiction and antithesis—what Walsh's mentor, Victor Hugo, called the "sovereign faculty of seeing the two sides of things"—is evident, first, in the design of the front credits and opening shots; soon after, in what happens where the intertitles cast speech into writing; and, notably in the later sequences, in the relation the montage and rhetoric of hypnosis establish with the experience of the film as a whole.[11] The effects are especially manifest in the remastered copy, in which editors replace damaged footage of its concluding minutes with still photos and a sequence from *Rain*, Lewis Milestone's remake of 1932. Given the discrepancies between the tale or stage play and the film, one of the aims of the paragraphs that follow is to discern productive contradictions inhering in the adaptation, singularly in how it deals with colonial policy at the time it was made; another, in line with this monograph, is to discern how, in a collaborative endeavor in which Swanson appears to be in command, the sense of a director's style and signature emerges.[12] Correlatively, as it happens in the study of cinema of times past, the wager is to displace a historical object that pertains to its own time and insert it into ours, where it might address (or betray) structural and ideological issues of longer duration. As seen in the first chapter, at the risk of belabored analysis, attention will focus on how the film works between what it writes or says in image and intertitle and what it puts before our eyes. Without placing undue emphasis on the plot, the nature of the adaptation, or the players' biographies, the reading will move from the opening minutes to the way bodies are depicted throughout the film as a whole and then to what it does with caricature and implicit obscenity, which appear implemented to offset hypnosis, which in turn is inferred to be a modus operandi of cinema. Finally, it will be worth seeing if *Sadie Thompson* might be a prototypical "woman's film" in a man's world, especially in the restored conclusion considered in the colonial context, in which an implied critique of the command of men over women could extend to a nation over its possessions.[13]

What Price, Gloria? Front Credits and Exposition

Like an enigma or a riddle whose solution is found in what it states, the front matter of a good deal of classical cinema tends to sum up what it heralds. The credits in the opening minutes of *Sadie Thompson* are no exception, in which the formatting seems designed to establish a field of tension. At the top of the first title card (fig. 2.1) stands (in roman majuscule) "Gloria Swanson Productions Inc" and at the bottom of the frame, as if in echo or counterpoint, "A Raoul Walsh Production." Set between inverted commas, the title (in italic) stands in deference to "Gloria Swanson," the name and surname (in roman) dominating the visual field in bold upper-case roman type that dissolves into the second card. "Adapted and Directed by Raoul Walsh" (fig. 2.2), set in bold, spells the name of the leading star seen in the previous card, while the mention of adaptation implies that the director is an "author" or, at the very least, a dedicated editor. The second card dissolves into a third, which signals

Figure 2.1. *Sadie Thompson*, first title card.

Figure 2.2. Second title card.

Figure 2.3. List of dramatis personae.

the eminence of art director William Cameron Menzies (following the masterwork of *The Thief of Baghdad* in 1924) who crafted the milieu of the hotel and interiors, photographers Oliver Marsh, Georges Barnes, and Robert Kurrle, and C. Gardner Sullivan (editor responsible for the copious intertitles). Finally (fig. 2.3), the order (or declension) of the lingering list of dramatis personae (01:12–49) shows more than what it enumerates. Counterpoint prevails at the *top* of the listing of the nine players and their names with "Alfred Davidson—*Lionel Barrymore*" while at the *bottom*, "Sadie Thompson—*Gloria Swanson*" sits below "Sergeant Tim O'Hara—Raoul Walsh." Over Walsh stands "Quartermaster Bates—*Will Stanton*," the onomastic (or, as it were, "onanomastic") drift of his rank and name suggesting the character belongs to a collective, to a chorus of players and viewers for whom pleasure is self-gratifying.[14]

The first image of the film is a piece of writing (01:41 indicating, as had the cast card, that jokes are the rules of the game. The front credits fade into a locative intertitle of long duration [01:40–54] [14 seconds]), alluding to the title of Maugham's story ("Rain," whose direct quotation permissions did not allow), while playing cat-and-mouse with codes of decency:

> Pago Pago—in the
> sultry South Seas—
> where there is no need
> for bedclothes—yet
> the rain comes down in
> sheets . . .[15]

Following the pun on rain and bedding, emerging from a fade, an iris opens onto a bogus seascape where, in the waters beyond the fronds of palm trees in the foreground, a cargo ship approaches the shore.[16] Natives and the foreign occupants, Marines in doughboy hats—for viewers of 1928, possibly refugees from Walsh's *What Price Glory?*—scurry about their business. In the middle ground a group of American soldiers in uniform walks to the right, a native woman ambles left, and in the corner a dark, muscular native wearing a lei, his torso bared, looks at the spectacle from behind, a standpoint mediating the spectator's point of view (01:53–02:05) (6 seconds).

Picking up on the ellipsis in the first intertitle, the second (02:05–16) reads:

> . . . and a detachment of
> U. S. Marines spend
> weary months of exile
> from white men—and
> white women.   [02:06–17] (9 seconds)[17]

The "detached" Marines occupy the island—because they are there. Nowhere is it stated they might be pawns of agendas reaching back to the Philippine War of 1899–1902 that included exploitation and development of interests in the South Pacific. The burden the US marines (or, in the film's graphic unconscious, "us" Marines) are shouldering, hardly of their own doing, is inferred owing to an absent cause. Linear scansion of the intertitle suggests that they starve, first and foremost, for white *men* and then, in second place, for white *women*. A nod to healthy homophilia? Perhaps: the medium shot that follows displays nine idle Marines clustering around a bale of goods (02:17–21) (5 seconds). A Marine on the left poses his hand on his belt buckle; another, legs spread, poses his left hand near his genitals; a Marine in the lower right corner of the frame, sucking on a cigarette, looks to the left with the others. One soldier wears an MP armband (in the center of the frame), suggesting that the military police are as famished as those whom they are assigned to surveil. All remain unfazed when three half-dressed natives dart by. A chorus of sorts, the soldiers form a masculine confraternity for which females serve idle pursuits of unwarranted "occupation."[18] The shot that follows suggests as much. Six Marines, seen along a diagonal axis, sit upon or lean against a bulkhead. Wearing neckties and doughboy hats, they look about their environs. Smiling and laughing in bright light, they invite viewers to do the same—to consider the off-screen space and its situation (2:21:23 [3 seconds], fig. 2.4).[19] An intertitle follows, suggesting that its words could be of a collective or anonymous origin, as much on the part of the imaginary viewer (the viewer the film is fashioning) as any or all of the Marines:

> That boat from San
> Francisco sure looks
>   good to me!   (02:21–31). (10 seconds)

In its long duration (vis-à-vis much of the montage) the shot begs us to ask who or what "looks good to *me*": would what is desired be the six Marines as such, or possibly the viewer they seem to address? *Me*

Figure 2.4. Idle Marines at the port of Pago Pago (02:17).

is not just those portrayed in the film. It refers as much to *we* who are told to note that whatever is coming—the film being advertised within the narrative—"sure looks good." The indexical vagueness (or "weakened deixis") of the intertitle enhances the potential of a willed confusion of things erotic and things exotic. Brief and summary, the sixth shot (02:32–33) (1 second), cutting back to the fifth, does not respond to the questions raised since the beginning. Now resembling a chorus in a classical drama, the soldiers mediate what the film is plotting and what it is doing with an unspoken (but collectively shared) agenda to pursue what "looks good." Shots of short duration are measured to conform with the serial disposition of the intertitles, which tend—herein the beauty of silent cinema—*not* to transcribe speech as might the words of a narrator who would move the film along its path.

The story gets underway with the arrival of the steamship, and with it comes the first of two decisive "scenes of writing" within the narrative.[20] The film cuts (back) to the Marines gawking at what approaches (02:33–34) (2 seconds). Suddenly, unannounced:

1. Long shot of the front of the boat where the captain and co-captain stand on the upper deck and, in shadow, four passengers (identified by their white hats) stand on the tier below. To the right a crewmember seems to be looking to his right, below, at a minuscule figure in the lower left corner of the frame, who wears a visor, whose forearms are posed on the railing (fig. 2.5) (02:33–37) (4 seconds). Eight shots below it will aver that, although isolated here, the person will become Sadie Thompson.

2. Medium close-up of Davidson (not yet named, whom a seasoned viewer would identify as Lionel Barrymore), wearing a bow tie and dark jacket and sporting a white cap, standing in front of an officer who looks directly at the camera from the left side of the frame. Barrymore turns toward a primly dressed female before looking at an officer who salutes him in passage. It is he to whom the words of the following intertitle seem attributed. (02:37–41) (4 seconds)

Figure 2.5. Long shot of the boat arriving in Pago Pago.

3. *Intertitle*:

   Would you please
   write something in my
       autograph album?   (02:41–47) (6 seconds)

4. Barrymore takes a pen in his hand and, with sanctimonious flourish, raises the pen and album. Then he writes an inscription (while the officer remains in shadow). (02:47:52) (5 seconds)

   The knife of reform is the
   only hope of a sin-sick
   world.
       Alfred Davidson.   (02:52–3:01) (9 seconds)

The shot dissolves from the hand to the finished script.

5. Now baptized with his proper name, Davidson hands the pen and album to his unctuously smiling wife, the camera panning right as she looks forward and enters her words in the album. (03:02–08) (6 seconds)

6. Dissolve from her hand that scripts a majuscule A (a scarlet letter) into the message in cursive:

   A righteous man will
   not hesitate to denounce
   evil.
       Mrs. Alfred Davidson.   (03:08–16) (8 seconds)

7. Mrs. Davidson passes the album to the steward (the camera panning right) who walks left, handing the pen and book to a couple who are now seen for the first time. The next personage in the shot, reflective, looks up for inspiration, nods, and scribbles some words (3:09–23) (19 seconds) dissolving into a finished and vertical cursive of a slightly different hand, whose autograph identified Mr. and Mrs. McPhail:

   Tolerance is such a splendid
   virtue it's a pity so few of
   us have it.
       Dr. and Mrs. Angus McPhail   (03:27–38) (11 seconds)

8. Cut to the McPhail couple, smiling, who look ahead as the steward picks up the pen and album and turns right (03:38–42) (4 seconds).

9. Cut to a view of the ship's railing, in diagonal, opens onto a bright and atmospheric view of the island and the space of a palm-lined harbor complementing the scene. The steward descends from the left edge of the frame, in the dark, along a passageway and a stairwell. The eye is drawn to the woman, who was barely perceptible in the establishing shot, leaning over the railing. She proudly displays her handsome rump. While two crew members in the background polish the railing, the steward descends and gazes upon her corpulence. He salutes and hands the items to the woman (still unnamed in the exposition). She bends over and arches back, turning to the steward (03:43–46) (3 seconds).

10. Medium close-up of the woman, now clearly Gloria Swanson, who wears a visor and sports a man's necktie. Her lips break into a voracious and toothy smile. The steward hands her the logbook that Davidson and his company have just signed. First putting the pen to her lips as if in search of words (objects of erotic fantasy), she then begins to write (03:47–55) (7 seconds).

11. Dissolve, as shown before, into the pen writing (now in a different cursive) and identifying its author who is the title of the film:

Smile, Bozo, smile, for no
matter how tough it is today
it's bound to be more tomorrow.
    Sadie Thompson.   (03:55–04:07) (12 seconds)

The conflicts and tensions to follow are graphically evident. More directly than the novella's exposition, the sequence anchors, as the credits have already made clear, another "scene of writing." Of Freudian facture, now seemingly peculiar to silent cinema, the words penned in the album appear and disappear, but in the film as such they remain present in their graphic impressions and, in view of other intertitles, they become memory-traces of images. In putting forward different styles—manners of doing and living evinced in writing—the personages map out the conflicts to follow. Vital for the exercise of colonial and missionary power, the acts of writing also belong to the greater configuration of interrelated images and intertitles that engage, convey, and divert the narrative—and ultimately call for critical engagement with the relation of writing (including cinema), authority and power.[21] Already, and surely on the mind of the director (who was said to abhor censorship), the sequence begs viewers to recall a formula whose formulation "deconstructs" the character of writing:

The *pen is* stronger than the sword.

Emblematic of the loathsome Christian mission he personifies, Davidson's *pen* is recalled in scenes in which his eyes become inscriptive instruments, which engrave guilt and remorse on his object of attraction. As the film proceeds, Sadie, under his spell, envisages herself (in a dream-sequence) a *peni-tent* locked behind the bars of a *peni-tentiary*, in the single and sole dream-sequence of the entire film (1:04:13–25).[22]

Faces and Rumps

The pictured writing in the exposition punctuates and fuses with the narrative. But so also, in accord with other intertitles, it points to a play of bodies that carry the story. The exposition continues:

12. Sadie smiles, salutes the steward. Turning about-face to look at a yacht in the harbor, displaying her backside, she refuses to acknowledge the camera that films her (04:08–12) (4 seconds).

13. Close-up of the captain gesticulating with his arms and hands. As if overseeing the mooring of the boat, his attention is drawn to what (a) seems to be the dock, and/or (b), in respect to the former shot, when the film is read both backward and forward, the hind side of the woman at the railing, whom he seems to be asking to turn around to display her maximal virtues. As the shot develops it appears that he is ordering his crew to dock the boat (04:13–17) (4 seconds) (fig. 2.6).

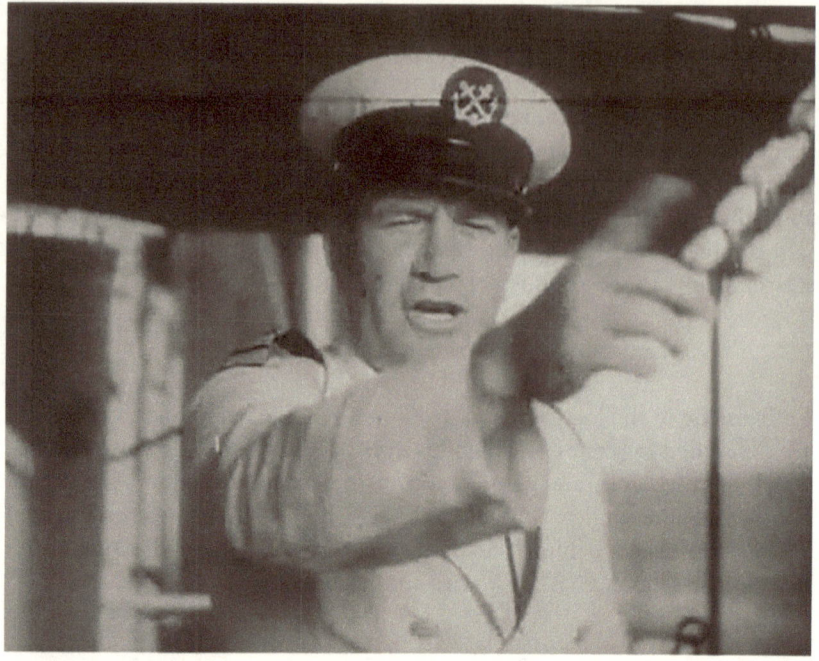

Figure 2.6. The captain orders the crew to moor the boat to the dock.

14. Quick dissolve, still from the captain's point of view, of the back and buttocks of a crew member, mooring the craft, who loops a rope around a piling. For an instant in the dissolve the rope appears strung over the captain's neck (04:17–20 [3 seconds], fig. 2.7).

15. Dissolve to a medium shot of two crew members arranging the gangplank the passengers will take to disembark. In the upper right corner of the frame the chimney of one of the boat's smokestacks seems to stare at the viewer (04:20–25) (5 seconds).

16. Cut to a medium shot, in three-quarter angle, of the gangplank, the dock and the upper deck of the steamship on which two pupil-like lifebuoys are placed. Wearing a broad hat with marabout plumes, brandishing a folded parasol, Sadie (with her rear end in eminence) looks toward the dock below. Turning right, Sadie struts down the plank in full glory (04:25–30) (5 seconds).

A Monkey Talks to *Sadie Thompson* 43

Figure 2.7. A crewmember ties the boat to the dock, following the captain's orders (13:56).

In the passage from the captain on deck to the dockside, three or four shots signal how the film portrays its characters from opposing angles, backside and frontside. The quick but decisive take of the stevedore's behind, possibly a cue for the comedy that follows, belongs to a network of images in Walsh's oeuvre, shots focusing on posteriors seemingly looking back at (or "mooning") the viewer, that challenge prescribed codes of decency. They bring into their narratives the pleasure not only of what critic Mikhail Bakhtin, apropos Rabelais, had called "the lower body" (or, in French, *le bas corporel*) but also, in the philosophical vein of Spinoza, awareness of the unlimited virtues of what the body can do.[23]

In many interior shots the camera aims at the buttocks and behinds of characters who move forward and away, as if on a stage, into arenas of conflict. Diverting attention from what they (and we) see from their standpoint, positioned in medium shots, their hindsides momentarily occlude—but also open onto—the field of view. The lower body becomes a site of visual pleasure that risks being overlooked when attention is placed on the narrative or, too, where the intertitles are read at face value and not in view of double entendre. When fat Trader Horn welcomes Sadie into the hotel, which lacks the space to accommodate her, he suggests that she lodge in a pantry (as he infers, with other victuals). He remarks, aiming his paunch at her face,

>   I've got a large store
>   room in back.   (13:49–53)

Shown in an intertitle following the two-shot opposing the one and the other, for an instant the words could be a fragment of indirect discourse. Would Horn be following the script, or would Sadie be reflecting on the virtue of her own lower body? A quick cut to the couple as they were shown facing each other gives way to an intertitle that identifies who has spoken. Sadie turns the words—Horn's—into a *quid pro quo*:

>   A nice one in front,
>   too.   (13:56–58)

In focusing on the hotelier and his paunch, the camera makes oblique reference to "Jim Conway"—if he is the same James Marcus—who plays the obese, drunken, and abusive spouse at the beginning of *Regeneration*.[24] Generously corpulent, evidence of pleasures past, Horn's body is set in counterpoint to Davidson's thin, lean, and vicious aspect.[25]

The captain's gesticulations prompt these and other carnivalesque or farcical effects. When Sadie walks off with the Marines in the direction of the hotel, the tracking shot focuses on the wiggling buttocks leading the men along their way. When cavorting with the noncoms by the Victrola, where she now and again mimes the famous RCA logo of a dog listening to its "master's voice," Sadie pins an advertisement for a nonalcoholic beverage on Quartermaster Bates's derriere that faces the camera (15:46–48, a detail nowhere in Maugham's novella).[26] The poster and posterior remain in place when he approaches the Davidsons at the dinner table (17:15–20). And so forth: when Sadie meets O'Hara, she backs into a beaded doorway, pressing his doughboy hat to the behind (22:40–49) she shakes to the viewer's delight and (in the next shot) to Davidson's angry envy (22:50–52). Playing hide and seek, feigning a fistfight, laughing loudly, O'Hara (in other words, Walsh, the past master of boxing films) gently pummels Sadie, pushing her through a doorway (22:53–23:04). Cut to Davidson, livid, in a primal scene, who is excluded from what he jealously beholds; cut to Sadie from the back, proudly holding the hat against her rear end. An intertitle declares that O'Hara has fallen in love with Sadie: in medium depth in a long shot O'Hara is portrayed from the back. Sadie turns around. Pulling and adjusting his pants, he readies to take her by the arms.[27] The couple saunters toward a hammock in the background. The camera follows the pair, emphasizing their *glutei maximi* as they sit down to page through the sergeant's picture album (25:57–26:03)—which in turn draws still images and intertitles, otherwise outside of the visual field, directly into the film.

Photographic Memories

In the middle of one of the many downpours, wearing a slicker, O'Hara enters the hotel. He meets Sadie—in a fitting two-shot—and listens to what she says (and we read) about Davidson being "creepy." In classic silent style, using sign language, O'Hara raises his right arm and flexes his muscles to signal he will protect her. The couple approaches the hammock. He picks up an album, then she strolls over to the arm of a chair on which she rests and invites him to join her. An uncommonly brief (two-line) intertitle follows:

> Sit, down, Handsome—
> I ain't a reviewing stand.   (45:52–54)

Seated side by side, shot along a diagonal axis, the couple shares a brief moment of intimacy when they flip through the pages (45:59–46:12). The book opens on a photo of the smiling sergeant's youthful face attached to the body of an infant sitting erect in a perambulator (fig. 2.8). Whose face is it? Is it O'Hara's, or is it Raoul Walsh's? The four fingers of the infant's chubby left hand hold the vehicle, while in his right hand he grasps a feeding bottle capped with an immense nipple. O'Hara points his finger (that displays a ring) to the legend below: "Greetings." To and by whom is the salutation addressed? Is O'Hara speaking through writing to Sadie? Are Walsh and Swanson bidding welcome to the viewer? Is it an invitation to take part in the mix of points of view?[28] The photo of the man-child at the nipple points to a sensuous mélange of orality and faciality—Sadie and O'Hara are obsessive gum chewers—that runs through the film.[29] Like an intertitle arresting the montage, the still image forges a myth of the actor-director in the film he is making or, as the photo collage suggests, in which he is born and nourished. An instance of an *auteur* function? Mythomania? Recalling Walsh's first major role in a film other than his own, playing John Wilkes Booth in *The Birth of a Nation*, the sequence signals what would be "the birth of a relation." As the disposition of the front credits had shown, a nod is made to the director in harmony (or perhaps in eager rivalry) with the star and major producer.[30]

Not by chance does the sequence appear riddled with writing. Immediately after she has enjoyed looking at the album and the photograph of O'Hara/Walsh as man-baby, in the best of all theatrical traditions, the plot takes a twist when a messenger delivers a letter. Sadie opens the envelope. Via a long intertitle in white (48:17–28), for a moment we are privy to the typewritten words of the letter and signature of authority that Sadie will read. The following shot (48:30–35) portrays Sadie (in an iris) deciphering the text, exploding in anger, arising, and exiting. Placed midway in the film, set in glaring opposition to the image in the photo album, the sight of the typewritten note and governor's signature marks a turning point in the narrative. If, as poetry is about poetry, and cinema is about cinema, the sequence indicates that Sadie "reads" the outrageous

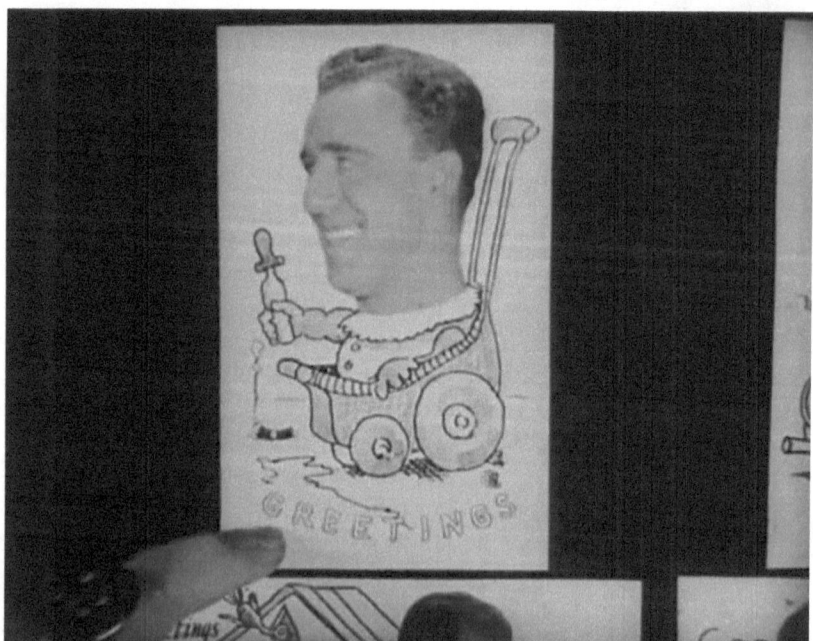

Figure 2.8. Portrait of the director as a grown baby: O'Hara/Walsh in the photo album (46:12).

letter, while the gesture of "reading" pertains to how the silent film is deciphered or decrypted, notably in the play of intertitles, that are to be seen and read, and to the reading of the film as such.

Sadie hands the letter to O'Hara, who then casts his gaze upon it (48:52–59), just as we, the spectators, having read the letter before, no sooner read (now in black) the intertitle that establishes the imaginary fulcrum of the narrative:

> I can't go back—
> I *can't* —— I'll go
> anywhere, but not back
>   there!   (49:03–08)

In a sudden shift in tone, Sadie confronts Davidson, gesticulating and shouting (in silence). Literally scripting the narrative, a cavalcade of three intertitles follows (48:30–52:00). Juxtaposed with shots of Sadie mouthing profanity, the intertitles imply that the Hays Code imposes unwished decorum to attenuate what lipreaders enjoy deciphering when focusing on Swanson's sensuous mouth. Adjacent to O'Hara, looking toward Davidson, she shouts,

> Was I doing you any
> harm? You bloodthirsty
>   Buzzard! Was I . . .   (51:11–16)

> Who gave *you* the right
> to pass judgment on
> *me*? You psalm-singing
>   louse!   (51:21–26)

> You'd tear out your own
> mother's heart, if she
> didn't agree with you,
> and call it saving her
>   soul!   (51:30–36)

So visible are the words that, nonplussed, the ladies (Mrs. Macphail and Mrs. Davidson) press their hands to their ears and exit hurriedly into the rain. O'Hara muffles Sadie's mouth with his hand (51:56–52:01) before dragging her outside into the rain. In the midst of the downpour he accompanies her under an umbrella and leads her through the turnstile outside the hotel. Calling in question the codes imposing prurient decency, the sequence touches on an emergent trope, resonant here, but running through other Walsh films of the late 1920s, that signals a proto-Brechtian "distanciation." As if she were an avatar of an alpha female or preempting the banter Sergeants Flagg and Quirt will share in *The Cock-Eyed World*, Sadie/Swanson challenges authority of masculine origin or inflection. "Who gave *you* the right . . . ?" *What* agency, exactly *who* ("in God's so-called name"), dictates the rules of behavior and decorum, and how and why in cinema?[31] In concert with Maugham's tale, she asks why Christian missionaries are meddling with the natives. By implicitly querying American foreign policy, in concert with the opening sequence the question begs viewers to wonder why and by the authority of whom a military force is granted privilege to occupy Pago Pago.

The ensuing section of the film uses the rhetoric of silent cinema to reflect on the political underside of the feature and on the character of cinema in the late 1920s. Convincing her to mend her ways, Davidson draws Sadie into his orbit. A modus vivendi of silent cinema, much as Jocko had been under the spell of Olivette's beauty in *The Monkey Talks*, hypnosis gains force, transforming the heroine into a penitent Magdalene. In the narrative three days pass before O'Hara happens upon the figure who is a ghost of herself. Looking like a refugee from the eerie illumination of Georges de la Tour's paintings, seen in backlit interiors, Sadie becomes pale, listless, zombified (1:13:45). Her condition is countered by her lover's common sense.

> No, Sadie! This old
> hyena's got you so
> hypnotized it's like
>   you're doped!   (1:17:40–45)

Now "penitent," abject, browbeaten into remorse and guilt, Sadie exudes an austere beauty enhancing a vampish charm that throttles the missionary's lust.

Suddenly and slyly, a decisive intertitle intervenes to subvert the moody scene and setting. Under Davidson's spell, dazed, as if outside of her body, Sadie shuffles to the quarters Horn had found for her. In chiaroscuro, in the light of a bright kerosene lamp placed on a table in the dark room, exhausted and emotionally drained, she slumps face down on a mattress. A dormer window reflects the rain, striking its panes (1:21–27). Cut to Davidson standing under a bright wall lamp in the lobby of the hotel, as if witnessing what we viewers are seeing.

Clasping and rubbing his hands in eager delight, he turns around while the Macphails exit (right), and Mrs. Davidson enters (left) (1:27–37). A two-shot portrays Davidson facing Sadie, solemnly raising his right hand, addressing her, and announcing through the intertitle,

> Sadie Thompson has
> been reborn —— her
> soul is   cleansed,
>   glorified!   (1:21:42–47)

Isolated, at the tail of the intertitle, *glorified!*, a curtsey to "Gloria," puts a tear in the narrative. Collapsing the melodrama, calling attention less to Sadie than Swanson, it momentarily "deconstructs" or "de-territorializes" the mise-en-scène.[32] Melodrama gives way to comedy—another indication that in taking a distance from its narrative the film draws attention to its "mode of production" and, if Hollywood is included in the scope of the frame, to its ideological machinery.

Soon after, in perhaps in the single most erotic shot of the feature, in close-up, supine, Sadie nightmarishly frets and tosses (1:23:35–44, fig. 2.9).[33] Slightly disheveled, her dark hair spread on a white pillow, eyes

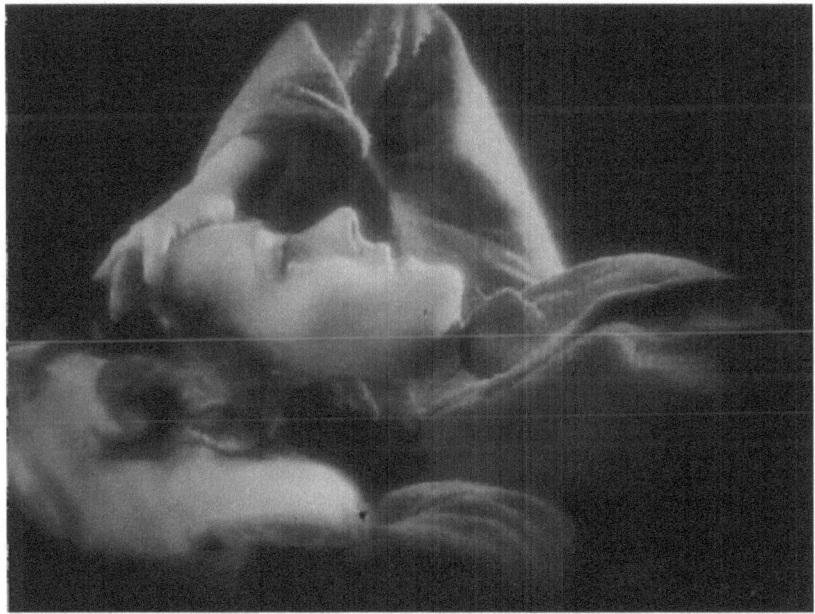

Figure 2.9. Sadie, abject, under Davidson's spell, ruminates in bed.

closed and mouth open, she could be dreaming as much of congress with O'Hara as she is (in the narrative) lapsing into abjection. Who could see her from this angle? From the vantage point of the narrative, it could be Davidson in his imagination, in the ecstasy of a wet dream but also, what the film projects in the tradition in poetry of the "dormeuse," in poetry the sleeping beauty the male contemplates alone, in complicated pleasure.[34] Sadie arises and soon encounters the demonic missionary who asks what she is doing. Pallid, a maiden of death, ruminating, she speaks (in the silence of the intertitle) of her fear while reproducing the conditions of watching a film in a movie theater.

> I was afraid to stay
> in my room—I got to
> seeing things in the
>   dark.   (1:25:47–52)

The relation of hypnosis and cinema is made glaringly clear. Soon the remains of the film give way to a conclusion crafted from production stills and some final daylight scenes taken from *Rain*, Lewis Milestone's remake of 1932, in which Joan Crawford is cast as Sadie.

The End

The preface to the remastered copy states that the history of the damage done to *Sadie Thompson* is tragic. To obviate the loss of the final scenes "from the sole existing print" (00:26), editor Dennis Doros coordinated the original script of the last scenes with "the stars' own collection of stills, and film footage approximating the missing section where possible." Grafted onto the film, the sequence from *Rain* depicting the discovery of Davidson's body begins with a fade-in to dawn (1:27:29–39) (10 seconds). Shot from a boat gently wafting at sea, beyond the harbor of Pago Pago, the scene dissolves to an establishing shot of the same port (in reality, on Catalina Island) exactly where *Sadie* had been filmed. Far in the distance and barely visible, in counterpoint to a barrel brimming with water from the night's rainfall, in the distance a minuscule fisherman casts a net in the shallow water (1:27: 40–50) (10 seconds). After so many sequences in the dark interiors of Horn's hotel, the outdoors and light of day change the tenor of the film: suddenly the day is bright, sunshine suggests dry warmth and, in sum, a return to life. An iris in medium close-up registers the native fisherman, his torso bare, pulling his net to gather his catch. Cut to a closer view (1:27:50–54, fig. 2.10): his bare arms, upper body, faint reminders of the natives seen in the very first shots, suddenly bring the film to life. Focusing on his muscular frame and the firm nipples of his chest, the shot makes visible what the story and the montage had been obliged to repress. The ensuing shots hold on the nude torso in recording the native who finds a clothed leg caught in the webbing. Discovering Davidson's cadaver, then with help from fellow fishermen, the indigene extracts the body from the surf. A friend runs off to the hotel to deliver the news.

Hardly detrimental to the tempo and texture of *Sadie*, the sequence introduces a sudden change in visual style that comes as a relief. In harmonic counterpoint with the dark rooms of Horn's hotel where much of the film takes place, however conventional it may be, dawn is a beginning befitting the ending. The suffocating atmosphere of the interiors and

Figure 2.10. A native finds Davidson's corpse in his fishing net.

cutaways of endlessly pounding rain give way to the welcoming sense of a *genius loci*. Without prurience or voyeurism, the clip celebrates the bare, muscular, and lithe bodies of the autochtones that everyone—Marines, tourists, missionaries—had refused to acknowledge. At this moment a cultural plurality is felt—one that had been refused, repressed, invisible, outside of the gated hotel, beyond the makeshift turnstile (a primitive variant of what viewers in 1928 might have associated with New York subway stations).[35] Paradoxically, the sequence taken from Milestone's remake brings a vital critical and aesthetic agency to both the film and its source of inspiration.

For the remainder of the restoration that ends on the promise of the new life Sadie and O'Hara will share (1:25:57–1:27:38 and 1:28:28–1:31:46), the editors mix images of previously seen film with production stills. Foremost is the final shot (1:31:25–46) (21 seconds), where, fading into view, in the style of Ken Burns's mode of closing in upon or moving across still pictures in his depictions of American history, the film fades into a photo-op of the couple who sit on the turnstile in front of the hotel (fig. 2.11). Whether identified as Sadie and O'Hara,

Figure 2.11. Photo-op of Swanson and Walsh on the set of *Sadie Thompson*.

or Gloria and Raoul, the pair strike a lively pose. In casual uniform, Walsh props his buttocks against one of its arms (fashioned from a canoe paddle) while Swanson sits on its opposite member. Holding the handle of an open parasol, its long rod resting on his left shoulder (to have its canopy double as a sort of halo), she wears a wide-brimmed hat and flaunts a fluffy stole—unlikely apparel for a torrid climate—matching her striped dress decorated with her monogram (ST). Smiling broadly, she looks into Walsh's eyes. Returning her gaze, as if eager and willing, he beckons with his right thumb to say they can spin off to Sydney and live happily ever after. His left hand grasps a long arm of the turnstile that thrusts forward diagonally, in trompe l'oeil, as if to indicate, ready as ever, he surely has the means and measure to satisfy her desires. The fur of the stole descends to her crotch where a slice of shadow implies that secret delights lie beneath the folds of the dress and, too, between the lines of the film and much more.[36] It may be that memories of this very moment and its situation inspired the making of *The Revolt of Mamie Stover* (1956) because of its resemblance to *Sadie Thompson*, which is the topic of chapter 4.

3

Eyes and Cockeyes

The Cock-Eyed World

We all gotta die some time. Me, you, whole cock-eyed world. [Don't] make much difference what kills us.[1]

Cockeye: Noun. An eye that squints or is afflicted by strabismus. (Apple Dictionary)

Cockeye, n. [*cock* to turn up + *eye*] A squinting eye

Cockeyed, *adj.* 1. Having a cockeye or cockeyes. 2. *Slang.* **a** Slanted or twisted awry; as, knocked *cockeyed.* **b** Slightly intoxicated. (Webster's *New Collegiate Dictionary*)

❧

It is strange to think that *The Cock-Eyed World*, a film touching on vagaries of sight and vision, was released on October 20, 1929, almost two weeks after Raoul Walsh lost his right eye while directing and playing the Cisco Kid in *In Old Arizona* (1928), a first "outdoor" western talkie shot in Utah, in the Zion and Bryce Canyon National Parks. In his memoir he briefly describes *The Cock-Eyed World*, a sequel to *What Price Glory?* (1926), before reminiscing about the production of *Sadie Thompson* (1928), which like *In Old Arizona*, premiered earlier. Walsh began working on *The Cock-Eyed World* when *The Loves of Carmen* (1927) was "still being cut and [also, or along with] *Women of All Nations*" (Moss 2011, 103), the latter eventually a talkie, that lay in wait before premiering four years later on May 31, 1931.[2] *Women of All Nations* would have been the third panel of the triptych, a final chapter of a saga that began in the feature of 1926 in which two professional soldiers in the trenches of northern France in 1917–1918, an odd couple, enemy brothers and spiteful lovers, bungle their lives and loves. Three years later, in *The Cock-Eyed World* (1929), they occupy Vladivostok before returning to the Brooklyn Navy Yard and the Bowery in lower Manhattan and then shoving off to the Caribbean before heading "home."

A Photo Op

Even if *The Cock-Eyed World* was finished before the director's enucleation, the ocular effects of what happened to the director in Bryce Canyon are spelled out in the title and so also in a photo op taken during the production (fig. 3.1). Tipped into *Each Man in His Time*, the poster cel-

Figure 3.1. A photo op: the players and eye-patched director of *The Cock-Eyed World*. From left: Victor McLaglen, Lili Damita, Edmund Lowe, and Raoul Walsh.

ebrates the film's release. Wearing an eye patch and a sailor's hat, Walsh stands beside the three leading players. He points a finger at a large globe behind Lily D'Amita, the leading lady who presses her right hand to her thigh and exposes her legs to the camera. Painted with eyes crossed, as if ravished by her knee and muscular calf, the globe is all smiles. To the right, sitting at one corner of the table dressed in military uniform, Flagg (Victor McLaglen) displays a top sergeant's insignia on the sleeve of his right arm. Pointing the index finger of his right hand at both the globe and Lily's buxom body, he grins with delight. To the left of the sphere, his legs astride the other corner of the table, with no visible rank and file, smirking mischievously, Harry Quirt (Edmund Lowe), points at the globe—or perhaps at Lily's bare knee. Her left forearm pressing on him, Lily aims her finger at the cross-eyed world beneath her.

The photo op suggests that the film has to do with things deictic and demonstrative—with indicative "signs," what volumes of film theory call "indexicality." The players' smiles tell us that because of its prequel, *What Price Glory?*, the film is a comedy or, in line with Shakespeare, a mixed genre that blends war with tomfoolery and barracks humor with bloodshed. And where Marines and the world are concerned, it also deals with post-1918 military policy. What the three players' fingers point at is anyone's guess: a cross-eyed or a cock-eyed world? At whoever or whatever agency—including the film—that names it as such? In the same breath, does the film question the authority or authorities whose "catchwords" or "order-formulas" appoint or assign functions to subjects as they deem fine and fitting? In this chapter, with *Sadie Thompson* in mind, the aim is to look away from the feature's legacy as a half-baked, half-assed cavalcade of adolescent antics and toward what it implies: in the direction of wit, farce, and political invective. In turn, we can consider in what ways, shot as it was in both silent and sound versions, the film plays on and off old and new technologies and "styles." Drawing inspiration from a "low norm," medieval satire harking back to the fabliau, the title asks viewers to consider a world out of joint or gone awry, whose sense (if sense there is) is best seen and heard in double entendre, jokes, and visible forms, masking others of a different order and hidden in plain sight, historians of art associate with anamorphosis.[3] We are invited to appreciate it, first, as a silent film (in which gesture is a spoken language, moving lips are seen to be savored as they are read, sound cues to make noise as "mute speakers") and, second, in the sense of an experiment in a new medium, where voice, music, speech, and noise scatter over the field of the image, by its disposition, which asks us to share a critical relation with what is being shown—in other words, as in the films studied above, a proto-Brechtian "distanciation."

Front Credits, Design, and Exposition

Set in bordered sans-serif majuscule, the title card (fig. 3.2) suggests that when C **O** CK-EYED is seen standing over W **O** RLD, the two **O**s suggest a presence of binocular vision. We are invited to imagine the vowels as two pupils, in slight asymmetry,

    l **o o** king

at the viewer from an angle perpendicular to the title itself, in a "cock-eyed" fashion. Standing at the top, "William Fox" is countered at the bottom (or the lower world of the card) by a "Raoul Walsh Production" (0:03–05). A man of means and muscle, Victor McLaglen (now in his second major film), a man of muscle and means, merits slightly higher point size than Edmund Lowe, Lily Damita, and El Brendel. In the space of two seconds the film dissolves into the card (0:06–08) announcing the director's name. Heralded and trumpeted with military fanfare, the third (0:09–21) acknowledges Laurence Stallings and Maxwell Anderson, authors

Figure 3.2. *The Cock-Eyed World*, title card and front credit.

of the Broadway play and screenwriters for *What Price Glory?* (starring McLaglen, Lowe, and Brendel), the source of Walsh's eponymous "smash hit" of 1926. With little ado the credit fades into a quotation of ribald innuendo. "And if sometimes our conduck / isn't all your fancy paints: / Why, single men in barricks / don't grow into plaster saints" (0:24–38). Memories of recent features come forward: Kipling's name cannot fail to prompt recall of the author known for the concept of the "white man's burden" at the core of *Sadie Thompson* and central to the tropical sequence crowning *The Cock-Eyed World*.

To the sound of martial music the first intertitle—much like that inaugurating the story of *Sadie Thompson*—is a joke. Conforming to the model of classical (Macrobian) geography,[4] it designates the first of the film's three thermal "zones" of activity:

Vladivostok, Russia—
Where the thermo-
meter registered thirty
degrees below zero, but
the U. S. Marines were
hot on the job.   (00:40–51)

A half-hour of skirt chasing in eastern Siberia (00:04:00–31:00) gives way to more of the same in New York City, an area of transit (31:00–53:30) before much of the film (53:30–1:55:60) takes place in the tropical or "torrid zone." In the first sequence the Marines are stationed on the eastern coast of the Soviet Union, sent on furlough to New York, and shipped off to the Tropics.[5] The film begins in Vladivostok, inferring that the Marines belong to the American Expeditionary Force (1918–1920), who were sent to the eastern border of the newly formed Soviet Union to fight the Revolution and sustain the Tzarist regime. Fresh with memories of combat on the battlefields of northeastern France and the war they waged with themselves over Charmaine (Dolores del Rio), professional soldiers, pawns of policies that order their lives, Flagg and Quirt go where they are ordered or told to go. They "lay over" in New York, an island whose rules and manners are not of their calling or station, before they are shipped off to occupy an unspecified region—the Caribbean (with innuendo of the Philippines)—where they don't belong.

Following the lusty epigraph attributed to Kipling, an intertitle, a classic sign of the lexicon and legacy of silent cinema, indicates that a military comedy will ensue. An establishing shot of a backlot Moscow in fake snow (00:54–01:11) is busied with horses and sleighs crossing an open square. A second and third shot pan left and right across a space where soldiers assemble (01:11–30). Cut to a superior officer, facing a regiment in winter dress standing at attention. In due protocol, he salutes and delivers an order to a captain who faces him. "Captain Griffith, your outfit will move out of Russia at 10:00 tomorrow morning."[6] The captain, timidly: "Yes, sir." "Destination: Brooklyn Navy Yard." Timidly again: "Yes, sir." Cut to a tracking shot of the faces of seven Marines (among them El Brendel), wearing fur caps who hear the order, smile, and giggle with delight (0:1:40–50). Cut to the captain who meets Sergeant Flagg, sauntering into frame and commanding the men to disband. Flagg gets mocked before he faces the camera, holding the straps of his rucksack, growling:

> Now listen you guys, when you got here, I ordered you mugs to *lay off the broads*. If any of you disobeyed my orders [now gesticulating with his right hand, indicating that the men scatter and do what he says], now go and settle your accounts before you leave. (3:18–34)

An official command turns into a double bind. A superior officer delivers orders to a captain, who passes them to a sergeant, who repeats them, inferring nonetheless that transgression is permissible:[7] "Lay off." Is Flagg inviting the soldiers to *lay* and in the same breath, *not to lay*, to pull back, away, and *off*? His order to settle accounts alludes to encounters where confrontation (with possibility of war) precedes, when it is successful, viable exchange.[8] The joke, an exercise in economy and settling of differences, would count among the many snatches of dialogue that aim at the Hays Code. Basically a *quid pro quo*, a "this for that," the joke is a weapon and a model of exchange. A "fable" of sorts, it asks its listener or spectator to see and read words and images with and against what they state.[9] Second, because *The Cock-Eyed World* is a sequel to *What Price Glory?*, a feature of strong political signature, we are asked to consider how the feature deals with stakes not only of power, capital, and military policy in a different venue but also of its strategic virtue in the moment of its making, at the cusp of the Great Depression.

Viewers who had seen *What Price Glory?* might have wondered how and when Quirt, Flagg's alter ego, lover, brother, rival, and enemy—or all at once—would enter the mise-en-scène. Flagg has just ordered his men to prepare for departure. He happens upon a soldier, his back turned to the camera, who has not been counted among the troops who had stood before the superior officer and the captain. Flagg, yells (*voice-off*), in classical interpellation:

"Hey Quirt!"

(03:36). Cut to the soldier, turning around while lighting and puffing on a cigarette, now recognized as (trickster) Harry Quirt, who responds: "Yeah?" Flagg's riposte, in his best Irish accent: "You heard them guys! And that goes for *you too*!" The innocuous exchange is doubled when, off and out of frame, Flagg's un-synched words are matched by a fist and an index finger, entering from the bottom right of the frame, aimed at Quirt (fig. 3.3). The sequence is crafted to imply that in its brevity the deictic (demarcating here from there and a superior from an inferior) begs a question of authority:

Who is empowered to order and why?

Figure 3.3. An accusative index finger points at Harry Quirt.

When Flagg puts strong vocal stress on *you too*, floating about the image, the words imply that they could be directed at the viewer (you, too) and at the couple we see from a distance (you two). What is the function of an accusative finger that enters the frame? The first of many in the film, the finger prompts consideration of issues of power. In close-up in two-shot (03:43–45), their noses almost touching, in profile, while each face a mirror of the other, Quirt barks, "Sez-who?" And Flagg: "Sez-me!"[10] Despite itself (or the legacy of the three features built around the Flagg-Quirt scenario), whenever the two men get at each other, their banter queries the nature of empowerment and the *absent causes* that legitimize it.

Seemingly of little relation to the question of who or what grants authority, the next sequence (03:49–04:20) asks viewers to consider how power is invested in what might be called sanctioned violation (or, in the idiolect of Michel Foucault, *illegalism*).[11] The camera follows a woman running after a soldier, contrary to Flagg's orders, who has not settled his accounts with her. As if rehearsing Freud's famous cauldron argument, the soldier says to Flagg while the woman pleads before him, "I don't know nothin' about it" (03:55). Flagg, between the two: "Wait a minute, wait a minute!" In medium close-up, in a two-shot that now *excludes* the woman who wails angrily, he looks at the soldier, the index finger of his right hand pointing (in her direction) off screen, "Did you do that?" "Do what?" Flagg, continuing to point: "What she said!" Soldier: "What did she say?" Flagg, resigned: "Oh, I dunno." Soldier: "Then I didn't do it!" Flagg, gesticulating, sending the soldier off (right),"come on, beat it, go on, get away!" The woman now addresses Flagg in Russian. He points at her with his right index finger, "Fine, you're all right, I believe everything you say. We'll see you again some time" (4:12–19). He leaves, the camera holds for an instant on the plighted woman. Shifting from Flagg to Quirt, the sequence doubles itself. In medium close-up, at a three-quarter angle, Quirt addresses a heavily garbed woman (seen from behind). Contrary to the Russian who was exploited or violated, the female, one of Quirt's lovers, gives him a piece of paper (a photo?), while insisting (in Pidgin English) that her memento is a gift. Smirking ("Quirt" rhymes with "Squirt"), he responds cynically, "Such a life, baby," as he puts the card into a back pocket by his rump, in a gesture shown as if he were wiping his backside with her image, while he adds, "I'll always wear it next to my heart" (04:29). The character of the male gender could not be clearer.

Pushing the Envelope

Before the Marines prepare to leave Vladivostok, referring to episodes in *What Price Glory?*, Quirt goads Flagg about the outcomes of their adventures behind the lines of battle. When they fought over Charmaine (Dolores del Rio), Quirt was a paragon of devious charm and his companion a delightful oaf. Spit-polishing his shoes while Flagg does his knitting, as if seeking the spectator's approbation, Quirt aims sarcasm (again) at the Hays Code and the prurience of the movie industry: "You call this war? Why it's even gotten so they won't even allow a gentleman to swear!" Flagg (then known among lipreaders for his profanity in *What Price Glory?*, when he looked at the camera, addressing Quirt and the audience, *you son of a bitch*) barks back, shifting from words eliciting speculation on the medium and its situation in Hollywood to the plot: "That's sure tough on you!" And Quirt: "Say, when they cut out swearin' they took out two-thirds of your language" (10:33–38).

The film assigns itself to swear otherwise, to push to a limit codified rules about what can be seen and what can be said. Walsh confirms this in his memoir, referring to *Sadie Thompson*, recalling his battles with censors over the duration of his embrace with Gloria Swanson. Emblematic, he recalls (as does Moss in her biography), was the moment in *The Cock-Eyed World* when El Brendel, in the company of three women who fawn over him, shows a topographical map to Sergeant Flagg. Unfolding the paper before the sergeant's eyes, he states, tongue-in-cheek, that he has "the lay of the land." The director's memory of the sequence affirms that here and in other films he had loathed censorship. A form of illegalism, censorship allowed the screenwriter, director, and producer to play with and against its rules in a game of hide and seek, much like what major media both cover and display in many magazines or newspapers: ravishing mannequins in silky blouses—erect nipples pushing at the fabric—while they stare at the viewer, their mouths slightly open as if heaving with desire at the sight of the viewing the reader. Or, in polymorphous appeal, handsome male models display great bulges in the midsections of tight jeans they are paid to display. The models on display elicit desire and fascination, and not, as in this film, laughter or satire that would turn them into ridicule.[12]

The Cock-Eyed World is so laced with double entendre that its play of cat and mouse with the Hays Code often overtakes the rivalry of the two Marines or the story of their itinerary. Here and there the novelty of the soundtrack in 1929 enables salacious comedy, while in others the arrangement of bodies in the composition turns pornography into farce. Three moments are keynote. A first and most robust episode comes with the two Marines hot on the trail of "Olga," a Russian prostitute of local repute.[13] On the eve of departure from Vladivostok, sneaking out of the dormitory where his troops are fast asleep and snoring, Flagg encounters Yump Olson (Brendel), who displays to the sergeant an alluring photo of a woman in negligee who displays a scantily covered breast (0.20: 39–42). Her name is not lost on Quirt who is in earshot. Deciding to pursue his quarry, he holds the photo high when, in a rapid dissolve that tells all, the image Quirt looks at gives way to a poster of a bare-chested wrestler on the wall of a nightclub (20:47–48) filled with song and merriment. When Quirt enters to inquire about Olga, a bartender wields a knife that slices Quirt's left eye (fig. 3.4). Oppositional montage: the camera dollies back to include the smoke-filled room that Quirt—and not Flagg—enters, then inches forward as he looks about apprehensively, approaching the bar to inquire of an "Olga" (20:45–21:10). He goes upstairs, meets, and soon charms Olga with magic tricks (for which he

Figure 3.4. Quirt's eye sliced by a knife in the tavern and bordello in Vladivostok.

had been known at the beginning of *What Price Glory?*) that define him, in the strict anthropological sense, as a *trickster*.[14] Olga's maid exits and then, as if in a peep show, opens a curtain to see what is happening. A shadow cuts down from her forehead to her cheek before her face comes into full view, slyly watching the seduction—as if to stress, first, a copresence of monocular and binocular vision and, for a second, a cock-eyed effect (fig. 3.5). Flagg enters and climbs upstairs. Cut to Olga, arched over recumbent Quirt, who shares a cigarette with him (25:12). Opening the curtains, watching the scene from behind, Flagg gazes upon Olga's capacious rump. Delighted, he fails to notice Quirt on the bottom. Eagerly removing his heavy overcoat, he knocks over a cup. The clatter surprises Olga, who raises her head from Quirt's midsection and turns around (the audible noise drawing attention to the new technology of the talkie). Grimacing, Flagg utters (as if referring to Quirt's antics in *What Price Glory?*) "So you're up to your old tricks again," to which, in a quick cut, Quirt responds, "No, I've got a lotta new ones" (25:34).

Figure 3.5. Her right eye sliced by a shadow, a maid watches a magic trick Quirt performs on Olga.

The banter continues. Quirt tells Flagg, "*Blow, blow,*" and Flagg retorts, "I don't hear her tellin' me to *blow*" (26:12). Finally exiting, Flagg wins the *quid pro quo* with an obscenely genial parting shot: "Hey Olga, you'll need a lotta face powder if you hang around with that guy" (26:44). So obvious is the analgesic "face powder" and the framing of the shots depicting Olga performing her blow job that it seems as if the Hays Code, far from imposing censure, was in collusion with screenwriters, producers, and directors.[15]

By virtue of design and point of view, the sequence is at the antipodes of cinema that exploits the trauma of an "originary" or Freudian scene in which, beholding its parents in coitus, a child—the ideal viewer of cinema—realizes that it is superfluous or excluded from the world it had felt to be its own.[16] Farce overcomes trauma. Frustrated but hardly devastated, Flagg goes downstairs to the cabaret where a famed "Lanavitch," a great muscle man wearing a fur cap and heavy overcoat, enters the establishment, salutes the clientele, and *turns directly toward the camera* (27:16–19, for three seconds), inviting us to join the party (27:00–27:53). Carefully composed, beginning *before* it catches Lanavitch entering the scene, the shot pans across a wall displaying posters that seem to celebrate the Russian Revolution and the triumph of the working class. Pulling the spectator into the space, the writing and images displayed on the posters flatten the depth of field. Like Lanavitch, an implied populist, they invoke a political situation to which the film makes oblique reference. The revelers in the cabaret belong to a community born of a revolution that promotes its spoils through broadsheets and printed images. Telling Flagg that the poster portrays "Lanavitch," "the strongest man in the world," a local reveler backs away so that only his hand can be seen with the index finger pointing at the poster (among the others, its legend the only one *not* of Cyrillic characters) (27:59–60). In concert, both men aim their fingers upward, toward what will be Lanavitch's encounter with Quirt and his lover.

Quirt's encounter with Lanavitch is crafted as if to fracture the effects of a "mirror stage." The Russian wrestler bolts upstairs, enters the apartment, suspects hanky-panky, and (like the maid and Flagg earlier), opens a curtain to peer at the scene from which he is excluded (28:39). In direct counter-shot (28:43–49) he enters while Quirt, his back turned to the Russian, takes a swig from a bottle. Cut to a close-up of Lanavitch watching Quirt, then to his point of view, that displays his buttocks before our eyes (28:52–29:01). Cut to Lanavitch in the background, viewing Quirt, glib and satiated, who looks directly at the viewer (29:04–09).

Back to Lanavitch, immobile (reflected in a mirror, still unseen) at which Quirt stares (his head, out of focus, in the right foreground): Quips Quirt (voice-off), mistaking one kind of image for another), "Hey Olga, who made this paintin'?" (29:09–16). Olga (voice-off, in a heavy Russian accent): "painting?" Cut to the scene from the point of view of the mirror (29:17–30). Quirt: "The paintin' with the mug with the mouth." Olga enters from left, pivots, looking at the viewer, suddenly realizing that Lanavitch stands behind Quirt. Aghast, she cries (voice-in but not synched): "[S]*anavitch!*" Quirt (-in and synched), implicitly identifying himself as the *son-of-a-bitch* he is: "Who, me?" Lanavitch enters, and bedlam ensues: a primal scene goes awry. A gag and a joke, the sequence is also about who sees and how, about reflectors, reflection and, via voice-in and voice-off, the invention of cinematic space.

Bedlam on the Bowery

Copresence of monocular and binocular vision marks an immediately transitional sequence (33:10–35:50) in which, sharing a stateroom on the ship delivering the troops to a furlough in New York, jabbing at each other as usual, Flagg and Quirt prepare for life at "home." Quirt will leave the service to become a "promoter" (a "promotah") and Flagg, professional soldier through and through, remains faithful—*semper fi*—to his calling. Flagg faces a mirror while shaving. Quirt sits behind him to the left, and between them an open porthole, an eye of sorts—perhaps the eye of history—bears witness to soldiers amassing and moving about in the space beyond. The men rehearse the usual question concerning authority ("Sez-who?"—"Sez me!," etc.) just as a "third" voice can be heard in Flagg's words touch on American military policy and its economy. Responding to Quirt's opinion that wars are over (recalling the slogan that the Great War was the "war to end all wars"), Flagg astutely observes (1) that war and conflict are sempiternal, ever unending and (2), anticipating the bombing sequence later in the film, that new logistics will require air power in coordination with the traditional deployment of infantry.

As if referring to the League of Nations, the diplomatic agency that will resolve all international conflict, Quirt states that countries now share among each other a "voibal agreement" (34:32). Flagg, mirrored, remarks almost intuitively, brandishing his shaver: "Why it ain't worth the paper it's written on." Quirt: "Sez-you!" Cut to Flagg: "Sez me! What are they fightin' for in China and Mexico? The fight's goin' all over the world." Quirt: "What's that have to do with us? We ain't gonna have no trouble." Cut to Flagg, turning away from the mirror while the porthole window stares at him (witnessing the conversation), his sleeves rolled up, displaying the tattoos on both arms and pointing his razor at Quirt, "So we ain't, ain't we? What are we men meant for? [. . .]. What are big battleships built for? And why [sic] are guys workin' on new poison chemicals for? [. . .]. Maim and destroy! Why half the dough that's spent on them aero-planes would educate the world." The film slips away from direct consideration of policy and diplomacy by equivocating military conflict with the men's battle for the women of the nations they occupy—but only to return later in the film, when Flagg affirms that war will be best waged with air power.[17] The film's ostensive smut is yoked to issues where cinema, military technology, and power are intimately correlated.[18]

New York becomes the setting of a second and joyously lewd episode. In a variation on the encounter with Olga, filching Quirt's address book, Flagg obtains a date with "Fanny" (Jean Laverty), first seen in a bathtub, whom he takes to Coney Island where they enjoy a swim in a crowded pool (44:05). Fanny prepares to take a dive. Seen from the backside (fig. 3.6), in extreme close-up at the right side of the frame, the cleft of her buttocks is thrust toward the viewer in trompe l'oeil while Flagg, standing in the pool with his arms outstretched and muscular torso on full display, awaits her leap. What *he* would wish to see in all his delight is what *we* see in soft focus: Fanny's bottom, establishing a comic play of "perspectival objects" in counterpoint.[19] The couple frolics in the waves. Flagg asks her to spread her legs before he swims under them and lifts her out of the pool. The pair soon walk by a scale where clients are invited to guess their "weight and fate" (45:35). Flagg discovers Quirt, hardly the "promotah" he promised to be, who mans the scale. Flagg breaks out, open mouthed, as he had in the Russian tavern ("Auf Magaw!"), laughing boisterously. Annoyed, standing under the scale whose arrow points directly at her, Fanny turns to Quirt who asks, "Do you want to get weighed, baby?" (46:14). In concert with the Olga episode, he hands the lady a rose, to which Flagg adds defiantly, "So you're still workin' from the back" while Quirt, smirking, whispers in Fanny's ear, "Anytime you wanna get weighed, come and see me, alone." Flagg pulls her away and, with a parting shot, yells, "Goodbye, big promotah!" Built on two flagrantly obscene puns, the episode repeats the pattern set in Vladivostok, indicating that the narrative, based on repetition and concatenating encounters of the same order, yields little or no resolution.[20]

Figure 3.6. Fanny readies to jump into the pool at Coney Island (44:05).

Following Orders

Well beyond the pale of other instances, a third and flagrant challenge to censure takes place in one of three routine sequences in which, following a chain of command, orders are passed from a superior officer to his top sergeant. Disembarked from the ship where he had exchanged impressions with another sergeant, Flagg arrives on the tropical island he and his troops are called upon to occupy. Carried in a horse and buggy, recovering from a hangover, he steps down and proceeds into the headquarters (56:06–34). A quick pan defines a typically bureaucratic setting where officers busy themselves with paperwork. Passing by a wall decorated with maps, the camera follows Flagg to the desk where two soldiers (one seated in a chair, the other at a table) interrupt their tasks to acknowledge his arrival (56:35–59). Voice, both -off and -in, mark the sound track. The backsides of the commanding officer and his adjutant who are speaking face the camera, indicating that the orders emanate from an unspecified source of authority. Flagg, however, facing the orderlies and addressing the audience: "Sir, Sergeant Flagg reporting for duty." Voice of the officer (from the table): "You're a little late, aren't you?" "Yes, sir." "Well, the major will take that up with you later. Get your company into shape. You're liable to moving out on short notice. [The seated officer turns his head down to read his papers.] That's all." *That's all*: Flagg turns about, the camera pans back to follow his exit.

The office and the arrangement of the men's bodies set the stage for an unprecedented variation on the same kind of scene only minutes later. As they were with Charmaine in *What Price Glory?*, Flagg and Quirt are rivals in pursuit of Mariana (Lily Damita), the voluptuous beauty of the island. In a rare moment of calm, outdoors, standing alone after being invited to serve as best man at the future marriage of one of his troops, Flagg is requisitioned by a soldier (1:22:59), first voice-in, who yells (in classic interpellation), "Hey, Sergeant Flagg!" Cut, now voice-off (hence of ungrounded authority): "Report to company command!" The camera responds, tracking the sergeant who struts off, donning a jacket and making haste in the direction of headquarters. Two shots later (1:28:18), Flagg enters the familiar space for a second time. Wearing a doughboy hat, the same superior officer, his back facing the camera, is seated at a table adjacent to a map on a wall. He sits calmly while two orderlies in the background, their faces visible, tend to their paperwork where they are seated. Accompanied by the Marine who interpellated him, Flagg passes between the camera and the officer. He turns toward the other side of the desk, at whose left stands, his back also facing the camera, a fourth Marine. His jacket open and unbuttoned, standing at ease, Flagg rests his right arm on the wall, holding his doughboy hat by its brim. For a moment his left index finger points toward the inner cavity of the hat and his groin and pubis (fig. 3.7). The voice of the person who seems to be the seated officer (both "off" and "in") utters tersely, "Sergeant Flagg, you've been down here in service before, haven't you?"

>**Flagg**: "Yes, Sir."
>
>**Officer**: "You know the country pretty well?"
>
>**Flagg**: "Yes, Sir."
>
>**Officer**, inching to his right: "Good. You and the company commander, Wagner, will be on a scouting patrol" (1:23:18–35)

Figure 3.7. Flagg receives orders to command a "dangerous mission" (1:23:55).

Cut to medium close up of Flagg, his jacket unbuttoned and wide open, standing before the head of the seated officer, shown in soft focus, first to the right of Flagg's midsection then directly in front of him. The accompanying Marine, to Flagg's left, looks intently at the officer who speaks. Officer: "You'll be gone between five and seven days. Now this is a very dangerous mission. But a very important one. . . . And if you have to make a forced landing [Flagg pulls his right hand out of his pant pocket]. Look out! Among Soreno's gang there are a lotta barbarians." [Flagg listens inquisitively.] And the last man they caught of ours, they buried him alive. [Flagg, as if a little more satisfied by what he hears, raises his left hand to the back of his head]. So if you have to come down, don't let them get their hands on the plane. Burn it. *That's all*. Good luck" [The officer turns his head away] (1:23:35–1:24:05, emphasis added).

Lasting thirty seconds, the briefing stages a fellatio. His jacket unbuttoned, Flagg looks at the officer whose face is at the level of his genitals. Dangerous mission or emission? What is it for Flagg to "come down" and to keep his "plane" (and its fuselage) from the hands of the enemy? Farcically obscene, the staging of the command is in flagrant defiance of good taste and, as the slogan goes, is an affront to "compulsory heterosexuality." Implied is that womanizing narrative sustains or is complemented by a gay (and joyous) order of queering that in 1929 the arts of framing and editing are enabled to convey.

A Politics

Early in the film the soldiers talk about their origins and the lives they lead. Opposing points of view in a way that aligns *The Cock-Eyed World* with a dialogical order tending to shatter thematic consistency or unity, the film asks us, first, to revisit what we think "home" happens to be and, in turn, to beware of media imposing the idea of a homeland, a national, or even an individual "identity."[21] The question about "home" is raised in the Russian sequence, in a laconic exchange between Flagg and a shy and "homesick" soldier. Smacking his hands to stay warm in the cold, Flagg looks around to see if his troops are in order (04:55–5:05). From the background where soldiers are gathered, the soldier comes forward and addresses Flagg, who stands to the left of a doorway in the background. Separated by the line of the door jamb between them, the soldier opines sadly, "Sergeant Flagg . . . how can I get transferred to a company . . . that's *not* going home?" Flagg: "What? In the Big War [in *What Price Glory?*] you was ravin' about gettin' back [he gesticulates with his thumb] and marryin' that gal of yours. Now what's the matter? Is she givin' you the gate?" The soldier: "Well, she promised to wait for me, but when I didn't get back, she married a pal of mine." Flagg, turning and grimacing, putting his arm on the soldier's shoulder, "What am I supposed to do, bust out cryin'? Aaagh, forget her, buddy, forget her. Maybe it's a break for us. [. . .]. I've been [turned away] loads of times. Listen! Between me and you [he points his fist and index finger at his interlocutor] right now! I'm sendin' twenty bucks a month to a jane in Joisey City. *And I know.* She's [with] a truck driver from New York. My good dough! Can you beat it? That don't say all janes are alike! The world is full 'o'good ones. I was once [taken] on a honey in Brooklyn." The soldier: "You mean you were nearly married once?" (5:00–6:04—one of the longer sequence shots in the film). Cut to a close-up of Flagg: "Once? [he turns his head away, smiling sarcastically, now pointing his finger at himself] 40 times! Some of 'em promised they'd stick and wait for me. Cause you can't blame them for changin' their minds. Cause what's the use of a man who's gone a month of Mondays? And sent for China on Thursday? You take it from me! When you've been in this racket as long as I have . . . you'll soon find out. [He raises his index finger high.]. There's only one . . . that'll stick by ya' . . . and wait for ya.' And that's ya' mothah" (06:05–38). [Almost mockingly, he pats the soldier on his right shoulder.]

The soldier, sadly: "But my mother is gone . . ."

Flagg, correcting his tone: "So is mine. [He pauses, looking for an answer.]. But that don't mean you have to forget her, does it? Forget the janes!" (06:38–47)

Perplexed, the soldier walks off and away. The matter is unresolved.

Toward the end of the exposition, readying for departure from Russia and on the heels of the communal, "last" meal that brought them together, the soldiers look forward to a layover in New York (09:36–49). Rubbing his hands, Quirt enters the barracks where (Mother) Flagg is sewing clothing. He announces blithely, "It'll sure feel good to get back home." Retorts Flagg, "Home, huh! Your home's in your hat!" Quirt: "Listen, flatface, I've got homes all over the woild, with a mama waitin' for me in each one." Flagg: 'Aaaagh, you ain't got no more homes than a frog's got feathers . . . [turning toward the third soldier to the left] how about it, [Bucky]?" Medium close-up of the contrite soldier: "You're right. We're here today and somewhere else tomorrow. We've never lived in one place long enough to have a home. Just roamin' and fightin' and preventin' fightin' to protect other homes" (09:49–10:03). The words uttered by a third or *other* voice breaks the sergeants' banter, attesting to homelessness as a total social and psychic fact, a condition to which Flagg subscribes ("That's our job") in a segue to Quirt's decision to leave the Marines and return to any one of his many abodes, clearly places where vagrant women are synonymous with home and hearth). To honor and emblazon military life, the sequence carefully avoids overstressing the effects either of rootlessness or the soldiers' relation to an imaginary motherland. A politics intervenes: the métier of the professional soldier dictates that apart from other men in the same order, no affective or sustained relation with anyone is possible. Thus, upon arrival in New York, if only for comedy of caricature, while other Marines of the regiment, two of different nationality (Italian) and religion (Jewish) briefly reunite with their kin, Quirt and Flagg have no one to greet them.

Arrival means departure. At the Port of New York, celebrating Quirt's decision to be done with military life and become a promoter, a diminutive Marine graced with a resonant voice intones "So Long," a lewd and politically incorrect song (that ought not be cited), which varies on "shoving off" (0:37:22–38:10). The melody becomes the feature's anthem. A medium shot centers on the little Marine who sings and the musicians around him. He chants, belting out what the lyrics describe:

> When Flagg discovered Sergeant Quirt,
> Walking down a road [was] a nifty little skirt
> The sergeant said [the singer cocks his fists], "lay off, you bum,
> Or I will knock you dead."
> But when he found out she was. . . .
> Now what do you think he said?
> So long . . . so long . . .
>
> This was once you was right and I was wrong!
> Now you're just the type for her
> So I beg your pardon, sir,
> So long, so long, so long, so long. . . .
> This was once you was right and I was wrong!
>
> [The camera dollies back, now revealing Flagg slouched on a table to the right, then panning slightly left to include Quirt, in civilian togs, who begins to clap.]
>
> Now you're just the type for her,
> So I beg your pardon, sir . . .
> So long, so long . . .

So long, a refrain of departure, goes with *that's all, scram, get away, lay off* or, as directors today would script the scene (one thinks of Quentin Tarantino), *fuck off.*

After all the merriment and mayhem in Manhattan, the third (or tropical) section of the film begins with a stock shot of a Cunard ocean liner leaving its pier on the Hudson River (53:54–59), fading into a crowd of soldiers standing on a lower deck, milling about, chattering and smoking, to the tune of "So Long." Rewritten for the occasion, the lyrics speak to the greater theme of perpetual departure:

So long, so long . . .
[We were off to win] the war,
And we were wrong,
Although we love the USA
We are glad to get away . . .
So long, so long . . ." (53:35–54:10, emphasis added).

And off they go. Cut to Flagg on a side deck, suddenly thrusting himself out of a porthole (an ocular form), intervening to stop the chatter and have his men get to business. In medium close-up, in a long take, from a diagonal angle a two-shot records Flagg and another sergeant (chevrons and ribbons proudly displayed) sharing impressions and wondering about the regiment's unknown destination (that could be the Philippines or Antilles as much as the Caribbean). Hungover and exhausted, delivered from jail, Flagg looks away, presumably at the New York skyline. Seated next to a taut chain behind his head, he casts his gaze on a sergeant to the right, smoking a cigarette, who remarks with snide irony: "How do ya' feel, Flagg?"

Figure 3.8. Flagg and a sergeant discuss their expedition to the tropics (54:20).

Flagg: "Rotten. When did I get on the ship?"

Sergeant, wryly: "Last night: on a shudder!"

Flagg: "Where's me company?"

Sergeant, puffing: "Left four days ago."

Flagg: "Where are we headed for?"

Sergeant: "Tropics. Nobody knows."

Flagg, turning left and right: "I know why! To protect big business! [gesticulating, pointing his index finger at the sergeant] Big business keeps us guys busy!"

Sergeant, continuing to drag on the cigarette: "Maybe you're right!"

Flagg: "I know I'm right! What's-His-Name has his interest in Where-Is-It. Who-Is-It comes along and makes a yell! Then Whaddaya-Call-Him butts in, and the next thing you know the marines are landed!"

Sergeant, wide-eyed, reacting in strong agreement: "I guess you're right!"

Flagg: "I know I'm right! I was down there [he points off] in 1910 . . ."

Sergeant, interrupting: "Is it hot down there?"

Flagg: "Sometimes it's so hot the hens lay fried eggs!"

Sergeant: "How is the grub?"

Flagg: "Okay . . . but great booze."

Sergeant, animated, smiling: "How long before we get there?"

Flagg: "Oh, about eight days on this dump, and two days over the trail."

Sergeant: Tell me it's a beautiful country. Beautiful scenery. Beautiful flowers."

Flagg: "And beautiful fever [the sergeant jumping with surprise] . . . and beautiful janes."

Sergeant, grinning: "Yeah?"

Flagg: "A little dark, but okay! [nudging the sergeant, and yawning] I gotta hit the hay." (54:20–55:48)

He disappears just before the friendly veteran mulls over his words. Flagg reiterates the point he had made about the Marines' rootlessness. Pawns of "big business," an absent, unsettling, and unquestioned cause, they are consigned to do due diligence in affairs of no concern to them. Unlike the "Great War" in *What Price Glory?*, when the rationale for American intervention convinced them they could fight with impunity "over there," in *The Cock-Eyed World* the occupation in Russia, the layover in New York, and expedition to the Tropics seem pointless—unless, as Flagg stressed earlier, the economy of war and conflict defines the human condition. Unspecified and without direct reference, Flagg's insistent remarks about "Big Business" could allude not only to the scandalous operations of the United Fruit Company; the obscene politics of intervention and occupation; American ingressions in the Philippines, Cuba, Central America, Vietnam, and elsewhere but also to the producers and distributors of the film itself. Although the names are floating signifiers, attributable to any number of referents, nonetheless "What's-His-Name," "Who-Is-It," "Whaddaya-Call-Him" and company accrue political resonance *before* Flagg reverts to memories of his tropical ventures of 1910. Given the tenuous links with the narrative, in their protracted duration the shot and the exchange imply that the expedition to the tropics is without reason or rationale.

The Cock-Eyed World may be best remembered for its trivial pursuits in the two-thirds of the film that follow. "Mariana" (Lily Damita), the female star who had been announced in the credits, finally appears on the heels of Flagg's first meeting with his superior officers. An erotic and exotic object par excellence, scantily attired, in cahoots with a duenna, she becomes a desirous point of reference. In tandem with—or avatar of—Charmaine in *What Price Glory?* or Carmen and her admirers in *The Loves of Carmen*, she flirts, cavorts, and baits Flagg and Quirt from beginning to end. Less a character than an icon, a physical specimen, she plays hide-and-seek with the Marines, ultimately mocking both the "gaze" they (and we) cast upon her. She defines a space where amorous conflict is a foil to the battle in the jungle.[22] When first seen (58:12–19), standing behind a caged parrot with Olson (El Brendel, the effeminate Marine who charms all the ladies), she embodies an unstated political stance. The bird-in-the-cage, generally associated with the condition of the female in a man's world, is altered. Psittacism is at stake: contiguity of the parrot and Mariana suggests that a colonized subject "parrots" the colonizers, seemingly conforming to their norms while thinking and living in ways unavailable or imperceptible to them.[23] A go-between or shifter in the conflict, in her dress and demeanor Mariana baits the censor and the viewer, while also using her mobility to disperse—or to mock—authority. She disappears when frolic gives way to war, but ultimately, in her raw beauty, she has the last and decisive parting shot.

It remains to see why. In a sequence foregrounding the battle with the insurrectionists Flagg pilots a rotary-engine biplane to reconnoiter the topography below. After a forced landing and three days spent in the brush he returns to headquarters with a map. In a scene that varies on the first meeting (1:23–24) at headquarters. Sporting a pair of goggles on his headgear (which stress the ocular issues in the film), Flagg gathers around a table strewn with maps. The mise-en-scène lays stress on acts of looking, reading, and deciphering, which implicitly ask us to do the same—hence to call the representation in question.[24] We learn that under their leader, Soreno, the enemy has gathered troops and armaments to counter the occupants of the island. A *voice-off* (in the twang of the officer who had spoken of the "dangerous mission" in the fellatio sequence) asks, "Where'd they get 'em?" Flagg, in response, voice-in: "big business, big business!" To which the unseen figure adds, "You said it!" (1:30:56–59). Flagg's mention of the unspecified cause prompts doubt: Have American producers supplied the enemy with ordnance for their own profit? Are the expedition and occupation a costly hoax? Like the film itself, is it a strategic operation designed to make waste?[25] Ensuing shots leave the questions unresolved. In sudden fraternal (and generously homoerotic) empathy, Flagg (a real hero) runs to the hospital to offer solace to Quirt (a coward) who is sick with malaria. Extending his arm to hold Quirt's hand, fearing the imminence of death, he leans over his friend, grieving as if to tender a kiss (in concert with the film's "cock-eyed" style), Flagg leaves the sick bay where, seconds later, grief gives way to aggression. News of insurrection arrives, reveille is trumpeted (as if to jumpstart the plot and in the film's silent version, to make the most of the sound cue).

Soldiers gather and march off and into the rainforest. Initially following the pattern of attack that had been shown in three waves in *What Price Glory?*, two successive tracking shots (1:37:25–54) record the Marines marching ahead (right to left), wading through swamps and jungle toward the enemy line, some advancing, others falling under rifle and machine-gun fire.[26] Point of view switches from the Marines to the insurrectionists (1:38:17–20), who operate a water-cooled machine gun, and back again to the infantry trudging ahead.[27] The drone of an airplane—another sound cue (1:38:15)—announces bombardment. The buzz on the soundtrack prompts a cut to a counter-tilt of the biplane above. Bombs (to which sirens are attached) are first shown in close-up, from the bay of the plane, from which they fall earthward (1:38:20–25) before three similar shots (1:39:9–11, 1:39:33, 1:40:26, perhaps from military footage) follow suit, the second depicting a landscape split by a river and the third the quarters where the enemy is gathered. This sequence cues on the noise and the whistle of falling bombs, opposing aerial and upward views, the montage setting in place what, not far from his words concerning the logo of 20th Century Fox, Paul Virilio (1989) had called a *logistics of perception*.[28]

After the bombardment the Marines sort through the wreckage. Responding to a soldier (voice-off), "This place looks my house after the mother-in-law called," Flagg, in medium close-up, his face and uniform sweaty and dirty, again raises his index finger, pointing skyward: "You said it! One of them planes can do the work of six battleships, four regiments, and [he spits almost contemptuously], a lot of generals." Voice-off (impossible to locate on any side of the frame): "I guess you're right, sergeant." Flagg, voice-in (repeating his own formula): "*I know I'm right. If it wasn't for them planes you guys would be in the muck for the next six months.*" Voice-off: "Yeah, it took that guy [the pilot, but also the sequence] "less than just six minutes!" Flagg, voice-in, gesticulating with his thumb raised, growling: "I'm tellin' ya! Them things make short wars! All of us foot soldiers will be out of a job . . . [pointing skyward]. Up there is where the next war 'll be!" (1:40:53–1:1:41:18). For a moment the narrative is suspended to promote reflection on cinema and the future of air power. The story intervenes, post facto, to mourn the dead: in protracted close-up Flagg tends to the homesick soldier, dying, for whom he was to be the "best man" at his marriage "back home" (1:42–1:43:13). In uncharacteristically extreme close-up, Flagg mourns him in silence before turning to the camera, breaking suspension of disbelief, ruminating over a waste of life (1:42:13–45): "Why couldn't it been me . . . , I ain't got nobody," his words dampening the celebration of coordinated air and ground power. The staging of the action scenes effectively discourages identification with winners or losers.

Shoving Off

And never more than at the conclusion. The narrative returns to the two soldiers who continue to battle over Mariana. They are surprised to discover she is betrothed to a diminutive and (to their *exorbitant* amazement) an effeminate *novio* named Capistrano. When the men ask her who he is, the camera cuts to Mariana at a doorway looking onto to a yard where a mule (or an ass) stands immobile. Suddenly a well-dressed local, carrying a cane, struts into the frame of action and embraces the beauty: a would-be primal, or at least, a disquieting scene showing the two Marines occulted or separated from their desired object (1:52–45–47) turns into farce. Mariana's duenna tosses the soldiers out of the household. Flagg cringes despite his size, and Quirt, half-dressed, trots off in a jacket and a pair of boxer shorts. Rescued by reveille, Flagg and Quirt hustle off to meet their troops at a bar where, awaiting departure, they joyously swill beer and wine. Unable or unwilling to foot the bill as he had promised, ugly American that he is, Quirt rips off the establishment and departs with the others. Oafs and nincompoops, the men don't belong where they are. The editing suggests that their departure is well taken.

The final shots and intertitle speak to the design of the film and its implications. Informed they will return to the Brooklyn Navy Yard (the site they had previously been happy to leave), the troops shoulder arms and parade away in fanfare (1:54:45–1:55:04; close up, 1:54:05–11). A cavalier view of the troops catches Mariana running alongside, jumping on a barrel, then standing, flanked by her duenna and Capistrano (fig. 3.9). Raising her skirt, waving her arms in proud display of her wet armpits, and raising her right leg (1:55:11–16), she bids them adieu. The last shot follows the troops marching away (1:55:30–41) before the last (and only third) title card caps the movie:

Figure 3.9. Mariana bids adieu to the marines (1:55:11).

Figure 3.10. End credit of *The Cock-Eyed World*.

Shove off—
That's all!

In place of an intertitle that would bring closure and resolution, the parting shot is open ended. It could be what it had been in the classical canon: *a Parthian shot*, a piece of wit, the last word of a *quid pro quo*, like an arrow fired by the fabled warriors on horseback, feigning retreat, who entice the enemy to advance, then shoot with their backs turned as they gallop off.[29] The final intertitle is cause for doubt: who orders the men to *shove off*? Would they be commanding officers barking "that's all"? And to whom is the intertitle addressed? To the soldiers, the audience, to a public at large? We are tempted to parrot Flagg and Quirt: *Sez-who*? If there is an implicit *sez-me*, who or what is the authority called "me"? William Fox and Company, ordering spectators to leave the theater and make room for the next showing? Mariana, flirting, telling the strangers to behold her thighs and no sooner get lost? From the standpoint of Hollywood in collusion with American foreign policy (in line with the Monroe Doctrine), does the remark beg armed forces to shove *off* the continent and occupy outer areas to better defend the mainland?

The unfinished end returns to what is stated in the exposition. In the first words he addresses to his company, standing next to a Jewish soldier named Goldberg, putting his thumbs to the straps of his knapsack, Flagg yells, "When you arrived here, I ordered you mugs to lay off the broads" (03:28–31). To *lay . . . off*: the statement invites transgression ("to lay") and, in the same breath, to stay away (be off and gone). A double bind: at its terminus the film prompts speculation on issues evident in the title. In a "cock-eyed" world masculine behavior is puerile, colonial designs go without saying, and authority is called in question. It is one in which sight is equated with lust. Despite its slapdash composition, beneath the bedroom farce, *The Cock-Eyed World* ends by posing questions about what it does and how it relates to a political and psychic malaise at the difficult moment of its release. The "Great War" whose carnage justified Flagg and Quirt's intervention is long gone. Now the two men simply go wherever military authority tells them to go. Yet, with the implementation of air power, wherever they happen to be, the stakes of combat will not be those they had known. As a tailpiece or an unfinished postscriptum, it can be ventured that *The Yellow Ticket*, appearing in 1931 on the heels of *Women of All Nations*, the dexter panel of the triptych that had *The Cock-Eyed World* in the center, the malaise is manifest in the prescient treatment of what would become, in the words Hitler pronounced at the Wannsee in 1943, early signs of "the Jewish question." Based on Michael Morton's play of the same name, that Victoria Morton reshaped in the form of a novel published in 1914, Anna Mirrel, a Jewess obliged to carry a yellow identity card, is the object of anti-Semite Baron Andreyev's lust. After being imprisoned and sullied, traumatized, she meets and convenes with Julian Rolfe, an Englishman, who becomes her savior. Far more lugubrious than its source, set on the eve of the First World War, the film makes clear the plight that is soon to come. Starring Lionel Barrymore in one of his most lascivious and evil roles, it also brings forward a dashing and handsome Lawrence Olivier, after playing in *Temporary Widow* (1930) and *Too Many Crooks* (1930), in an early and decisive role in his illustrious career. Photographed by James Wong Howe in *noir*-like style, we can say by virtue of hindsight, and at the cost of leaving closer inspection aside, *The Yellow Ticket* addresses what the men in *The Cock-Eyed World* would later confront and, as the following chapter contends, features shot in 1932 and 1933 would prefer to avoid.

4

From Sadie to Mamie

The Revolt of Mamie Stover

Adepts of auteur theory contend that great writers and great directors constantly alter, redo, rethink, and even invert themes and styles inspiring their creations. Greater than any of its individual works and rich in its mass and totality, an author's oeuvre is defined by variety, contradiction, and—paradoxically—an overriding coherence. In 1939 Jean Renoir famously stated that filmmakers of mark and measure spend their lives making "one film," a film in our collective imagination that could be a composite of all those they had ever made. Like Balzac, whose ninety-plus novels amount to a great "human comedy" of many facts, spaces, and places, so also, they say, when the term had currency, are *auteurs* of the stamp of Hitchcock, Ford, Hawks, Anthony Mann, Allan Dwan, Walsh, and others.[1] Quite often a director will produce a variation on or even consider reprising a work to fit—or to make sense of—different cultural conditions than those that had informed the original or ignited its spark of inspiration. In anticipation of broader treatment of Walsh's work in the later sound era, I would like to entertain the thought that *The Revolt of Mamie Stover* (1956), while not a remake of *Sadie Thompson*, appears born of its memory. A different and now revised or rounded reflection on masculinity unlike what marked the early years—or the director's "adolescence"—the feature of 1956 harks back to the force of attraction inspiring the late silent feature of 1928,[2] especially for the way the "man's world" of the late 1920s is rethought through the prism of femininity that perhaps Walsh first developed in his collaboration with Gloria Swanson.

Somerset Maugham's "Miss Thompson," the template for *Sadie Thompson*, we recall, ends when a community is finally rid of the lascivious Christian zealot who had violated and abused the unlikely heroine of its title.

> You men! You filthy, dirty pigs!
> You're all the same, all of you. Pigs!
> Pigs!

Sadie's invectives could have been in the thoughts of the heroine at the beginning of *The Revolt of Mamie Stover* (1955). The film tells the story of a prostitute, like Sadie, banned from San Francisco, who faces the challenge of making her way in a man's world. Unlike Sadie, however, Mamie doesn't have bevies of Marines rallying around her; nor, in the name of a Handsome Tim O'Hara, does Raoul Walsh come to Mamie's rescue. Sadie has resilience, ambition, and ultimately a sense of autonomy.[3] Unforgiving, cruel, self-indulgent, the men of the films of both 1928 and 1956 have little to do or share with the women who have brought them into their world—those who nourished, fed, or raised them before they became the piggish creatures they are. It can be said that *The Revolt of Mamie Stover*, recalling and rewriting *Sadie Thompson*, proposes a woman's film that fits for a moment, with some exceptions, in which postwar Hollywood seemed to assign itself the task of defining sexual difference, of establishing highly coded divisions of labor, and (as Jacques Rancière would have it) establishing unequal distribution or sharing of sensitivity. Mamie is the embodiment of a woman who makes herself and who realizes her potential as she goes.[4] An admirably *self-making* and eventually autonomous woman, in the context of what then were almost concurrent words of Simone de Beauvoir, the story of Mamie, who is not born a feminist, tells us how she implicitly becomes one. It may be that Mamie carries into a difficult time and space the spirit and will of her glorious forebear of 1928.

Set in a world light years from *Sadie Thompson*'s Pago Pago in the 1920s, following the Depression and World War II and shot partially on Oahu, *The Revolt of Mamie Stover* turns on its title: the heroine's revolt is at the threshold of a revolution. While conforming to an established pattern of "rolling back" front credits inaugurating a good deal of Hollywood features of the 1950s, the first shots suggest how and why. Prior to the display of the title, a "teaser," a snippet of narrative, locates the hour and place where the film begins and then identifies its central personage and where it might end. Amidst a dull bleat of foghorns and the sight of a cityscape in crepuscule, a first title card tells us (in both 1956 and here and now) we are in San Francisco in 1941. Seeing the Bay Bridge extending across the wide frame (its aspect-ratio 2:66–1:00), we realize, looking east, that we are at the *Embarcadero*: as if the name embedded in the image would indicate, the beginning is a point of arrival and departure. "Embarked" as Blaise Pascal had embarked us on the famous "bet" (*le pari*) in his *Pensées*, we are carried from "life" on the outside (ending when the requisite studio logo comes into view) and sail toward the darker realm of what the movie thinks and does.

A police car comes to a halt at the entry to a pier where, to the left, an oceangoing freighter is moored. After a cavalier (or crane's-eye) view of the scene, in a medium shot the left rear door of the car opens. A man and a woman step out. The camera dollies in, following the woman as she proceeds toward the boat. She stops at a fenced barrier, *turns around*, and stares intently at the viewer who might, we suddenly realize, be both ourselves and the policeman. Printed in bright red, the title of the film suddenly extends across the wide frame of Cinemascope (fig. 4.1). In concert with the subsequent title cards, a series of tracking shots accompanies her walking along the pier, a "woman with a suitcase" in one arm and a jacket in another. She strides down the pier in the darkness, boards a gangplank, and finds her way into the freighter. The plot begins to unfold in the sequence seen *through* the screen of credits, which include the title, the names of the players and listing of the agents, and agencies responsible for making the film. Attention is drawn

Figure 4.1. *The Revolt of Mamie Stover*, front credit.

to how the disposition of the words—their typography, point size, and spacing—relates to what seems to be shown behind them.[5] The woman's initial about-face, which could be taken as a refusal to be part of what ensues, stands independently of or opposed to the cards placed over her listing among the *dramatis personae*, the editors, managers, musicians, director of photography, producer, and finally the director—whose name appears when she enters the ship, the vehicle we assume to be a mode of transport, in other words, a *metaphor* of the movie as a whole.[6]

An Overture

At the risk of repetition, a closer and calibrated reading of the sequence reveals how the credits summarize and determine what follows:

0:01–10 20th Century Fox logo, a megalith of sculpted writing, extends across the screen while five moving beacons beam shafts of light into the aquamarine sky.[7]

0:10–18 Set in *cul-de-lampe* perspective enhancing the depth of field of the writing, stretching across the width the frame, in sans-serif typography:

> twentieth century-fox
> presents
> A
> C i n e m a S c o p e
> p i c t u r e

The majuscule A at the center of "Cinemascope" points to the A above, in slightly smaller point size, which draws the eyes into an imaginary depth of field and, laterally, across the broader and flatter horizon, what in 1956, three years after *The Robe* (1953) and subsequent features such the *King of the Khyber Rifles* (also 1953), rivaling 3-D, became the novelty of the wide screen. Sculpted to fit the framed space they create, the letters spelling "Cinemascope" both extend and amplify the image-field.

0:18–28 Cut to black, then a quick fade-in to an intertitle, now in Garamond, in fire-engine red letters,

San Francisco
1941

on a black background out of which sparkles of city lights emerge before the Presidio and Embarcadero become visible. As if chosen for Cinemascope, the outline of the Bay Bridge extends across the broad frame, suggesting, first (by way of allegory) that the film will deal with two areas or affective surfaces that may or may not "connect" with one another and that the new and uncommon wide-angle view will be one of the major elements, areas of tension, or even a player or "actant" in the film to follow. The scene is marked by a distant scream of sirens cutting through the darkness.[8]

0:29–34   In opposition to the preceding wide-angle view, a straight cut to a long shot in deep focus of a pier. An oceangoing freighter is moored to the left, and to the right stands an imposing building of tan concrete. A white fence blocks entry to the pier. On its ground the railroad tracks reach into the distance. A police car (now seen as the source of the siren) enters and comes to a gentle halt. Mellow trumpet music goes with the scene.

0:35–55   Cut to a medium shot of a plainclothesman in a trench coat, exiting from the left rear door of a 1941 Ford. Exiting the car, lugging a tan suitcase, he is followed by a woman with fulsome black hair. He hands her the baggage. In the background a tugboat toots a whistle twice to announce her entry. The camera dollies in to record her from the back, departing, leaving the plainclothesman in the intermediate space and out of view. She crosses the barrier at the entry to the pier, holding the suitcase in her right hand and a tan overcoat in her left. In the center of the wide frame, all of a sudden she turns around. Her red lips pursed, she stares at the camera directly, accusatively, angrily. Quickly emerging from the dark blue and black background of the dock and the ship in twilight, the title appears in bright red letters

The Revolt of

M A M I E S T O V E R

and extends across the frame. As if branded by the title, the woman looks back at the viewer contemptuously (fig. 4.1). The portrait and the title hold for six seconds (0:49–55) before quickly fading away. Then:

01:18–32   Medium tracking shot of Russell/Mamie walking right while the credits continue to dissolve in and out of the moving images.

01:33–02:26   Quick dissolve to a medium long shot, still tracking right, that goes with the walking woman and then stops to follow her along the pier. In the distance, she boards the boat, goes upstairs to the right and then along the deck to the left before exiting *into* the boat. The last title card signals the director's name against the diagonal view of the moored freighter. The woman disappears into an area between "Raoul" and "Walsh." Fade-out in blue-black. We behold the Bay Bridge stretching across the very wide frame, illuminated by a string of streetlights, standing against blue-black cloudy sky. Splotches of red light punctuate the skyline below the bridge while soft trumpet music continues.

0:02:26   Abrupt cut to a stateroom: a portly officer in khaki uniform enters a door from the left side of the frame where, in the middle, sitting at a round table, a man—clearly "Richard Egan"—listlessly reads a newspaper. The narrative begins over and again.

The play of the title and its background suggests that the beginning is an ending, or perhaps that at the outset for Stover *it's over*. A dividing line is drawn between a here (San Francisco) and a there (who knows where). In the first of the front credits her eyes tell us to *shove off* and so too does her abrupt turn when, dismissively, she shuns the camera and does the same. Looking at the viewer, her *right eye* is almost slivered by the extender of the letter *e*, like a sickle, that cuts across the top of her nose and joins the curve of her eyebrow.[9] Covering her left ear, a bar of the letter *v*, following the line of her hair, frames the portrait. Now named by the title superimposed on her defiant portraiture, Mamie moves ever so slightly to indicate that we are not viewing a still or dead image. We behold her in a critical relation she establishes with what the writing is stating. Stressing the ocular character of the film to follow, the credit sequence suggests that Mamie's *revolt* could be both contestation and revolution, the latter an itinerary that either returns to its point of departure or, in upheaval, reverses a condition of things.

And Another

Mamie is on route to Hawaii but not to Pago Pago where the rain had come down in sheets. She is going to Honolulu, in 1956 the capital of a utopian archipelago three years before Hawaii became the forty-ninth state of the union, a place Americans dreamed of visiting but also a site recalling what Walsh had filmed in 1923 in his *Lost and Found on a South Sea Island*. While aboard the freighter (that carries only two passengers), Mamie meets Jim Blair (Egan), whom she sees sharing a coffee with his older officer in a "man's" quarters, the latter having spoken of her with caution ("she means business!"). Mamie retreats to her cabin where (similar to the rhetoric of Jane Russell blockbusters), she unbuttons her blouse and goes to bed.[10] The next morning, apologizing for the importune words the men exchanged, again identifying himself as a writer, Jim strolls beside her on deck. Mulling over what he believes might be her "life story," he is eager to gather material for a future novel. While she tautly holds a strut line, after posing some leading questions, he learns of her difficult past that began in Leesburg, a rural town in Mississippi.

They find mutual attraction in playing horseshoes. It is not long before the pair embrace in front of two eyelike portholes that seem to be looking at them (fig. 4.2).[11] After arrival in Honolulu, despite living with Annalee (Joan Leslie), presumably his wife or partner with whom he shares a sumptuous villa overlooking the city, Jim lends Mamie enough money to get a fresh start. She meets up with Jackie Davis (Jorha Curtright), a former lady friend who obtains employment for her in a cabaret-seraglio where commissioned soldiers on the island (like the Marines on Pago

Figure 4.2. Mamie and Jim embrace in front of two portholes.

Pago in *Sadie Thompson*) eagerly buy tickets to spend calibrated time with ladies under the strict rule of the well-named Bertha Parchman (Agnes Moorehead), whose ways of living and being could not be more arid. Caged as it were, the ladies are forbidden to leave the area, to share any relations with men, to frequent Waikiki Beach and, moreover, to open a bank account of any kind.

Mamie quickly becomes Bertha's favorite and a jovial member of the women's community. After dyeing her hair red, soon known as "Flaming Mamie," Mamie begins to transgress. She picnics with Jim at the beach and accompanies him to his country club. Getting wind of her peccadillos, Harry Adkins (Michael Pate), Martha's bouncer, thrashes her in her stateroom. On the morning of December 7, 1941, a "day of infamy," Honolulu suddenly crashes into history when squadrons of Japanese planes bomb Pearl Harbor.[12] Amidst the pandemonium, Jim desperately seeks Mamie, who already speculates about investing in real estate in the wake of the attack. Catching up, breathless, he informs Mamie he has joined the Marines. Mamie begins buying properties devalued after the bombing that no sooner, by virtue of irony, she rents to the US military forces. Upon return to Honolulu during a furlough Jim proposes that she leave the club and marry him as soon as the war is over. At the country club (a *locus classicus* in this film and others of the 1950s), Harry finds Mamie sharing a table with Jim. Challenging Jim, a soft-speaking, muscular American who carries a big punch, Harry gets decked (and a black eye) in full view of the club's members and the military police. Firing Harry for his run-in, knowing that Mamie is a star attraction, Bertha convinces Mamie to stay with the club, first offering her half and, after Mamie hesitates, 70 percent of the club's commission. Mamie buys into the deal and, along the way, holding to the illusion of marrying Jim, rejects the advances of a married officer who promises to take her away. Meanwhile, in his barracks at the front lines, Jim is slightly wounded when a Japanese airplane drops a bomb that strikes the barracks where he and his soldiers have gathered. He takes a brief medical leave that allows him to return to Honolulu and retrieve Mamie. Finding her in the slough of the bungalow, dismayed at the sight of what she is doing and nonplussed by her success, he bids her goodbye. Initially heartbroken and disillusioned, she gives her money away and returns to San Francisco. When she disembarks (fittingly, at the Embarcadero) the plainclothesman who had driven her to the same spot at the beginning of the film reminds her that she is still banned from San Francisco. He amicably promises to drive her to the airport where she can catch a flight to Mississippi.

Like Sadie, who had been banished from the same city, Mamie lives in transit and exile. And like Sadie, although no longer the figure she had been in *The Outlaw* (shot two years after the "day of infamy"), Mamie is taken to be a voluptuous object of attraction. But unlike her avatar of 1928, clearsighted and calculating, Mamie attracts men whom she defies and exceeds. Sadie had arrived on Pago Pago with panache and pizzazz; when she forsakes a life among citizens who wear brightly colored shirts, Mamie returns to a world where it will be up to her to realize her promise. Another parallel: where Sadie had danced around a Victrola with admiring Marines, at the apex of her success in the Bungalow, Mamie, swinging her hips, sings "Keep Your Eyes on the Hands," a dazzling number telling the Marines to take keen note of a woman's signs—to acknowledge but not to touch. Where Sadie had been under the spell of a lascivious missionary in the alteration of Somerset Maugham's novella, before its turnabout (or "revolt"), the narrative of the later film stages Mamie as prey to the illusion she can lead a conjugal life with a man. Where (in guise of Handsome Tim O'Hara) Raoul Walsh comes to rescue Sadie and take her to an island where they can live happily ever after, Mamie turns toward an unknown future. Contrary to Sadie, who is hypnotized, Mamie is not. Nor does she, in the sequence when she breaks off from Jim, need to be remedied on a psychiatrist's couch. And like Sadie, who correctly dismisses men as pigs, Mamie returns to San Francisco, free of the men (including those of higher station) she had encountered in her earlier and recent life. Challenging the policeman who apprehends her, telling him he would be unable to comprehend her life story, Mamie's fresh eyes indicate that, well, for Stover *it's not over*. Mamie turns about again and goes off, revolt becoming the promise of a revolution. A woman's story is in the making in a man's world.

A Woman in Men's Quarters

Much like the overture, in anticipation of what the story delivers and congruent with the anamorphic aspect of Cinemascope, what is told in the first sequence spells out the tensions that run throughout the film. In conjunction with tracks and pans that draw attention to the flat and wide frame, the narrative begins when two men, an officer and a writer, meet in a compartment furnished with a table and, by a wall, a coffee machine (coffee being the universal solvent of life in postwar cinema). The staging and sweep of the camera tell much about what follows.

0:02:28–3:10: Medium shot, interior (forty-two seconds), which follows from left to right an officer entering through the door of the "Ward Room." Seated in the middle, dressed in a white shirt and holding a cup of coffee, Jim Blair (Egan) reads a newspaper plopped on an ashtray. An empty armchair is to the right: pan to the stout officer walking over to pour himself a cup of coffee from a pot on the right (while walking, he defines the width of the frame, indicating that the narrative may cue (as had *The Big Trail* in its 70 mm version in 1930), on the extended distance between personages and things in the horizontal aspect of the frame. "Jim, it's you [he slaps him on the back]." Jim: "Hi, captain." Captain: "How long you been on the mainland?" Jim: "Too long. Honolulu's goin' to be good to me." Captain, who fills his cup: "Where ya been?" Jim: "Hollywood. I sold them my book." Captain approaches and sits down, snickering, his words folding the film upon itself: "Did you, ah, write'em a movie?" Camera dollies in. Jim, distracted, eyes still on the paper: "No, I didn't want to stay." Captain, now seated, from the right side of the frame: "Oh, ha, huh, you're punchy [he raises his arm and drops a pill in his coffee]. You're goin' home to the islands when you coulda' stayed in Hollywood with all them actresses around?" Jim, looking up: "I gave it some thought." The captain takes a deck of cards and shuffles it: "How 'bout some [ca]sino?" Jim: "I'm your pigeon."] He hands the deck to Jim who cuts and shuffles, uttering, "How many passengers this trip?" Staring at his coffee, grimacing as if it were fetid but potable only when the other passenger comes to mind, the captain, now matter-of-fact: "Ah, there's just one beside you." The captain arches over: "Hey did yah ever meet Marlene Dietrich up close?" Jim, looking frontally, at the end of the table: "Oh, about from here to there."

03:10–21 (eleven seconds): Cut to medium close-up, across table. The captain smiles, "Ha! Yah know, I saw that picture of her three times." He pulls back, imitating Dietrich: "She sang this song, with those long black stockings and that black garter belt! Ah, ha, huh!" Close-in: "That gal's not got a thing outta place!"

03:22–27 Counter-shot of Jim smiling, reading the cards in his hands, and raising his arm. He adds, "Say, you know, that other passenger isn't so bad."

03:27–33 Counter-shot of the Captain, looking at his hand: "Ummm." Now changing his tone: "The company's got strict rules. Business and pleasure don't mix." He drops some cards. "Gimme tens."

03:34–50 Two-shot of the men, each on either side of the wide frame, rehearsing a time-held scene (since Cézanne, Lumière, and Méliès) of cardplayers at opposite sides of a table. Jim: "Why'd the police bring her aboard?" Smirking, the captain flips the front side of a card in view of Jim: "Look at this big [card] to see her." Holding the coffee cup, he adds: "The cops just wanted to see that she got outta town . . . [almost presciently], whaddaya wanna do, put her in a book or somethin'?" Jim, smiling: "Maybe." Captain: "Hmm. Stay away from that one, son, it'll cost ya!"

03:51–4:03 Cut back to counter-shot (as in 3:10–21): "She'll take guys like you to the cleaners." He picks up his cards. Jim: "It might be worthwhile." Captain, uttering, "Too expensive," then sipping his overcooked coffee and retching, "You know when a lady's down to her last five bucks."

03:53–4:11 Cut to a two-shot. Captain extends his arm and brandishes his cards as if signaling the width of the frame in which the shot is taken. "A landlubber like you [he drops a card] was made to order for her." Jim looks at the captain inquisitively. The captain rises and turns to the pot to refill his cup, uttering (as the camera follows him, leaving Jim out of frame, stressing: "*And this lady knows her business.*" He turns right, to the counter, putting a spoon of sugar into the cup: "Except this ain't no lady!"

04:11–13   Abrupt cut to the doorway, in medium close-up, where Mamie leans against the wall, wearing her tan overcoat and standing in front of a fire extinguisher behind her. Her lips red as ever, much as she had in the front credit, Sadie stares accusingly at the scene. To the right, on the wall, a plaque reads "Ward Room." She utters, with seductive disdain, "Mind if I have some coffee?"

Now that she is suddenly *seen*, her words simulate a need for stimulation, be it oral or visual. Rehearsing what she will do at the end of the film, in exiting Mamie *breaks off*. The initial dialogue inaugurates, develops, and almost summarizes what will follow. We don't know exactly *when* Mamie intrudes to hear and peer at the men who talk about her. Leading into the feature, the dialogue begins in reference to the movies, ostensibly, to Dietrich, either before 1941 when, renouncing her German citizenship in 1939, she helped Jewish refugees or, more likely, when she was making movies to support the American war effort in the years 1942–44, *after* the date noted in the front credits.[13] When the captain remarks that "business and pleasure" don't mix, that the woman on board *knows her business*, and that she is not a "lady," he could be describing an entrepreneur of the postwar era, like a Hollywood producer, for whom fabrication of *pleasure is business*. His words become the thread that ties the woman's part to the greater economy of the feature. Thus, when Jim mutters offhandedly that "it might be worthwhile" to be "taken to the cleaners," he predicts what his destiny will be. The card the captain holds high could be any of the pinups that will later bear Mamie's image (and the high spade of a winning hand). The fire extinguisher next to Mamie's face indicates the "hot-cold" effect she brings to the setting: igniting desire, she also douses it with crisp words and an icy stare.

A Writing of History

Today we might wonder what the effect of the sequence representing the bombing of Pearl Harbor (roughly, 41:51–48:20) would have been like in 1956. A turning point in the timeline of the film, the incursion of history (that had been anticipated in "1941," the date noted in the intertitle following the front credits) marks the moment Mamie becomes aware of her entrepreneurial savvy and the beginning of her rise to power. Shot in 1954 and seen in 1956, the representation of the bombing is a sugary simulation of what black-and-white photographs and newsreels had shown hours after the Japanese air force had sunk, as Christopher Marlowe had described the face of Helen of Troy, and "burnt the topless towers" of the American fleet. At the time of the film's reception, the attack (the author of these pages was born on December 7, 1943) had hardly been far from collective memory. Pearl Harbor Day was marked on calendars. What Franklin D. Roosevelt announced to be the "day of infamy" in American history became the title of Walter Lord's exhaustive history of the event. Shortly before *Mamie* came to movie theaters Pearl Harbor had been at the core of melodrama and romance, first in *From Here to Eternity* (d. Fred Zinnemann, 1953) and long after that, when its impact had faded, the bombing became grist for features that include *Tora, Tora, Tora* (1970, d. Richard Fleischer) and *Pearl Harbor* (d. Michael Bay, 2001). The most telling testimony to the event had been—and perhaps still is—Movietone News, placed at the beginning of single and double features alongside serials and trailers, whose footage brought (and continues to bring) to viewers the discomfiting and even traumatic recording of the bombardment and wanton loss of life. In all likelihood, contrary to what Roberto Rossellini had done when inserting stock material in *Roma, città aperta* (1945) and *Paisà* (1946), the designers of *Mamie Stover* preferred not to include ocular testimony in the narrative. For one, in the midst of *Mamie's* carefully executed chromatic spectrum, like the history of the event itself, recursion to black-and-white material would have been unsettling and unduly distorted if made to conform to the aspect-ratio of Cinemascope. In view of the format and coloration, inclusion of photographic evidence of the event within the narrative might have risked untimely shift of tone and temper—nor would the plot have been enhanced if the characters were shown looking at documents of the event in which they were enmeshed. In the mid-1950s, much like reference to the Holocaust, reminders of recent history, traumatizing to a public already vitiated by what the Allies discovered in the German death camps, tended to be consigned to archives, made difficult to find, or considerably edited.[14]

Mamie Stover is no exception. Yet, in view of the woman at the center of the film, perhaps in the vein of Douglas Sirk's concurrent features, the cloying imagery emphasizes how much the film is a saccharine *writing of history*. For Michel de Certeau (author of the eponymous study cited elsewhere), historiography is by its nature and definition a "fiction" of truth and science.[15] In *Mamie Stover*, copied from photographs and newsreel footage, executed in miniature and slow motion, colored representations of the sinking of the battleships *Arizona* and *Utah* (along with the damaging of seven other juggernauts of the Pacific fleet) prompt immediate comparison with collective memory-images of the morning of December 7, 1941. The film puts cream and glaze on what newsreels had been showing to prompt the United States, at long last, to enter the war. Yet, in keeping with the smooth continuity of the montage, and in harmony with concurrent psychoanalytic practice, the film can be seen avowing it *cannot* represent a traumatic event, if only because trauma is impervious to representation or semiosis.

The historical fiction superimposes audio-visual practices of the Hollywood postwar era—discernible in terms of what Michel Foucault called "visible" and "audible" formations—onto earlier events of different facture and mentality.[16] If, too, the "free indirect subjectivity" of the episode can be inferred declaring that the "history" it represents is a fiction shaped for postwar ideology, *Mamie* summons us to consider in the same breath a critical relation it keeps with the story it tells. Two instances are key. In a first, on a bright morning Jim fetches Mamie to take a ride around the island and enjoy the amenities it offers (implicitly, to tourists in the 1950s). At the end of a blissful day they have spent on the beach, he drives her to the Bungalow in the early evening. They kiss each other goodbye. Standing in front of the establishment, identified from the back by his cream-colored suit, Harry notices Mamie exiting from Jim's plush convertible. As usual, when she gets out of any of the vehicles in the film (Mamie is forever embarking and disembarking), anxiety ensues. She dashes into the Bungalow. Witnessing her transgression, Harry follows down a corridor where, in front of the ladies, he sadistically enforces house rules. As he is wont, he removes his thick horn-rimmed glasses, grabs Jackie, Mamie's close friend and confidant, and pushes her to the floor. He then enters Mamie's quarters and goes to work. Three women restrain Jackie to keep her from coming to Mamie's aid (41:35–42:20).

The violence at the Bungalow gives way to what would be its historical counterpart. In a second instance, in a brief dissolve (42:21) from night to the next day, civilians in their Sunday best gather and walk toward an "Oriental Church." Hearing the buzz of aircraft that promise more excitement than prayer, children look up and misidentify the planes under the clouds. Focusing on a soldier who prefers to buy a cup of coffee rather than go to church, the camera pano-tracks to the right, stopping at the window of a local diner (42:22–47). Explosions prompt him to remark (as shadows of passing aircraft shoot through the image), "a fine time for target practice!" In line with early sound cinema, history—or the "real"—intervenes in voice-off: a radio in the café announces that Oahu has been attacked. The second is the shift to the reenactment of the carnage, panic, and the citizens' desperate flight to the hills. When the USS *Arizona* topples in flames, a brief cutaway catches crew members jumping from the decks into the flames and smoke below (43:26–29). The three seconds force recall of the extras jumping from the pyre of the *Shamrock Queen* three decades earlier, the centerpiece in *Regeneration*, of which Walsh had spoken vividly in his memoir.[17] A sign of the auteur (or at least of the film of 1915) is born, too, in an unsettling detail in the montage of evacuation. A brief pan follows a family of Hawaiians descending from the veranda of their modest dwelling, a father with a nude baby flopping on his left shoulder, running to pack the infant into the back of a station wagon (44:26–34). Frail, inert, bouncing on its father's back, the sight of the infant begs us to assume its point of view—to think of the trauma to which the major players seem inured. And more so contrastively, earlier in the sequence when the event finds Jim wondering what is happening. Above the melee, in earshot of noise and din, Jim runs to the balcony of his villa to see what is happening far off and below. As he looks at the seaside in the distance his bare torso and magnificent musculature capture our gaze more than what he is witnessing. Showing him at the threshold of cleanly clipped hedgerows, for an enduring instant the film asks us to choose between gazing upon history or taking pleasure at the sight of Jim's body (fig. 4.3). Or else to see how they mesh: abandoning his sculpted pose, to the surprise of Annalee and his factotum, Jim rushes from the empyrean of his villa to extricate Mamie from the pandemonium in the city below. Before the sequence ends, when the girls pack up and flee (46:15–37), Mamie momentarily stays behind, speculating on what she can make of what she sees. Pulling Jackie to a window, pointing to the confusion outside while holding a roll of cash

Figure 4.3. Jim looks at Pearl Harbor from deck of his villa.

in her left hand, she looks out, sensing what can be made of the chaos, exclaiming, as if *seeing* were believing (or telling viewers to take note of the contradictions the film sets forward), "Look Jackie, see!" (fig. 4.4). Cut to the crowded bustle in the street. Countershot, Mamie declaring, "Scared, gettin' out, but not me! [cut to interior] I'm gonna buy real estate with every dollar I can raise . . . there's 10 cents on the dollar!" While the building shakes, Jackie quips (in a lilt recalling Eve Arden's Miss Brooks), "Keep stalling and you'll wind up buying real estate in a cemetery" (46:30–33). Mamie finally meets Jim in a setting where contradiction could not be more manifest. Juxtaposed in a two-shot, they stand in front of a background that displays, to the left, a poster

Figure 4.4. Mamie sees a future in the pandemonium of the bombing of Pearl Harbor.

making a pitch for WACS (American women in military service), asking women to give themselves to their country, and to the right, a board on the door of the Bungalow: "Champagne, $5.00 a glass." In implicit dialogue with the two signs, Mamie and Jim face and hold each other, in conflict over personal interest and commitment to the nation now at war with Japan. Betwixt and between, Jim seems closer in spirit to the WACS, who give their lives to their country, while Mamie tilts toward the business of pleasure.

Numerous shots in color reconstruct the black-and-white footage of the Japanese attack on the American naval base. Clearly done in miniature or by way of special effects, they imply that the reality of the event cannot be reproduced. What they display are simulacra, or "dummy" images that soften or even edulcorate the violence of the event, in a deliberately contrived fashion fifteen years after it had taken place. One of the telling shots of the film—perhaps for cinephiles its most significant—caps the sequence simulating the disaster. Like Jim in his convertible, their status identified by the cars they have driven to a promontory not far from his villa, groups of well-to-do residents of Honolulu witness from a distance what has happened over the course of the day. The carnage and smoke on the horizon in the afternoon hours seem to indicate that although devastating, the event is becoming history. Standing below the camera that takes a bird's-eye view of the scene, the residents are more like "tourists" who look at the remains of Pearl Harbor as if through binoculars or pay-for-view telescopes installed at roadside vistas. A calming shot that assures the carnage is over, it is also one of the most unsettling (fig. 4.5). Between the fades and dissolves we are told that Pearl Harbor is

Figure 4.5. Spectators behold the devastation of Honolulu.

elsewhere, or rather that, when the narrative begins again, it will become a ground for a new economy and new development, closer to the Cold War than to December 7, 1941.

Ontology of the Pinup Girl

The new or postwar economy comes in medias res with Mamie, in the days after the debacle, when she trades in pictures. Like what the film is bracketing (and asking us to look at, perhaps with tongue in cheek), her futures are in the pinup, the item whose "ontology" or "entomology" was made famous with her—or Jane Russell's—debut in *The Outlaw*, but no better "theorized" with consummate hilarity than in *Gentlemen Prefer Blondes* (1953), Howard Hawks's feature that became (or remains) a compass point for what André Bazin considered the major currency in the erotic economy of American 1950s cinema.[18] In the opening sequences of *Mamie*, in transit from San Francisco to Honolulu, Jim stresses the point offhandedly, even dismissively. In Hawaii, he asserts (clearly while coveting Mamie more than he would like to believe), the horseshoes partner with whom he strolls on deck by the moonlit sea would become "Mamie Stover, the Anglo-Saxon bombshell among the Honolulu hula-hulas." In response to his remark that could be both a come-on and a slur, in *quid pro quo*, Mamie's laconic words suggest that her entrepreneurial talents are greater than her romantic designs. Mamie, spot-on: "It's all right with me, as long as the money rolls in" (12:00–02).

The episodes that follow the moonlit evening the couple shared on board the cargo vessel demonstrate how Mamie becomes what Jim (tried and true phallocrat that he is) had imagined but wished she would not. An keynote sequence depicts Mamie "becoming-pinup" (or "becoming-bombshell") when she is turning not just into an image but into *an image of an image*, into a mechanically reproduced fetish (fig. 4.6) the film everywhere "de-fetishizes." It begins in comic counterpoint: first with scenes of soldiers rising and slogging their way through the jungle [a clear reference to Walsh's *Objective, Burma!* or *Distant Drums* (1951)], and then, from the rainforest to the bedroom: the film dissolves (1:15:07–08) into the staging of a photo-op in a shot lasting fifty-eight seconds that does great honor to the long take (1:15:09–16:07).[19] First in medium depth, in deep focus, Mamie, shown dressed in a diaphanous, black sheath with a low bodice, sits at the corner of a pink-toned mattress. The camera

Figure 4.6. Mamie becomes a reproducible image.

draws back, revealing that the bed has been placed in the lobby of the Bungalow where other ladies are watching passively from the bar in the far background. Her right knee and calf bared, feet in fluffy slippers, lips painted bright red, arms pressing the mattress, she stares vapidly at a camera mounted on a tripod to the right. The photographer busily sets it in focus. Wearing a white skirt and pink blouse, elevated on white high heels, Bertha (ever a reminder of reality) enters from the left, then stands in profile, looking on glacially. Holding a newspaper in her left hand (1:15:13), she approaches, asserting matter-of-factly: "More of a lonely-hearts expression, Mamie." To the right, arching over the camera, a stout photographer intercedes. "Madame, if you please! Hold still, but not the lonely hearts." Bertha steps back, folding the newspaper she had just displayed. Bending down, sticking his fulsome buttocks toward the spectator, he adds in delicious double entendre, "Now gimme that 'come hither' look . . . yes, yes, that's it, provocative, definitely provocative . . . steady, steady [flash], excellent!" (1:15:30). Bertha proudly raises her arms and then scans the paper as the camera dollies-in: "I'll have this photograph blown up so it'll be six or seven feet high!" Mamie, squirming, her straps bothering her: "Finished?" Thrusting her (famous) chest forward, she rises to meet Bertha who has opened the newspaper: dolly-in, tightening the two-shot, when Mamie takes the paper from Bertha, opens and agitates it, scanning it distractedly, looking up, refusing to engage eye contact with her interlocutor, "You know, I wonder how I'd do if I opened a place on my own" (1:15:43–45).

Figure 4.7. Holding a newspaper, oblivious to the headline, Mamie bargains with Bertha.

Once again history again intercedes (fig. 4.7). Announcing

VICTORY AT MIDWAY

the headline of the paper infers that the date is June 7, 1942, exactly six months since the bombing of Pearl Harbor. In the time that has passed Mamie has gained immense fortune and agency. Neither she nor Bertha sees or takes note of the recent naval battle involving ships, damaged at Pearl Harbor, that had been repaired almost miraculously and in time enough to engage the Japanese fleet. More than a locative sign, a passing reference, or realistic effect, "VICTORY AT MIDWAY" in boldface could be a lure marking, first, a "turning point," a trope pertaining to the War in the Pacific, that in 1956 was known to be a first victory in a campaign so long and draining that it prompted Harry Truman to use nuclear means to devastate Hiroshima and Nagasaki. Like or unlike the Allied forces winning the first of many battles to follow—the film implicitly asks the viewer to consider which "victories" are in question—Mamie succeeds in obtaining a commission of 70 percent, thus taking control of Bertha and the Bungalow. The newsprint might be making oblique allusion to John Ford, colleague and friend of Walsh, whose inspirational documentary, *The Battle of Midway* (1942), winning an Oscar, had further spurred the nation's commitment to defeating the Axis. Between one point of reference and the other, the announcement begs us to take a critical relation with a narrative obliged to teeter-totter between the Cold War, memories of two world wars, and a perennial war of the sexes. Mamie, like the M's of her name that are at the center of the alphabet, is *Midway*, between fantasy and history, bearing attributes of both male and female valence, and between one aspiration (success) and another (illusion of romantic or conjugal bliss). In the same sequence, when apart from Mamie and chagrined at the state of her condition, Bertha stands next to a mirror. Gazing upon it, she seems to realize that she is no more the fairest of them all, while also staring accusatively at the spectator, her eyes adjacent to a sign on the wall that affirms a woman's project: "Let no man *waste* our time."

Mamie becomes immortal in the form of the pinup, the portable image *within* the film Allied soldiers purchase, exchange, and carry into combat as a fetish-object and, *outside*, or along the margins, in posters behind vitrines at the entry to the movie theaters where the film is shown.[20] In one shot, several soldiers enter the Bungalow by a doorway that could imaginably lead into the lobby of a movie theater. Like stills from a film to be screened, black-and-white pictures tacked on a surface are behind a corporal whose holster and .45 automatic pistol are adjacent to his crotch. He looks about, like the MP at the beginning of *Sadie Thompson*, to keep order among the troops, while to his left, seen from behind, a soldier takes a photograph of the color picture manufactured from the photograph the professional photographer had made of Sadie sitting at the corner of a queen-size bed. The film doubles itself in picturing its own picture, and all to the delight of the ogling troops who enter the establishment.

The pinup, the war, and the battle of the sexes take precedence in two late sequences that portray the heroine finding her autonomy.

Figure 4.8. Soldiers ogle a pin-up photograph of Mamie.

Mamie has performed "Keep Your Eyes on the Hands," a Hula-Do dance capturing the hearts of a throng of soldiers. She takes "golf lessons" with (the well-named and even "poisonous") Captain "Eldon Sumac" (Richard Coogan), whom she slaps in the face when his indecent advances and slurs slight her character. After a rendition of a "golfing lesson," pushing toward her midsection, Sumac shows her how to hold the handle of his driver. A married man, the captain becomes aggressive in his pursuit. Attraction gives way to repulsion. The couple's strife on the links leads to strife in the Pacific. The film dissolves into a counter-tilt of palm trees bending in the wind. Panning downward, it travels across a lush setting where tents and barracks indicate that men are at war. Dissolve again to a medium close-up of Jim reading a letter; a pan right, across a bunk and a table where three men play cards (the men are killing "time" instead of "Japs"). As in Senecan tragedy, the chorus of indolent soldiers comes to life when a messenger arrives with news affording a turn to action. Brandishing a black-and-white pinup of Mamie, the carrier quickly finds himself surrounded by seven Marines huddling around him):

> "Get a load of my new pin-up! Get your old man, get your own, Flamin' Mamie belongs *to me*." (1:19:06–10).

Cut to Jim, wearing a sergeant's chevrons, who looks with condescension at the soldiers who gather to see the pinup. In accord with the words of Mamie's "Keep Your Eyes on the Hands," one soldier shouts:

> "Lemme look, boy! Lookin' ain't touchin'." (1:19:14)

The exchange addresses (or touches upon) the ontology of the photographic image, which in the famous essay inaugurating *What is Cinema?* (in French as "Ontologie de l'image photographique" André Bazin had considered *real* because it simply *was* (in Catholic terms)—and did not "represent" (as it would have for Protestants)—what it put before its viewer's eyes. An ogling soldier steals Bazin's words: "Hey, for *real*, it can't be!" But it is: another says, gesticulating, "That's the *realest real* you've ever seen! Hey, Mike, where'd you get it?"[21] A soldier in the back bends over: "That's the Honolulu broad." Cut to Jim, frustrated. Back to the group: "A C-company [a *see-company*?] replacement had a lotta prints made when he was in Honolulu last month." Cut to Jim, perturbed. He hears the soldier add, "He's sellin' them for two bucks a copy!" Cut to the group: sucking a cigarette, another soldier (to the right), "Boy, he must be makin' a million!" Another: "I gotta buy one of those for my lonesome nights!" Back to Jim. Holding a picture, a hand enters the frame from the right. Voice-off: "How do ya like it, Sarge?" Jim arises, takes it in his hand, and looks closely. Pan right: in the center, a soldier adds, "Boy, if I ever get to Honolulu I'm headin' straight for Flamin' Mamie's and see if she is *real*!" Jim looks up contemplatively when, suddenly, planes in the air announce a bombing. An explosion throws everyone and everything askew and awry.

The sequence conflates pinups, the "real" (as that which cannot be reduced to language), and "bombshells." In "En marge de l'érotisme au cinéma" ("Entomology of the pinup girl"), Bazin correlated the erotic photograph with the platitude of the "real."[22] It is as if, like a 500 lb., nipple-nosed explosive dropped from the sky, the picture of Mamie baring her knee was enough to throw the soldier's world topsy-turvy. Capping the sequence, the shot that carefully arranges the soldiers looking at the photograph (fig. 4.8) becomes a hilarious study of the male gaze and its force of self-gratification. Seated in the foreground, three men share a privileged view. One soldier in the center purses his lips and draws on a cigarette while the partners who surround him smile with glee. Standing in the back, four men (wearing soft caps) peer at the image. Wearing a brief undershirt that enhances his musculature, the soldier to the right is oiling his M-1, the erect barrel of which thrusts into the frontal space in trompe-l'oeil. Caressing the bolt-action component and chamber of the rifle with a white cloth, he could be enacting what his companion wishes to do to remedy his "lonesome nights." The farcical underside of the detail offsets the plotline that follows Jim's confused and morose longings. The collectively shared pleasure of looking and laughing at an image shatters the self-gratifying economy of the "pinup."

Revolt and Revolution

Before (or in order to) get the narrative underway, *Mamie Stover* begins with departure, but hardly a departure, as Walsh had shown in the opening of *The Big Trail*, of the kind that bears promise or travel to new and unforeseen realms and regions. The feature begins as an eviction that turns into a story of success at the end in the name of romantic disillusion, which the heroine (so suggests the final shots) has courage enough to throw away. It seems that when Jim breaks off from Mamie (1:22:11–22), as it happens with so many "problematic" relations of men and women in postwar melodrama, schmaltz reigns supreme. Or does it? Prior to when Jim, his demeanor pensive and doleful, enters Mamie's sanctum, a comic sequence depicts a diminutive sailor eagerly throwing his money away in a card game. The sight of the sailor who empties his pockets for the pleasure of spending a few minutes with an attractive card shark stresses the difference between an economy of dispensation or waste (congruent, say, with the finale of Marcel Mauss's *The Gift* (1925) [in French as *Essai sur le don: Forme et raison de l'échange dans les sociétés archaïques*] and another of accumulation and enterprise. Flashing a wad of tickets that faintly resembles a strip of celluloid, the soldier eagerly buys into getting ripped off. Would he be reproducing the economy of American postwar melodrama? Or else, especially in its proximity to Jim's final meeting with Mamie, is he showing how much his *waste* responds to the poster in the Bungalow, carefully arranged to be seen behind Bertha when she negotiates with Mamie ("Let no man *waste* our time")? Their encounter is a delightful expenditure of affect. A two-shot of the sailor and the shark gives way to Jim, reduced to the status of a client, entering Mamie's den through a Hawaiian curtain in the company of a hula girl. She turns around, then puts the arm of a record player to a disc that turns at 78 rpm, before setting the time clock that calibrates the length of the meeting for which Jim has paid his money. As in much of classical sound cinema, the lyrics of the song serve as commentary on the action: "If you can, with Mamie take a chance, with Mamie, the chances are you'll find romance, with Mamie, there are no stars in the sky [a second hula girl returns with a bottle of watered-down champagne], for the stars are all in Mamie's eyes, and for all that, a man with Mamie, for all he ever had, with Mamie, for those who try to resist . . . are the pyre of psychiatrists . . . for . . ." Having heard enough (also wasted or feeling he has been "taken to the cleaners"), Jim lifts the arm and shuts off the record player. He shuffles to the right, to a window at the other side of the room (the width of Cinemascope stressing the effect), tossing a piece of paper (a ticket?) to the floor. The camera almost swish pans to the left to catch Mamie entering the room and, in surprise, suddenly discovering "Jimmy!" The camera soon records the dialogue from *outside* the window (at an angle perpendicular to the establishing shots) that reframes the interior, now affording a distance on the romance, even as Mamie looks away and upward (presumably at the "stars" noted in the lyrics). He turns around and leaves the room. Mamie about-faces and goes to the record player, sets the arm on the disc and, sobbing, lets the lyrics play.

Continuing after Mamie exits the room and walks down the corridor, the lyrics could be her thoughts, or else a third voice that extends to the finale when, after a fade-out in black, the camera returns to the setting of the Embarcadero (1:27:24–29). She descends the gangplank, looks at the skyline of the city as it had been shown at the beginning, then tears up and tosses away the shards of a ticket as song continues ("if you want to see Mamie . . .") and fades away. She meets the same plainclothesman, recognizing her (in another face-to-face two-shot made for Cinemascope), who says, "Mamie, nothing's changed, Mamie. You're still not welcome in San Francisco." In a friendly gesture she challenges him to believe a story about her fortune won and given away. A gentleman who listens (another intermediate spectator), he agrees that he cannot. He amiably opens the door of the car, offering her a ride to the airport.

Whether or not the fortune has been thrown away is of less import than the record player, an emblem of the film, suggesting that what comes around turns around. Like the source of the song just heard, the revolt spelled out in bold red characters in the front credits becomes a point of reference for what has been an audio-visual "revolution." The unspoken and almost unnamable, indelibly present moment, the Pacific theater of World War II in which the narrative has been situated, would seem to be forgotten when the end credits (1:28:47) are set over the freighter—a mode of transport, thus a metaphor—seen at the beginning. Embarkation and debarkation underscore the "turning" or, crazily, the locomotion that drives the film ahead. In the narrative an arrival can go one way, in reverse (toward disillusionment, waste, time spent and lost, both in the film and in the theater where the paying customer has spent almost an hour and a half), or another (ahead, toward a new life, new promise) that viewers might see in Mamie's frontal gaze reproducing what was seen in the front credits, but now, however, altered, not only because she talks, but also in the lilt of her voice and in the assurance of her movement. Refusing to turn her back on the viewer, she steps forward and into the vehicle, in a direction that bears a resemblance to what viewers see through the damaged celluloid when Sadie Thompson, Mamie's other, awaiting Handsome O'Hara, looks toward other islands and new continents. But with a difference: Mamie does not need a man or men to accompany her wherever she decides to go. The *Revolt of Mamie Stover* is a woman's film, to be sure, whose roots are embedded in the feature of 1928. Other films of feminine leaning in the oeuvre tend to be associated with the postwar years, in *The Man I Love* (1947) and

Band of Angels (1957). Yet inklings are to be found in the early cinema, in *The Yellow Ticket* (1931), but especially three others in which a blonde Joan Bennett takes command, including *Wild Woman* (1932) and *Big Brown Eyes* (1936), that sit well with *Me and My Gal* (1932), the feature studied in chapter 6.

5

Big Trees, Tall Men

The Big Trail

Historians can smile in recalling that *The Big Trail* had been a big flop. Shot in five languages and in 35- and 70-mm versions, the epic western may have been victim of a time lag. In the early years during the diffusion of sound cinema, it stood between the technology that made it possible and the settings in which it was shown. In its modest format, in 35 mm, the feature circulated in theaters that were new to the use of sound apparatus (or perhaps those not equipped with the technology could have shown it as a silent film), while its wider counterpart, done in "Grandeur process," of an aspect ratio anticipating Cinemascope, was limited to plush movie houses, no doubt in urban centers, equipped with the modes of projection the film required. No less, seasoned viewers in the fall of 1930, expert in lipreading, familiar with sound cues and the lexicon of gestures in silent cinema, would have been especially alert in hearing the din of dogs barking, wheels creaking under the weight of their rickety wagons, the rattle of bridles and hennies of horses, grunts and groans of oxen under whiplash, war cries of chanting Indians, gunshots echoing across landscapes, and shards of speech, both random and synched, lost in the frame—in sum, aural material heard all over and everywhere, both for effect and in correlation with an exodus and long voyage. *The Big Trail* may have been designed to appeal both to older audiences and, in the same measure, a then younger, "millennial" generation thirsting for synchronies of sight and sound. Seeking proceeds from worldwide distribution, in accord with current practice, using different casts, in the year following its premiere in America, Fox released 35-mm versions in French (*La Piste des géants* / The trail of the giants), German (*Die Grosse Fahrt* / The big journey), Italian (*Il grande sentiero* / The big trail) and Spanish (*La Gran jornata* / The big journey). In 1980, more than fifty years after its completion, appealing to a public "of a certain" (or antiquarian) age, to an audience appreciative of early cinema, the Museum of Modern Art completed a difficult and costly restoration of the wide-screen version. Now on YouTube in its wide-screen format, in crisp definition, the film is available to one and all.

A sumptuous, still unparalleled visual and aural spectacle, *The Big Trail* begs us to wonder why it failed. In the Depression were urban settings more fitting than the mythic spaces recorded in *The Oregon Trail* or tales of travels west? Did the annoying simplicity of its plot blind viewers to what its cameras were doing?[1] Were they (as we no doubt are) put off by the so-called comic sequences where Gus (El Brendel) squabbles with his mother-in-law (Louise Carver)? Or else, preferring complexities of human relations, did viewers overlook the Aristotelian poetics on which so much early cinema, Walsh and the western in particular, were based? Did they forget that for the Greek philosopher drama moves forward on the basis of *action* and not psychology? From this angle, given a striking contrast of moving forms *within* many of the long and often uninterrupted sequence shots and tableaulike takes, initially so contrary to the disposition of montage, would viewers weaned on Griffith's and Walsh's earlier films have felt shortchanged? Or would they have overlooked the way the film deploys stasis to stress effects of relentless movement and forward motion?

A film about an invention of space, place, and passage, *The Big Trail* weds vast breadth and depth of field to an almost primal wonder of the unknown. Tapping into a disquieting mix of awe and fear we feel when we find ourselves lost in the world, the film encourages today's viewers to consider the shrinking beauty of immensity. For cinephiles (generally of French extraction) weaned on auteur theory, the sky and space of Walsh's western would forcibly recall Blaise Pascal, who wrote of agoraphobia with the advent of Copernican science, when the earth was no longer at the center of things: *the eternal silence of these infinite spaces frightens me.*[2] Where it portrays its travelers in landscapes far beyond the measure of what they can see or comprehend, the film unsettles. Seen today, the quality of the landscapes it records attests to ninety years of unparalleled environmental depredation.

Geography, the Eye of History

Geographia, oculis historiae: such the maxim of Abraham Ortelius, reformer, cartographer, and entrepreneurial author of the first atlas of the world, *Theatrum orbis terrarum* (1570). Walsh's feature is as much about the eye of human geography in recent history as it is a narrative of love spurned and won; of pursuit, revenge, and vindication; of fantasies of manifest destiny, outside of movie theaters, when none were to be had. *The Big Trail*, as some have noted, is about *vision* and what it means to be in and behold the world in its immensity.[3] Ninety years after its premiere (in October 1930), the film spins off the lectures Frederick Jackson Turner delivered at the turn of the twentieth century, who charismatically told Americans to look *west*. *The Big Trail* may have been scripted to appeal to a public, living as best it could, its producers believed would pay to behold the greater space that lay beyond.[4] Possibly taking note of the path Douglas Fairbanks takes when he heads west in *Wild and Woolly* (1917), a story about the end of the frontier, rolling back to an earlier moment, the epic isolates its players in situations and spaces they would never have seen before. Dressing its travelers in the canvas and woolens they would have worn in the 1830s, setting them aboard and beside Conestogas and prairie schooners, having drivers tighten reins and put whips to teams of oxen, the film sets itself in tandem with the concurrent development of automotive culture.

The spectacle of 1930 blazes what was by then what James Akerman (2006), in research on early Rand-McNally Road maps, alertly called "a well-trodden trail." Circulating not long after the initial planning of the Interstate Highway system, the film turns the clock back to a time before the Depression, to the moment prior to the desperate journeys John Ford would portray in *The Grapes of Wrath* (1939) and other features.[5] A "myth-history," it sustains a dialogue with silent films of comparative scope, including *The Covered Wagon* (d. James Cruze, 1923), *The Vanishing American* (d. George Seitz, 1925), *The Iron Horse* (d. Ford, 1924) and, although not about manifest destiny or the conquest of wilderness, Ford's *Three Bad Men* (1926). The film internalizes a silent style while making much of the novelty of sound, especially in the 70-mm version, where aural signs are scattered across a wide frame in an immense depth of field. Its speech and ambient sounds behoove us to "look for" what we are hearing or glimpsing, both actively and passively, when our eyes travel through a cavalcade of tableaus. Hence the errant noise of travel, of bovines pulling wagons, settlers trudging beside creaking wheels (in close-ups) pushing through mud and sand, yapping dogs trotting not far behind, oxen straining in harnesses, children crying and laughing. The sequence shot becomes fitting for experiment with the sound within the extended frame. As if each were a painting or a diorama, mixing classical and colorful styles—a model for Heinrich Wölfflin's enduring distinction between the classical and *malerisch* or painterly aspects of a work of art—the film invites us to see the blend of soft and deep focus, pictorial stasis, and montage or kinetic process.[6]

From this angle *The Big Trail* encourages us to see the film as a film and not simply to pigeonhole it as the first feature in John Wayne's career. Nor can it be assumed that the happy ending tends to paper over the fears and anxieties of viewers seeking relief from the travails of the Depression "only yesterday."[7] A variety of motives may have been at the origin of its creation.[8] Hal Evarts, author of the story and a "pioneer serial" in the *Saturday Evening Post*, met with Walsh to chart the outline and select locations for what they wanted to be an imposing project. After directing and acting in *Sadie Thompson*, when filming *In Old Arizona* (1928), for which he had been tagged to direct and play the lead role of the Cisco Kid and not long following the loss of his right eye, the director's thespian career was over. He had to learn to "see" again. Depth of field that went without saying in films shot before the accident of 1928 suddenly became "a depth of surface."[9] *The Big Trail* may have had much to do with a mentality and vision of the world that had taken a new direction. The use of 70-mm film stock and deployment of a scale of a 3 (vertical) x 8 (horizontal) aspect ratio could have been, as Moss (2011, 116) has remarked, an appeal to a great depth and breadth of vision when the director was possibly at odds about how to see the world around him.[10]

The narrative is refreshingly rudimentary. Gathered at the shore of the Mississippi, a party forming a wagon train with plans to settle in the west has little inkling about where it will go. Brett Coleman (Wayne), a young scout coming from Indian country, catches up Zeke (Tully Marshall), and old trapper friend, and makes the acquaintance of Pa Bascom (Frederick Birton), the devout leader of the troupe that wants to find "another Missouri off yonder." Knowing the lay of the land, Coleman recommends that they aim north of Oregon. Gruff, stout, and surly, Red Flack (Tyrone Power Sr.) has been hired to be the ramrod. With him come two rogues in an otherwise tightly knit community bearing strength, courage, and infinitely good will. And so forth: surely Francis

Parkman's *Oregon Trail* (1849), reprinted time and again in the twentieth century, a paradigm for the westward movement Frederick Jackson Turner had been championing, was in the mix. The initial shots inspire recall of the opening paragraph, as if appealing to the memory of a work that in 1930 had been grist for the mill of manifest destiny. In both the film and Parkman's account a steamboat and its passengers travel upstream and disembark at Saint Louis. Thus begins Parkman:

THE

CALIFORNIA AND OREGON TRAIL.

CHAPTER ONE.

THE FRONTIER.

Away, away from men and towns
To the silent wilderness.

SHELLEY.

Last spring, 1844, was a busy season in the city of St. Louis. Not only were emigrants from every part of the country preparing for the journey to Oregon and California, but an unusual number of traders were making ready their wagons and outfits for Santa Fé. Many of the emigrants, especially those bound for California, were persons of wealth and standing. The hotels were crowded, and the gunsmiths and saddlers were kept constantly at work in providing arms and equipments [sic] for the different parties of travelers. Almost every day steamboats were leaving the levee and passing up the Missouri, crowded with passengers on their way to the frontier.[11]

And so also, following the front matter extending across the broad width of the frame, *The Big Trail*. Announcing the scope of the epic to follow, the title cards say much about how the film emerges from accounts of Parkman's grist and grain, and in what ways, too, it will become a study of how it is cinema can teach us how to see.

Credits and Intertitles

The frame and graphic disposition of the front credits, identical to the ten intertitles that punctuate the film, each bearing considerable iconic force, remind us that we are in the frame of a silent film. Fading into view before lap dissolving into the next, the title card displays a panoply of western paraphernalia (fig. 5.1). Attached to emblematic figures at each of the four corners, two strands of rope extend along the frame to enhance the novelty of its aspect ratio. Tied to four decorative items, the filament suggests that it encloses a promising story, a "yarn" whose threads are tied to the corners: to the upper right, a shield enclosing the portrait of a Native American, in profile—reminiscent of the figure on the reverse or tail side of the Indian Head Cent (in production from 1857 to 1909)—who stares at the shield of the United States, studded with stars and stripes, that occupies the upper left corner of the frame. Directed toward the shield, his gaze draws attention to cultures in opposition. Of unique design (no other concurrent film is quite like it), they are the shorthand of an American exodus. "Voices of silence," they become "legends" to the sequences that surround them. And initially, before the narrative is established, fading in and out of darkness, dissolving credits (fig. 5.2) turn the writing into an enigma. Taking shape from the final credit bearing the name of the director (0:33–49), the first intertitle,

Figure 5.1. *The Big Trail*, title card.

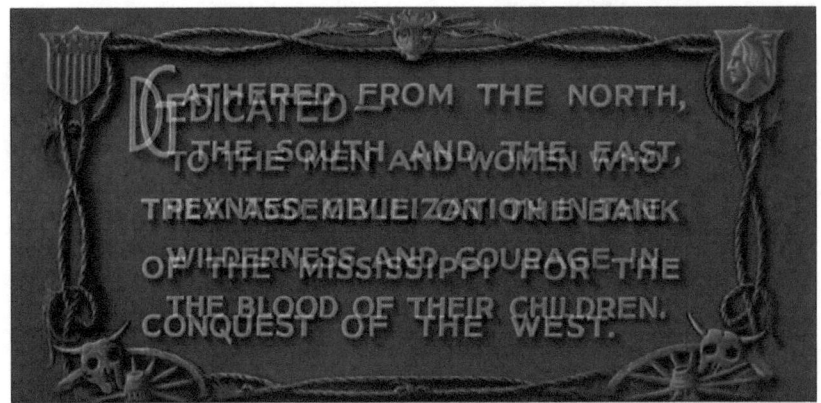

Figure 5.2. An epic takes shape: title credits in dissolve.

Dedicated—
  to the men and women who
  planted civilization in the
  wilderness and courage in
  the blood of their children [.]

dissolves into

Gathered from the north,
the south and the east,
they assemble on the bank
of the Mississippi for the
conquest of the west [.]

(0:51–1:05) before quickly fading to black and then straight cutting to the first shot in bright daylight. The first two intertitles, moving in and out of legibility, promise a language of myth appealing perhaps to viewers literate and illiterate alike. The stasis of the written material, which is read or scanned from left to right (or west to east) stands in counterpoint to the prevailing movement of the images from right to left. However, where the title cards dissolve into each other, an intermediate, quasi-unconscious zone of overlapped picture writing comes forward, suggesting that a myth is in the making.

The intertitles that follow point to the visual design of the sequences they herald. Interceding only after thirty minutes (31:26–33), following the magnificent treatment of collective departure, the third title, that comes in silence—"Prairie schooners rolling/west. Praying for peace—but ready for battle"—stands in contrast to the fracas and noise of passage that precede and follow. Cowhands shout, whips slash and crack—but above all, in the communion of humans and animals in what follows, dogs bark incessantly, in cadence with the men and women who walk alongside the wagons. Inserted unpredictably into the film, the intertitles simulate the words of a demiurge, an *aède*, a bard or a great storyteller while the soundtrack reproduces the noise and din of concurrent movement. And, because the inserts never specify where the film is taking place, the geography becomes metaphysical. Although the film was shot in fifteen locations, the narrative never reveals quite exactly the path the wagons follow nor, apart from general regions (prairie, desert, badlands, etc., before the ending in a forest of sequoias) where its episodes take place. At the beginning the only clue is that the wagon train will be going *north by northwest*.

The Journey

The story, "its adventure and romance," having "little complexity of plot and character" (Moss, 2011, 20), turns on the designs of scout Breck Coleman (Wayne), who destines himself to kill an enemy he feels is in his midst and to obtain the graces of a charming young widow and her child. Although he is familiar with the trail, he initially turns down the invitation to lead the caravan. He changes his mind upon catching sight of its bullwhacker, Flack, in every way a rough, tough, but reliable wagon master whom he immediately suspects to be the scoundrel who had murdered Ben Griswold, a lifelong friend, and (as Coleman recalled him), a surrogate father. Leaving a cluttered trading post where he learned that a man named Lopez (Charles Stevens) had just bartered bundles of wolf pelts that a crony of many moons is putting in order, Coleman exits. He no sooner finds a stray knife lying on the ground. Looking at the instrument, he is led to pause and ruminate: the film dissolves into the unique flashback (16:33–17:10) in which Coleman discovers the same weapon near a cliffside at the edge of what might be the Grand Canyon. Accompanied by a Native American (who quickly disappears), Coleman encounters Griswold's skeleton. A white man's arrow is shot through its sternum, and beside the bones lies the same weapon. The sequence dissolves into the present (17:09–11) in which, still ruminating, Coleman stares piercingly at the world around him. Now, pursuit and revenge in mind, he returns to the trading post where he learns that Flack will be the troupe's bull whacker. Setting his cap lock rifle aside, casually leaning on bolts of cloth fur (with the inimitable feminine grace for which Wayne was known), Coleman informs the trader he'll lead the train after all. Obliged to reframe itself laterally—the scene is already too broad for the wide-angle lens—the shot in the dark space of the trading post records the trader raising his arms, describing Flack as "pretty ruffian, but he can maul the toughest trader on the plains into a pulp without workin' up a sweat" (17:59–18:18). A two-shot in medium close-up of uniquely silent facture, holding for over twenty seconds (18:25–47), opposes lily-skinned Coleman to the grizzly faced Flack: a graciously muscular youth, an ephebe in a cowhide costume, stands before a rough beast. The latter grumbles while the former listens. The mesh of two styles of cinema, one established and other nascent, admirably fits the action. His physiognomy fitting well the role of an evil presence, the stuff of the western in the silent tradition, formerly famous on stage, Tyrone Power Sr. reminds us of the villains he had portrayed in dozens of earlier films, including Griffith's *Dream Street* (1921) produced with synchronous sound), and famously *The Red Kimono* (1925) before appearing, shortly before his death, in his first and last sound feature.

With Flack opposed to Coleman, so begins the film at one of the many bifurcations it faces on the "trails" it will blaze. Dissimulating his suspicion, Coleman closely monitors Flack and Lopez while leading the train and—as every western requires—setting his eyes on Ruth Cameron (Marguerite Churchill), a widow and a single mother with her adolescent son, who has spurned him in favor of Bill Thorpe (Ian Keith): Thorpe is a dandy and a ne'er-do-well evading justice who teams up with the villain and his henchman. As the wagons move west, Flack and company twice fail to kill Coleman. After trials and tribulations—crossing a swirling river that pulls its chattel downstream, cutting a path through a forest of weeping willows, descending a precipitous mountainside, encountering death and starvation in the desert, withstanding an Indian attack at the cost of many lives, pushing ahead in mud and mire under torrential rains, and surviving blizzards—under Breck's good guidance the community reaches the promised land. They settle while Breck takes leave to pursue and kill his archenemy in a frigid and snowy setting in the sequoia forest in the High Sierra. The film ends in spring when, upon the recommendation of Zeke, Coleman's companion and sidekick (and, as it were, spiritual advisor), Ruth leaves her cabin in search of the man she now knows she loves. Under the great sequoias, following a long path leading into the shadows under the majestic trees, they meet and embrace. As in a Homeric poem, the characters are one with a world of force and beauty beyond anything they and, no less, we might have known. No one lives in guilt or remorse. Appealing to a world prior to what György Lukacs calls the "lapsarian condition" in the modern novel, the film aspires to be a founding myth at a depressive moment, when quite possibly the studio felt that a film of the genre would be welcome.

But, as the film arcs toward its end, it is a founding myth with a difference: when the party reaches the hilltop over the valley where will plant its roots, pointing to the path the group can follow, Breck becomes an alluring leader, a tender Moses, who brings love to the world around him. "Yonder, stands the great white mountain, and down below lies the valley I've told you about" (1:49:30–38). Almost delivered in falsetto, his words mesh an odyssey with a vulgate exodus. At the terminus, two traditions, two visions coincide.[12] Instead of dying at the threshold of the promised land after crossing the Red Sea and desert, bent on pursuing another trail, Coleman becomes a variation on Ulysses, a character who is as generous and giving as he is astute. Not that he encounters Flack in a great hall among a throng of suitors but rather, in a snowscape under the veil of towering sequoias. In a sequence where myth and silent cinema converge, leaving Lopez to freeze to death, Flack traipses off into snow and blizzard. In patient pursuit of his archenemy, climbing to the top of a monumental trunk of a fallen sequoia that reaches into the forest on which it rests, Coleman finally confronts and kills the brute. When the film returns to the settlement in spring, at a time implied to be months following the murder, myth turns into romance, romance into pastoral, and pastoral into mystical dazzlement. In the shadows of rows of sequoias that would be the vaults of a long nave, in a cinematic variant of any of the spiritual canticles of Bernard of Clairvaux, the lovers approach each other from afar, meet and embrace in the nave of the cathedral of sequoias.[13] With nothing left to tell, the camera tilts up in awe and admiration of the sheltering landscape and the light above.

Tableaus

The picture is composed as a cavalcade of arresting tableaus. The voyage begins on the western shores of the Mississippi, a site where, as the cavalier angle of first shot makes clear, wigwams housing native Americans stand in the background of a landscape where masses of wagons are assembled for their westward journey (fig. 5.3). In deep focus, a long take (1:06–20) depicts a flurry of action that extends far into the distance. Followed by a horse and a foal, carrying a young woman and a child, a wagon in the center rumbles into the scene. Initiating movement across the wide expanse the shot, a team of eight dappled oxen plods from left to right. Behind them, their faces hidden by the bonnets they wear, women scurry in different directions. Would-be travelers wander into the action from the bottom of the frame. Ambient noise, chatter, words bellowed and garbled: din is everywhere. Repeated viewings disclose scenes of everyday life on rear decks of at least seven covered wagons. Sporting a bowler hat, a child—an ideal mediator to relay the wonder and confusion about what is on display—comes forward to survey the action before catching sight of two girls approaching the platform on which he stands.

If a narrative there will be, so far it is nowhere to be found. The plot might already be seen as "an open totality," fraught with promise, a fragmentary whole or a summary assemblage signaling that the world viewed is in a state of *becoming*.[14] Whatever the ensuing narrative may be, it can only be of lesser magnitude than what is shown. The shot implies that the tableau and tableaus to follow are to be seen and read together, deciphered, walked about, worked, and traveled through from different angles in multiple viewings, so that a broadened sense of *point of view* can come forward. From the given cavalier angle—cavalier implying a perspective from horseback—the shot implies that from the get-go the viewer is at a standpoint where *all possibilities* of narrative development in the mass can be discerned at once.[15]

Figure 5.3. Voyagers prepare for travel: the first shot of the film.

Anticipating what André Bazin called the "image-fact," each tableau (or "tableau-image") is arranged in paratactic relation to those that precede or follow.[16] The simplicity (or frailty) of the story draws attention to how shots work autonomously, as much by juxtaposition as by concatenation or continuity.[17] Often resembling *tableaux vivants*, drawing (consciously or unconsciously) on European and American paintings, they invite contemplation and patient reading. Multiple "worlds" unto themselves, sometimes they follow one another in the fashion of Frederic Remington's paintings a viewer sees in haphazard montage when walking through the Amon Carter Museum of Art in Dallas. A picture of sorts, a composition that sets different objects and forms in contrast and dialogue with each other, each take is a "plastic" entity.[18] A detail, a fragment, or even an errant sound in the image field of is enough to cue what follows.[19] The spatial parataxis reminds us that a story, as the classics understood it and insofar as *narratio* is coextensive with *dispositio*, primarily works as a function of its distribution into manageable spatial units. Juxtaposed, the "scenes" are so autonomous that the film seems to beg viewers to pay as much heed to the unity of each tableau as to the storyline and intertitles that tether them.

The ordering of the exposition attests to the tableau effect. After the first shot, where no sign of narrative is visible, in the second (1:21–32) faint indications of a storyline are heard in voices floating in the image field: "I wonder what time is that [sic] . . . don't worry about that, father, we'll be going soon." Our attention is drawn less to what the youth is saying than to a strong woman in the foreground to the left, wielding an axe, who chops logs, each her of blows resounding as it were the beat of a metronome. A woman in the center assiduously washes clothes in a barrel set on a platform while, in the shadow of the wagon, seated, an older woman tends to her knitting. Behind them, two men mount a wheel on wagon's front axle, and behind them others mill about. Lethargy to the right counters the action on the left: a child (among others in the sequence, future director Robert Parrish) plays with the bars of a wooden cage while a woman under a shawl sits in the foreground and a man leans by an ox adjacent to another, the rear end of which unceremoniously faces the camera.

Then, suddenly, speech floats freely: "Hey, did you feed them hounds?" "Yes, grandpaw, yes," while the shot—and many to follow—display women performing the majority of chores and tending assiduously to daily labor. Only with the third shot (1:33–45) does the film begin to "turn": in a medium shot a woman washes in the center and, for the sake of continuity, the forearm of the woman wielding an axe is visible, while the men mount the wheel (the time-held icon of fortune and the sign of montage) to the axle of the wagon. The words of the older man who picks up a pail bear on the story and the wheel, its metaphor, or "mode of transport": "Well, all right, take her up son, she'll take us where we're goin'." To which responds the woman washing and wringing her hands, uttering (not in visible lip-synch), as if referring to the vagaries of the narration: "But where are we going?" Her question addresses the film as much as her interlocutor. The older man replies, raising his arm and pointing to somewhere off-screen, "Now Maw, they're hashin' that matter over there right now." Establishing a pattern for the ensuing tableaus, the configuration could lead the film in any number of directions. By design and necessity, of uncommonly long duration, the shots require ample time to be explored and worked through.[20]

In the shots recording Coleman's entry on horseback and his description of the "great white mountain," movement and hubbub are everywhere—cut only when Coleman turns around and rides through the traffic of men and bovines in the background (4:30–39). Guffawing, a voice somewhere in or out of the frame utters, "Hey, hey, maybe he's telling us a fairy tale." But whose? Coleman's about a land at the end of the rainbow? An interpretation of the film as a piece of wish fulfillment? It could be in the next tableau (4:40–5:01) that suddenly brings the viewer into an exclusively women's world, whose duration invites us to study it as a painting. Four pioneer women wash or comb their long and ample heads of hair extending to their midsections. Dogs (off-screen) continue to bark; a man in the background carries a heavy burlap bag on his shoulders; steers pass by men filling a wagon with provisions; in the background ladies meet and talk to each other. Only after five seconds, when Coleman rides into the scene, dismounts, and walks to the right (*behind* the women washing their hair) are we reminded of a story being told. Our eyes focus on the studied elegance of a staging that could belong to Edgar Degas, whose paintings eroticize (or annoy us) simply because, busy with themselves, their women could care less about who looks at them.[21] In its last seconds (4:54–59) Coleman's gestures underscore the irony. While a covered wagon moves past in the same direction as the hero (left to right), looking at the women from behind (whom we behold from the front, in portraiture), his hand on his rifle, perplexed, in a strange and other world, he scratches his head, then moves forward and away. Absorbed in their washing, busily moving their hands about and through their long locks, the women are the topic of the scene that does not cut with Coleman's exit. Holding for an instant, it affords the pleasure of its composition (fig. 5.4).

Many of the tableaus establish or finish the sequences they either define or to which they belong. Here, the woman's world is separate from and even alien to the hero. In the long two-shot that follows (5:01–36), from the outset Coleman, in frame, meets "Mother Riggs." Standing next to a well and the lever of its pump, the elderly lady bends over and tends to a dog by a fountain. She utters (from behind, not in lip-synch, her voice floating in the frame), "Now don't be a pig, you know" (5:03), as if addressing the canine drinking from a pail of water but also the viewer—or even, unbeknownst to herself—Coleman who is behind her, while to the right, two chickens, avian doubles of Coleman and the woman, strut about to the left. With bumbling grace of a gifted youth, the hero announces, "Howdy, Mrs. Riggs!" Looking up, she exclaims, "Land sakes!" He replies, poised with her in profile, as they shake hands, in the same tone and tenor, "You sure look fine, Mother Riggs." "It's sure a long time since I've seen you." Between them, while they speak, stealing the scene, the hind end of a dog wags its tail, while in the back horses and wagons move across the scene. As the dialogue continues, two frisky dogs, as if miming the pleasure of Coleman's encounter with the mother, wag their tails. They establish what becomes a generous rapport among living forms in the many environments of the sequences to follow.

Figure 5.4. A painting of sorts: caring little about who sees them, the westward women comb their hair.

Intermediaries

Median figures announce and define many of the tableaus given to landscape, which often supersede the epic of exodus or foundation of a community. In the 70-mm version intermediate figures, calling attention to an implicit phenomenology of perception, portray the birth of visibility taking place within a given field of vision.[22] Looking at what we see from their point of view, they draw our gaze to the tableau in which they are players or staffage. For this reason, in the manner of writers from Rabelais to Dickens or from Henry James to Proust, children are ideal mediators because, with fresh eyes, they gaze upon scenes and situations they cannot put in language.[23] Two tableaus depicting the departure of the wagon owe much to the child or children who view them from within. When the departure gets under way, in the middle of a great perspective in which the teams of voyagers, oxen, and wagons begin their journey, Flack (always squinting, always of an evil point of view) directs traffic westward (28:46–52). Three shots later (29:13–25), drawn by a team of six mules, followed by four men on foot, a wagon carrying women turns right and rumbles ahead. Near the right corner of the frame, wearing a bowler hat, his face turned away and toward the action, a child looks on at the scene. Statuesque in poise, he stands erect, budging backward only slightly. Seen from aside and behind, his point of view on the scene alerts us to the marvel of its action and the great expanse ahead. The child would be a passing detail were it not that the scene is reframed two shots later (29:36–52), when he looks directly into the landscape while a trailhand approaches an ox in the lower right corner, and a woman on a horse is followed by a couple, also on horseback, who relentlessly move ahead (and to the right, contrary to the major of shots in which wagons move from right to left, implied to be from east to west) (fig. 5.5). A team of six oxen pulls a larger schooner while men and women walk alongside. On the soundtrack pigs are squealing, dogs barking and yapping, voices mumbling, wagons straining and creaking. The shot cuts when the boy raises his arm to acknowledge a rider on horseback just before other figures occlude the view. Without the child witnessing the scene within its frame, the tableau would arguably be of less or little wonder.

Both within and in the margins of the narrative, the tableaus become sites of contemplation. Because the film belongs to a "classical" mode, its rhythms must mime the body that acts, expends energy, rests,

Figure 5.5. Wearing a bowler hat, a child watches the movement of the wagons (and the movie).

and begins again. Enhanced by the punctuations of the ten intertitles, the many fade-ins and fade-outs lend the effect of a film that breathes.[24] Early on, after the excitement of departure, a shot captures a multitude of wagons moving away from the camera, converging from both sides of the frame in the direction of a setting sun at the center (36:30–43). When night falls the film fades into the fourth intertitle that announces respite: "The caravan halts. Some dance because they know what is coming—and to forget. Others in blissful ignorance"). An evening of polkas and merriment in a dark setting offset and modulate the longer diurnal sequence (37:00–45:12).

Functioning as cues or modes of entry into the tableaus, mediators gaze or point toward what we see from other angles. Placed in the foreground or midway in the depth of field, like staffage in the foreground of classical painting, what they see (and what we believe they are seeing) amplifies the magnitude of the settings. The landscape of the Indian attack (1:25:42–1:34:42), a topos requisite for all wagon train movies, is as epic as any ever made in Hollywood.[25] Taking place on what seems to be the eastern plains of Montana, the conflict begins with shots of warriors preparing for battle amidst agglomerations of wigwams. Portraits in the style of George Catlin or Remington lend a "tableau-effect" to the sequence. In a shot reproducing the Indians' call to action (120:23–26), as he would be shown in a comic book, a Native American in full headdress, in profile, beats the drum of war. Before him a dark and wizened comrade of many years, one feather protruding from

Figure 5.6. While Native Americans beat drums in preparation for battle, in the center, an elder contemplates the fate of his people.

his thick and fulsome head of hair, sits in an air of stoic resignation (fig. 5.6). A physiognomy of suffering, his face and skin hardened by years of exposure to sun and wind—and, so the image implies, to depredation and murder at the hands of the white invaders, the Native American is indelibly authentic, unspeakably *there*. Set in front of a palomino horse and another Indian, the grim beauty of his portrait brings forward the underside of manifest destiny, prompting us to wonder if he and his coequals are on display to enhance verisimilitude, or if a politics can be felt through the scene.[26] The brutality of history is underscored in shots where the Indians rush to their horses and gather for battle. One cutaway includes a squaw, facing the gathering of warriors, wearing a bright leather papoose in which a dark-skinned baby sleeps peaceably, entirely unaware of the fate that awaits it. Stressed here, the nobility of the Native American is shown in an earlier and passing portrait when, aghast at the company to her left and right, of lilywhite aspect, Ruth is framed between two wise and stoic Native Americans the camera seems to hold in awe and admiration (fig. 5.7).

Which is not all: toward the end of the sequence, as it was at the beginning when the wagons drew into a circle, shots in counterpoint depict the battle from opposite and coequal points of view. From within the circle, reminiscent of Griffith's *The Battle of Elderbush Gulch* (1913), young mothers and children hunker down and hide while men and women, crouched under the wagons, fire away at the men who fall acrobatically from their galloping horses. Marginal to the narrative, extreme long shots

Figure 5.7. Frightened, Ruth stands to the left and right of two noble Native Americans.

of the circle of battle include hundreds of scared horses that scurry left and right within the enclosure of the wagons. As the battle winds down, three chiefs in the lower corner of the frame look on the action from a vantage point not far from where the camera stands overhead. In full headdress, seen from behind, holding their feathered spears high, mediators, they gaze upon the scene far beyond. The shot asks us to wonder what they see or think. Could it be to stress the history of their decimation? To imply an unspoken solidarity with the Cheyenne tribe's fortitude and bravery? Or, with little interest in winners or losers, to view the battle simply as a battle on a great vista? The final images refuse to answer the questions they raise.

The shot that caps the episode might be the most telling and enduring tableau of the entire film.[27] Seconds before, posing his arm on Zeke's shoulders, walking toward a wagon where women are wailing, Coleman announces what he plans to do. His back facing the camera, the words do not emanate from his body. His horse stares straight at the camera and, in the background, Ruth follows him with her eyes. At that instant he iterates a piece of the title of the film for the first time since his first appearance:

> Well, Zeke, I'm gonna trail the injuns and make sure they go back to their villages. You scout the train ahead and I'll pick it up in a week or so. (1:34:05–13)

After Coleman's departure, heading westward, the party leaves behind the graves of the victims they have just buried and mourned. In the final shot and its dissolve, almost lost in the landscape, a dog turns a conventional image of grief into searing plight and loss. The obsequies done, the party packs up. Suddenly, cut to a long shot of the graveyard in the foreground from which the members of the party, many arm-in-arm, evacuate the scene. Their heads down, they walk away and toward the wagons (1:34:19–42). In the foreground a family member goes to a grave at which two children mourn with a dog that sits at its side. The parent gathers the children, draws them away, and leads them into the crowd ambling westward. The dog settles down to stay with its dead master. In the passage of eight seconds, in the foreground of an infinitely vast landscape, in a shot of painful duration, a minuscule detail commands the scene. Refusing to leave with the collective, remaining at the sepulture, a dog becomes the embodiment of grief and fidelity (fig. 5.8).

Perspectives

It is said, rightly, that the sequence recording the party lowering wagons and chattel down a great cliffside (1:02:40–1:06:58) counts among the most daring and visually stunning tours de force the western has known. Of short duration, between two intertitles that set it within and apart from the narrative, aside from demonstrating the words announcing it ["Cliffs ahead, canyons on all sides, block the way; but there is rope, muscle and

Figure 5.8. A dog remains at the grave of its master as the wagon train departs.

determination and the big march pushes on" (1:02:40–48)], its relation to the storyline is tenuous. If it is part of the tale, it is not unwarranted to think that the block and tackle with which the oxen are carefully lowered over the cliff (1:04–11–37), or the rope the men and women hold when they inch down the steep slope (1:03–17–22; 1:03–39–1:04–06) can be seen as the narrative thread itself. In a series of takes in extreme tilt and counter-tilt, a vertiginous panorama alters conventions dictating the representation of landscape. Nineteen shots depict the event in the space of five minutes. Shown from four principal angles, the sequence begins on a horizontal plane, atop (and slightly above) the crest of the cliff where, in the background far off and away, a chain of unspecified snow-capped mountains cuts across the horizon. Three shots (1:02:58–04:02) depict the operation. In the din of men and women chattering, the first and third, close to eyeline level, compose a tableau where different (both complicated and delicate) operations lower the schooners earthward while, in the same take, squeezed together, the men and women (some with infants on their shoulders) inch their way earthward.

Throwing visual rhetoric askew (1:03:16–21), the camera points downward vertiginously (fig. 5.9).[28] Stressing the precarity of the operation, a fourth shot displays a man, fearless but fearing for life, who descends with a child who has her arms around his neck. Although subsequent takes pick up the love story by having Ruth cling to Coleman as they shimmy and scratch their way down the cliffside, the close-ups lend greater visual impact to the extreme long shots in counter-tilt that register wagons falling

Figure 5.9. Holding to ropes, the travelers descend a vertiginous cliffside.

earthward, smashing to bits (at twenty-four frames a second, and not in slow motion). Three sublimely humane shots depict how the chattel are handled. Trussed and tied, then dangling over the crest from struts and guard ropes, the frightened oxen are lowered, helpless, no less frightened or unnerved than the humans (1:05:35–36, 1:05:47–52), eliciting empathy and concern when the camera turns upward (from the point of view of Coleman and Zeke who have landed safely) to watch wagons breaking off their ropes, tumbling, rolling, and shattering. Contrasting the rhythm and measure of the montage, a long sequence shot (1:06:38–52) buckles the chapter. Now seen from far below, by a shallow and rocky river, the cliff stands behind Coleman who leads the way on horseback, and after him, two Indians who ford the current. Action is everywhere: the shore in the distance, women fill buckets with water while the three men ride along a diagonal course across the river, from background into foreground, underscoring the height, width, and depth of the mise-en-scène.

The film reaches unparalleled visual sublimity. No less breathtaking is what the montage does with proximities of life and death. Belonging to the category of intermediaries, companions in a community of beings and things, animals give credence to a sense of shared immanence. An intertitle puts an end to the party's descent from the cliffside, and a new chapter begins: "The last outpost, the turning back place for the weak; the starting place for the strong" (1:06:58–1:07:08). The words bookend relief, repose, and deliberation before the party faces the hardship of crossing the desert (1:07:08–1:22:57). Wagons approach the post where Coleman arrives on horseback (1:07:23–34). Flack, sipping a jug of moonshine, tells Pa Bascom that with five hundred miles ahead they can face hardship over the arid range or simply turn back (1:07:34–59).[29] Cut from Flack and company to the camp (in considerable depth of field) where women feed their children. Only when Coleman enters from front and center does the narrative engage a wondrous (and, in the genre, unique) scene of nature and nurture: a woman breastfeeds her baby—hardly an image in the visual lexicon of the western—while another holds her infants by her side (1:08:03–14); a foal ambles to its mother mare in search of her teats while a pig stands by its cage in front of four men and women who are picnicking (1:08–14–22); lying on an outstretched blanket, a dappled Dalmatian welcomes its puppies to suckle, their tails wagging in delight (1:08–22–27); searching for milk, three kittens approach their alert mother who watches over her litter (1:08: 27–33); a magnificent sow gives her teats to nine piglets that crowd around her belly for nourishment (1:08:34–39). Regeneration abounds.

"Tell me what you eat, and I'll tell you who you are:" The most memorable line in Anthelme Brillat-Savarin's *Physiology of Taste* would be a primer for these and the next shots recording a gamut of etiquette and table manners. In a take that reaches deep into ambient space, Flack and company sit around a mess where, growling and groveling, they tear into raw meat (1:08:39–47). One of three dogs, sniffing around for scraps, pulls a steak from Lopez's mouth before the scene suddenly cuts to Ruth, who gently stirs a *dinde au pot* while a girl cuddling a dog in her arms approaches the fire. Leaning over the stewpot, Ruth opposes Thorpe, reclining and waiting to be served, who invites her to return with him to his fictive plantation in Louisiana. Words recalling the narrative—Thorpe mendaciously beguiling Ruth—pale in view of the scene and its savory context. A carefully set table is placed behind a child and her pet next to the heroine who looks over the casserole; men and women in the background speak peaceably to one other while oxen fill out the scene with elegance and grace.[30] When Coleman enters, Ruth's son or next of kin (David Rollins) invites the hero to share the food that in fact he had delivered to the family (three shots, 1:08:59–1:09:47). Sighting Thorpe, Coleman exits. The camera cuts to Zeke and company between the wagons. Flipping pancakes over a fire, he welcomes into the men's world the lover who again has been jilted. Once the scene is set and the conversation engaged (the men have cooked and consumed eighty-five flapjacks), Coleman enters, spurning the invitation to share the fare when able only to taste the aroma of braised turkey (1:09:47–1:10:21). In the mix of the hero's tribulations, three gastronomic styles, three perspectives on civility, are juxtaposed to animals who feed themselves and nourish their young with elegance and loving care. Soon after, the sequence finds a grisly complement where horses and travelers face death and dying in the passage across the desert (1:23:35–1:26:04). An elderly member of the team falls sick and is buried in the sand by the side of the trail. The cadaver of a mule is seen on ground where bones and skulls are scattered.

Big Trees

The most commanding perspective of the film, of implication and visual measure equal to maneuvering the wagons over the cliffs, not unrelated to the civilizing process at the campsites and trading post, or the extremely long takes of the Indian attack, is shown in the sequoia forest in the film's final minutes. "We all get off on the wrong trail once in a while"

(1:42:49–50), Coleman asserts: the expedition has fought through mud and diluvial rain and is finally on a path toward the mountains on the horizon. He learns that Ruth's wagon has been left behind. Knowing that Zeke killed Thorpe while attempting to kill Coleman, Ruth finally turns her affection toward the hero. Admitting she had been misled, then he informs her she had "taken the wrong path." From then on, *trail* becomes a password. In clear allusion to the history of the Donner party in 1846, the wagon train takes refuge in the mountains at the onset of winter. Forge ahead or turn back: that is the question. Coleman implores the party (and the viewer, no doubt alluding to the Depression) to keep a stiff upper lip and hold to "the trail." The hero declares with pulpit oratory, repeating the movie's title,

> We can't turn back! We're blazin' a *trail* that started in England. Not even the storms of the sea could turn back those first settlers. And they carried in on further. They blazed it on through the wilderness of Kentucky. Famine, hunger, not even massacres could stop them. And now we've picked up the *trail* again. . . . We're building a nation. No *trail* was ever blazed without hardship. You gotta fight! What do you want to do? Lay down and die? (1:45:15–22, emphasis added)

He soon brings to the collective fresh evidence of Flack and Lopez's murderous designs. Standing by an emblematic elk carcass the men are skinning and dressing, Coleman informs the group he will kill the animal he has been pursuing. "I'm off on their *trail*" (1:48:33). "Well, Zeke, I'll see'em to the end of the *trail*. Then I'm pickin' up a new *trail*" (1:49:00). He plods off in the storm. Upon discovering Lopez's cadaver frozen in the snow, he follows Flack's footsteps. Flack climbs a ladderlike branch leaning on the left side of an immense fallen sequoia tree, shown in chiaroscuro, that fills the center of the frame, its trunk projecting toward the viewer as if it were a recumbent giant (fig. 5.10). Using tree limbs as a makeshift ladder, he climbs over the top and slips down to its other side. Coleman follows, climbs the trunk, and confronts Flack, who shoots and misses. The time lag allows the hero time enough to aim and throw a knife into his adversary's belly (1:55:20–24).[31]

Sequoias become the final and defining forms of the film. In the space of a fade the murder in winter gives way to life and growth in the spring (1:55:20–34). In a bright landscape construction of cabins is underway (where the hefty woman who was chopping wood in the second

Figure 5.10. Brett and Flack on either side of the monumental trunk of a fallen sequoia.

shot of the film is now chopping in the background). A fittingly timed butterfly flitters across the frame (1:57:24–25) when Ruth, in close-up, looking toward the screen, contemplates Coleman's absence. The film becomes a landscape when, as if mystically, the personages the narrative has destined to bring together are dwarfed under the sequoias where they meet. The cue to the event could not be simpler: while readying to pack off, Zeke hears a whoop, knows well that it is the voice (or spirit) of Coleman, then tells Ruth to find happiness in the woods beyond. She exits the cabin and community (to the left) (1:58:20–22). Cut to the majestic sequoias for three decisive seconds (1:58:23–26) *before* Ruth enters the forest. The sight of the trees implies that although their duration and grandeur humble the humans among them (witness Scotty [James Stewart] in *Vertigo*), they are nonetheless delicate. Given their adventitious roots (shown by the dead tree just seen), they are victims of their own immensity. The water that nourishes them—melting snow, dew, fog, and morning mist—is not always available; the sunlight they need is high and far above: a fragile grandeur reigns. As the shot continues (1:58: 34–39), far in the distance of a forest path in extreme depth of field, a minuscule Coleman appears (1:58:39, fig. 5.11). Approaching Ruth (or the camera), he disappears in shadow, emerges into light, then (in counter shot) sees Ruth standing by the trunk of a sequoia to her right (1:58:51). From an extreme distance, in dappled light and shadow, Coleman and Ruth approach each other (1:58–58–2:08). In the mode of a spiritual canticle

Figure 5.11. Brett meets Ruth in the great forest of sequoias.

they meet, embrace and, still humbled by the grandeur of the trees, they amble out of frame, leaving the camera to pan toward the sky above. The film ends in reference to a duration and immensity of forms and forces far beyond the scope of its players or the story just told. Unlike any western or epic film in the American canon, in its legacy *The Big Trail* can be imagined, like the fallen sequoia Coleman scales to kill his enemy, as a sleeping giant. Unlike any of the director's many westerns, it has no equal. It seems well reasoned to think that after the failure the film witnessed at the box office Walsh would turn to projects of smaller or modest proportion. Such is *Me and My Gal*, the topic of the next chapter, that brings the viewer back to urban spaces in the midst of the Depression.

6

Me, My Gal, My Brother

Me and My Gal

So you waited until they locked my brother up, and then you ran out on him, eh?

—Baby Face Castenega (Noel Madison)

Oh, What's this? A brother act or somethin'?

—"Pop" Riley (J. Farrell McDonald)

What about my brother?

—Duke Castenega (George Walsh)

❦

ALTHOUGH SMALL WHEN SEEN next to *The Big Trail*, without a doubt *Me and My Gal* (1932) stands high and strong among the features Walsh directed at Fox Studios in the early 1930s. A pre-code film, a far cry from the epics and the war trilogy Walsh had directed at the cusp of the silent and sound eras, it emerges from a group of remarkable features, now in near oblivion, historians and cinephiles may be most likely to appreciate. Titles include *The Man Who Came Back* (1931), *The Yellow Ticket* (1931), and *Wild Girl* (1932). *Wild Girl* begins in the shadows of the sequoias where *The Big Trail* ends. *Me and My Gal* can be said to begin where *Wild Girl* leaves off and to end where *The Bowery* (1933) begins. *Wild Girl* features a racy Joan Bennett, the not-so-bashful blonde of "Salomy's Jane's Kiss," the driving character in a memorable short story by Brett Harte (1836–1902). A stunning *ingénue* endowed with a shapely frame (displayed in a daring sequence of skinny dipping) and caustic wit, Salomy never minces words with her suitors. When she finally wins Billy (Charles Farrell), the lover of her choice, whom she saves from being unjustly hanged, her dreams come true.

Shot immediately afterward, *Me and My Gal* pairs an urban wild girl who makes good, another blonde Bennett, with a young Spencer Tracy, who meet in a diner (where else in the Depression?), perhaps around Fulton Street (or where young Owen Kildare had been an ice crusher in *Regeneration*), in Lower Manhattan. Where *Wild Girl* casts its players in the shadows and clefts of redwoods, *Me and My Gal* places its dramatis personae in confined or contained spaces: the edge of a pier, at the tables and counter of a crowded chowder house, near the doorway to a police precinct, at the entry and counter of a haberdashery, in a modestly furnished apartment, or in a crammed loft. Like *Wild Girl* and other titles of this moment in Walsh's career, *Me and My Gal* takes inspiration from the novelty of sound along with the visual style and manner of silent cinema. In this feature, at once immediately and accessibly (and very soon after in *The Bowery*), signature effects emerge from what the director does in mixing the two modes and their technologies.[1]

In "The Evolution of Film Language," a canonical essay of the postwar era that considers epochal transformations—the rift, reversal, and revolution—the seventh art is said to have undergone in the shift from silent to sound, André Bazin (1999, 63–80) contends that great directors, the real auteurs are (or now were) those who adapt silent composition to sound film. For Bazin, trained in land science and geography, the long take and deep focus define the spatial and temporal virtues of the seventh art. For this reason, the cinematic upheaval that came with *The Jazz Singer* (quoted in *Me and My Gal* and *The Bowery*) was less a "geological metamorphosis" or revolution than, as proposed in his analogy, an "evolution" of cinematic form.[2] Silent cinema, an "old" testament may have ceded to a "new" testament, but in the traditions of typology and figural realism that Bazin follows to the letter, the former anticipates the latter, and the latter often glosses the significance of the former.[3] Elements of the *old* live within the *new*. By dint of comparison and contrast the one endows reason and truth to the other, and vice versa.

> In fact now that use of sound has amply shown that it did not come to annihilate [*anéantir*] the Old cinematographic Testament but to fulfill it [*l'accomplir*] we can wonder if the technical revolution the soundtrack introduced truly corresponds to an esthetic revolution, in other words, if the years 1928–30 are effectively those of the birth of a new cinema. Envisaged from the standpoint of editing, the history of film does not indeed reveal a solution of continuity between the silent and the talkie so clearly as we might have thought it to have been. (1999, 63, my translation)

In *Me and My Gal*, in 1932, it is still "less a case of opposing the 'silent' to the 'talkie' than, in both the one and the other, bringing together families of style, of fundamentally different concepts of cinematographic conception" (64) to foster a distinction between the "plastic" and narrative effects of the filmic image. For Bazin, the decoupling of the sound and image tracks promotes a diagonal, differential, or transverse approach to the medium that in silent film had gone without saying. Accustomed to taking note of sound cues, to reading the moving lips of characters in the action, viewers who had been weaned on silent film were quick to see that synchronization of sound and image, at the crux of cinematic illusion and representation, often drove ideology.[4] A creatively critical appreciation began—or begins—where the silent and the talkie overlap and also where economy and the transgressive potential of the play of sound and image, when recognized as such, supersede the narrative, thus effectively "emancipating" the spectator.[5]

From this standpoint, *Me and My Gal* folds a "love story" into the new and fresh experience of a sound film withheld in the tradition of a recently silent past. The context of the Great Depression is of consequence—if only because in 1932 the effects of severe economic downturn (including, in America, as *The Monkey Talks* had shown, the misery pauperized or invalid veterans of World War I were facing) could not be disregarded. The moment of its making is everywhere and nowhere in the screenplay: the difficult years following the Wall Street crash, the effects of the Volstead Act (along with the Hays Code), the eve of the transition from the Hoover to the Roosevelt presidency and, overseas, the growth of fascism. In sum, with respect to what surrounds it, the economy (in a Freudian sense, which includes the wit and invention) of *Me and My Gal* bears strong critical and historical implication.

From Depression to Merriment

The screenplay Arthur Kober prepared for *Me and My Gal* is based on "Pier 13," a story by Philip Klein and Barry Connors, which in 1940 Eugene Forde would remake in a feature under the same title. Telling of loves won and lost, the movie of 1932 is a mixed or motley genre, principally about a cop's courtship of a street-smart cashier whose weaker sister, engaged to (and soon marrying) a nincompoop, is enamored with a former lover, a thug—having eluded the police on two occasions—who returns to New York rob the bank where she is employed. The weaker sister falls for the criminal and harbors him. The cop wins over the cashier he first met in a dockside diner. With her assistance he eventually finds and confronts the gangster. He engages in gunfire and is slightly wounded in the exchange. Winning the shootout, he watches his adversary teeter-totter and then plummet to his death from an attic storeroom in a modern apartment building. The thug now out of the picture, the policeman and the cashier can marry. The forlorn sister and witless husband join the celebration and send-off of both the story and the film. An occasionally gripping and often riotous plotline alleviates the depressive condition of its circumstance, which the comedy clearly takes its task to elide. The sorry state of the world in the exposition becomes, as the narrative thread unwinds, what it "prefers not to" remember and, at its end, almost succeeds in forgetting.[6]

The time is 1932, when much of the United States is still under the dictates of Prohibition. Four years after the advent of sound cinema, the novelty of new technology is marked time and again, emphasized in passing remarks ("you haven't heard anything yet" is uttered in reference to Al Jolson), in the sight and audition of sound machinery (in an apartment a console radio conveys information that carries the plot), and some historical reference (allusion is made to the election of 1928 that saw the defeat of Al Smith, the year after which Jolson's vocals inaugurated the new medium in *The Jazz Singer*). Recalling the force of wit and attraction Beatrice and Benedick share in *Much Ado about Nothing*, the story veers toward reflection on the nature of fraternal and sororal relations. The leading lady, Helen Riley (Joan Bennett), a strong and clearsighted woman armed with creamy lips and a razor-sharp tongue, has as a foil her weaker sister, bank clerk Kate Riley (Marion Burns), who is conflicted over a past love for a criminal who returns, "out of the past," as it were, with a trio of gangsters. The thug, Duke Castenega, happens to be Raoul Walsh's brother George. Between plot and production, the film plays delightfully on the well-worn theme of enemy brothers, as if the director, thumb-in-cheek, were taking pleasure in extending the motif of fraternal rivalry and brotherly love begun six years earlier in *What Price, Glory?*, and then, because of the fame George had known in the silent years, in having his younger sibling killed.[7]

Many episodes are tenuously tied to the story line: in two sequences the antics of a drunk (Will Stanton, who was Quartermaster Bates in *Sadie Thompson*) at harborside and in a diner divert and distract. Two raucous marriage ceremonies and their send-off are a paean to populism. Jake (Bert Hanlon), a detective who is assigned to shadow the hero, resembles a marionette or a dummy who listens to and doubles the words spoken by his "master's voice." In his role of repeating his superior's words, Jake confirms that the film is indeed a "talkie." During the party celebrating the betrothal of his daughter Kate, Pop Riley (J. Farrell McDonald) enacts violence on an electronic sound-producing mechanism when he tosses a console radio out of the second-floor window of his apartment.

Of variegated design, antics and non sequiturs mark the film's four principal spaces. (1) A dockyard by an unseen pier where workers go about their duties gives way (2) to the interior of Ed's Chowder House, a diner, revisited on four occasions where slapstick and banter mix, but also where Helen and Danny first meet each other, test each other's wit and later, where the couple, whose force of mutual attraction resembles that of Rosalind and Orlando in *As You Like It*, soon agree to marry. (3) A spare apartment on the Lower East Side, in which Helen lives with her father, Pop, has a counterpart (4) in Kate's dwelling, in which "Sarge" (Henry B. Walthall), an invalid veteran of World War I, is confined to a wheelchair below an attic where the escaped convict and criminal, Duke Castenega (brother George) hides out and, as noted, whom Danny, wounded in his shootout, drops with a bullet when the villain tries to escape through a skylight. The camera enters a precinct adjacent to the dockyard, a hat shop, the lobby of a bank, and an apartment over its vault where a family of immigrants dwells. The action tends to move in and through compact worlds populated by individuals having the lucky fortune of being employed. Rife with wit, individual scenes initially stand apart from the narrative that carries them.[8] Banter, riposte, and *quid pro quo* become matter and substance. By virtue of sidelong speech, protagonists and antagonists turn the *places* they occupy—the diner, the haberdashery, Pop's apartment, and so on—into memorable *spaces*.⁹

Title and Exposition: A Busy Dockyard

The film begins with a drum roll heralding 20th Century Fox's newly designed logo, the sculpted megalith of its name surrounded by moving beacons (0:04–0:10), a reminder of antiaircraft technology developed during World War I, projecting beams of light into the evening sky. The logo gives way to the title card, where "Fox Film presents" stands above *Me and My Gal* in cursive, over the names of the two leads, Spencer Tracy above Joan Bennett, in roman majuscule, set over (in lowercase cursive) "A Raoul Walsh Production" (0:11–24), which dissolves into the filmmaker's name ("directed by *Raoul Walsh*"). The names appear in accompaniment with perky music (0:25–31). The attribution dissolves into a card acknowledging the authors of the screenplay, the director of photography (Arthur Miller), the sound recorder (George Leverett) who ranks over the art, wardrobe, and musical directors (0:31–44). The card dissolves into the names of the players staggered across the screen, Tracy on top and Stanton on the bottom (0:45–57). In the credits the director's name has gained eminence and presence.[10]

A hierarchy is given, and so also an indication, as in the silent tradition, that the film is to be both seen and read. The last card dissolves into a close-up of two hands donning and eagerly adjusting a pair of white gloves. Inaugurating the sequence, a time-held convention cues on a detail, a visual synecdoche, that follows the gloved hands as they move upward, spiffing up a policeman's badge atop the visor of a familiar cap.[11] The camera draws away when the gloved hands place the cap on the head of the person it identifies. The first of two "hat tricks" (the second taking place in a haberdashery), the exposition establishes the profile of the yet-unnamed character. Swish-tilting upward, the camera happens upon the face of the star (or the star-to-be)—Tracy—before engaging surrounding bustle and action where men scurry about to the left and right (0:58–1:08) (fig. 6.1). Cut to the dockyard that now situates the cop: having turned about-face, he proudly struts before coming back toward the camera (1:08–1:21). Two shots later he meets an idle (unemployed?) and unshaven dockworker Frank (Frank Moran, known for the raucous voice Preston Sturges would make famous in the role of a sarcastic

Figure 6.1. Proud of his uniform, Danny opens the film when he dons his officer's visored cap.

chauffeur who drives a land cruiser in *Sullivan's Travels*), seated, somewhat disgruntled (perhaps unemployed), who reads a newspaper.

Cop (snappy): "Hi Frank!"

Frank (gruffly): "Hello, Dolan."

Dolan (cop now identified): "How's it goin', buddy."

Frank (almost growling): "I see the where the Metropolitan Opera House will open with Palliaci." [In the process-shot behind them a crane hoists a load of goods onto a boat, while men at work carry full burlap bags on their shoulders.]

Dolan, promptly revealing his social status: "Reminds me, I think I'll go to a burly-cue show tonight."

Frank, in close-up, changing the topic: "How do ya' like this? Mr. Brisbane says that the capitalistic Depression spasm is only a slight chill."

Dolan, in close-up, his lips tightening and puckering: "He does, huh. Ah . . . those politicians are all alike, they're all of 'em crooks." (01:22–44)

Cut to medium shot: a worker bearing a heavy load of bananas on his shoulder passes across the frame. In defiance of the law he is employed to defend, Dolan nonchalantly steals one from the bunch the worker is carrying. His white gloves evident, he turns, looks around (assuring us that he is nonetheless "vigilant"), then listens to Frank. Like the politicians he calls crooks, Dolan is of the same fabric. The pot calls the kettle black.

Frank: "Here's a piece [which could refer at once to the article before his eyes, to the banana, and to the film itself] about social economy."

Dolan in close-up: "Social economy, huh? They're nuts, the social economy. What's on the sportin' page?" (1:45–51)

Cut from close-up on Dolan to the dockyard where another worker, bananas slung over his left shoulder, marches by. Dolan steals a second banana—a priceless gift in times of need—that he hands to Frank. His jowls full, he speaks through the pulp he masticates, as if he were the law incarnate: "Here . . . wrap your kisser around that."

Dolan exits frame right. The camera cuts to Frank in close-up from a diagonal angle, who methodically peels the banana, tosses the skin behind his back (that we hear plopping on a metal drum, followed by two toots of a tugboat), stuffs it in his mouth, and takes two bites (1:44–2:11) (fig. 6.2). *Here, wrap your kisser around that*: the words are spoken as if, in the weak deixis, Dolan is ordering Frank to enjoy the fare but also inviting the spectator to *suck* or *chew* on the movie. From its beginning, fixating on oral pleasure, the film makes much of eating, chewing, puckering, spitting, coughing, hacking and, in sum, that its "money is where its mouth is."

Severe economic distress, indigence, and famine are briefly but decisively manifest in the next sequence. Facing the entry to the precinct where he customarily reports, Dolan notices and follows an old

Figure 6.2. Frank (Frank Moran) gobbles a banana.

man walking his dog along a pier where a cargo ship is being unloaded (2:11–21). Seen from behind a massive mooring post (2:21–26), then in medium close-up (2:27–36), the old man (Roger Imhof) puts the dog on a piling, sighs, then utters, "We've missed many a meal together." Caressing his best friend, he puts a heavy rope and weight around its neck, adding, "You'll never miss another one." Readying to drown the dog, he bemoans, "well, good-bye." (2:37–46). Dolan enters from the right, behind, then (*not* in lip-synch), as if speaking to the old man—while accusatively addressing an unemployed or indolent audience having paid money to watch the film, in two-shot: "Is that all you've got to do?" (2:46–49). Medium close-up of the old man, for viewers today an avatar of Domenico Ferrari (Carlo Battisti) in De Sica's *Umberto D*, continuing to caress his companion, responding to Dolan's words: "It's all that I can do . . . for him."

In the background, bending over and lifting freight, a busy worker displays his bottom in the middle of the field of view, suggesting that because he is employed and is laboring, the old man's plight—or the movie itself—is unworthy of attention. Holding the mutt in his arms, the old man says wistfully: "If I had nerve enough, I'd go with him" (2:49–56) (fig. 6.3). Then, in two-shot: the dog, still in the old man's embrace, faces and smiles at the spectator. Dolan extends his arm, pats the animal, uttering, "Looks like a pretty good pooch. Maybe I can find a spot for him." The old man: "You can? You mean that, officer?" (3:04–06).[12] In medium close-up, from a diagonal, the old man embracing the dog: "Ohhh, you've got a home, boy. Maybe, maybe a real home!" Conveying an unsettling visual effect, a long chain in the background, not visible beforehand in the composition, extends from the deck of the ship to where the dog is sitting, along a line of the dog's leash in the foreground, suggesting that it is attached to the world again (3:05–17).[13] Cut to a medium shot registering the old man, speechless, limping off toward the camera before a close-up of the smiling dog seemingly watches his master depart to commit suicide (3:18–25).

Cut back to the old man in close-up, looking left, wiping his eyes in front and turning right and away, "Good-bye, old pal" (3:26–30),

Figure 6.3. Amidst laborers in the background, the old man leaves the dog he will drown before Officer Dolan intervenes.

revealing in the background—continuity and visual economy being of the same measure—the signboard of the "Harbor Precinct." The old man exits frame right when, immediately in the next shot (in extreme continuity) Dolan brings the dog to the door of the precinct and enters, handing the leash to a seated friend. "Hey Joe, take care of the mouse hound here and I'll go over to the [diner] on the corner and get him somethin' to eat" (3:31–42). The dockside has become a site where work and wit are one.

Ed's Chowder House

The episode, which lasts less than three and a half minutes in the film, refers obliquely and in passing to an aggravated social milieu. Stevedores work along the docks, going about their business, without paying heed to a useless and penniless old man who considers suicide. Relief is found in the odorous warmth of the local chowder house, a *locus amoenus* where the Depression is elided or transformed into the space of a masculine community. In the next sequence, the first of five in the same setting, in direct counterpoint, famine gives way to feast, plenitude, and succulence but also to a verbal economy in which wit is legal tender, the art of placing a sharp word in a sparring contest, a *quid pro quo*, a "this-for-that" being evidence of egalitarian exchange as it rarely occurs in everyday life.[14] Dolan's voice cue signals an abrupt shift from the threshold of the precinct where Dolan leaves his canine friend to the inside of the establishment to which the film returns on three other occasions.

A carefully blocked establishing shot makes for flawless continuity. Directed toward a corner of the room where ample windows to the left and right display its mirrored name, the setting is busy (03:41) (fig. 6.4). In soft focus, in the immediate foreground, a mound of food—it takes a moment to realize that it is steamed lobster—commands the front corner of the frame, in front of a counter where a speaker-telephone is placed next to a sizable cash register. A waiter wearing a white apron hurries across the middle ground. Seated on the swivel chairs at the front of the counter, two men are speaking with a cook who is identified by his toque. To the right, a blonde cashier, her right hand resting on her neck, leans over a book. Seated behind a register and a telephone, she is oblivious, so it seems, to the ambient bustle of the working men who come and go. Busily chewing gum, engrossed in reading, she is in front of a chef (wearing his toque), in the background, who talks to two customers at their

Figure 6.4. A plate of lobsters in the foreground the interior of Ed's Chowder House (03:41).

stools. Scurrying from right to left, a waiter attends to three customers at two tables adjacent to a wall telephone and a gas lamp, while moving behind the window and then opening the door, Dolan enters the scene. In the foreground, to the right, though not immediately commanding any interest, a seated man (Stanton) pours a bowl of sugar onto his victuals. Only when Dolan speaks does the scene tie in with the dog's aborted drowning: "Hey Bud, give me a half a dollar's worth of bones" (3:41–50).

The drunk stands up to challenge the cop, slurring, "You're a policeman, aren't you?" In the background, a client seated at the counter (seen from the backside), impervious to the action, signals a sense of routine. Chewing her stick of gum, Helen (Bennett), the comely cashier, bemusedly looks up to watch the action that cues on a pun: when Dolan asks for bones the fool believes he has "bones" to pick with the policeman. Dolan, at no loss for words, addresses both the company around him and the viewer, snapping, "Here's an argument for prohibition!" Cut to comic dialogue between Dolan and the inebriated client from the perspective of the establishing shot that includes the cash register. To assuage the drunk, pointing at the plate of food, Dolan—his mouth full, as he had with his banana, chomping on a piece of food he has taken for himself—draws our eyes again to the *mouth* and *kisser* that marked the words shared with Frank. He tells him: "Now, come on, sit down, *put your puss* in that."

Mouth, puss, kiss, and kisser: Dolan catches sight of the cashier who seems to taunt him with her moving lips. While the transaction takes place over the register the visible cost of the dog bones he purchases for his new love—60¢—seems correlative with the worth of the wit. When Dolan makes his purchase, the exchange speaks to the general economy of the film. A panel on the wall in the background reads "Clam Sauce" above "Crackers," which implies that the fare in Ed's place includes well-wrought jokes. Food would be equivalent to wisecracks, to words exchanged and paid for at the "register" or sent through the telephone adjacent to the open book below the cashier's shapely body. Exchange of money and of goods finds analogy in snide remarks, in one-liners where words—tidbits like *amuse-gueules* or deep-fried clams—are served and followed by quips and rejoinders. The shot suddenly cuts to a close-up of the register that Helen rings up to read "No Sale": unlike coffee and "chowder" (in derivation of the contents of a heated cooking pot or *chaudière*), the lady is not for sale. Is it because the cashier (as cash here), having spirit the others lack, knows how to say no? Or because, alluring, equipped with a sharp tongue, she is beyond any measure of exchange value? Where Dolan and company are concerned, the register displays their estimated worth (60¢, in the Depression, a sizable sum). But, as Mastercard would put it, Helen is *priceless*. Given the greater economy in the film and its broader context, orality signals once again that the *mouth* is where the money is. In the early moments of the narrative, enticing the clientele but, above all, flirting defiantly with Dolan, chewing gum as a cow its cud, Helen endlessly puckers her lips. Close-ups call attention to oral pleasure where eating is syncopated with talking, and where, a sight to be seen, a lock of her hair on her forehead curled to resemble the arc of a circle, she stands in front of an eyelike porthole behind her (fig. 6.5).[15]

Clams and Wisecrackers

The second sequence (11:14–13:54) in the diner begins, like the opening shot of the film, with a synecdoche. In close-up two cups of coffee are being filled. Suddenly, in a cut to a medium shot, they are brought to

Figure 6.5. In front of a porthole, Helen smiles to conquer.

the counter where Dolan and Al, his shadow, have repaired to dry off after jumping in the water to "save from drowning" the drunk who had fallen off the nearby dock. Behind the ruckus at dockside, Duke Castenega (George Walsh), his brother, "Babyface" (Noel Madison), and his henchmen have managed to slip away from the eyes of the two detectives (or, in the slang of the moment, the two "dicks"). At Ed's Chowder House, coffee, a universal solvent in Depression films, comes with an attractive waitress who works on the other side of the counter. Dolan confirms laconically—hence thriftily—in the words he shares with Al when sipping coffee at the counter (Dolan: "Whadjha' think they were gonna do? Hop in after us to keep us company?"). Once again, a diagonal shot (11:40), now in the evening light, frames the men talking, the chef who listens and, in the foreground, Helen, a mischievous Eve, reading a book, biting into and ostentatiously chewing an apple. The community in Ed's Chowder House turns to pandemonium when the drunk, teeter-tottering into the diner for a second time, is told to leave. Exiting, he knocks over a waiter burdened with a tray of dirty dishes, whose clatter allows Helen reach for the telephone to contact her sister. Only then, like whipped cream, does the plot thicken.

A third sequence (29:58–34:47) in the diner is even more tenuously attached to the narrative. While by their car Dolan and Al hear a dispatcher's voice (whose authority is greatly enhanced when heard-*off* or cannot be located in the frame), informing them that a disturbance is taking place at Ed's. The drunk who had caused a ruckus earlier wields a flounder to slap the face of an adjacent client. Excited that Helen may be there, Dolan arrives, witnessing three inebriates arguing over the name of the fish the drunk continues to brandish by its tail. The man whom the drunk has threatened insists it is a "bloater" (a "bloatah"—but what is a bloater? A smoked herring? A cisco?). Seated, a drunken Englishman (Ralph Sipperly), raising his index finger, says, "You're wrong, actually, the fish is a salmon." Riposte: "I know what it is, it 'tis a bloatah." Cut to the Englishman (behind whom is Helen, who steals the scene chewing her gum, her moving lips having an uncommon erotic charge), who insists, "I do not like to be contrary, but you were struck with a salmon." "What's the use of wrangling, I know the difference between a bloatah and a salmon!" The drunk, who slaps the fish on the table: "You're both wrong, it's a halibut." The Englishman, bending over, sniffing it: "Pardon me, old boy, you made an error. It's not a halibut, it's a striped bass" (31:07–09). Synched with the pun (the drunk responds, "Call me that again," one man's bass being another man's bottom) when Danny, wearing a bowler hat, enters with his assistant—thus returning to the narrative. "Wait a minute, wait a minute, what's goin' on here?" All the while chewing her chiclet, feigning disinterest, Helen (now named, her cheek bedecked with a beauty spot near her moving lips), dressed in a checkered blouse matching the tablecloths and curtains, looks at the antics with detached amusement. The camera continues to cue the dialogue in focusing on the mouth. Dolan asks those present (and, as if tongue-in-cheek, the viewer): "Now, cut out the comedy, so who slapped who and with what?" But whose comedy is it? In his signature rasp, seated behind Dolan, Moran growls,

> I was sittin' here with my beak in a bowl of chowder and this dude comes into the stew with a big shad in his mitt. This Chinaman here says, 'waiter, where's my fish?' and this stew bum says here and wraps it around his puss.

In the thick of the quarrel Dolan and Helen manage to flirt, eventually sharing a couple of winks. Returning to work, she notices a newspaper announcing Castenega's incarceration "up the river," in other words, Sing-Sing. As if by happenstance, the film returns to the business of its narrative.

The fourth sequence (56:05–26) has Dolan entering the café at night, closing, while a sailor and dockworker, exiting, cast *noir*-like shadows on the window. The camera tracks into a two-shot that sets the lovers in profile (the poster for "clam juice" and "crackers" is squarely between them), where objects of superb oral fantasy are eminently visible: a rotund jar filled with doughnuts, the button handle on its lid the virtual nipple of a breast, and a bowl of candies (fig. 6.6). The longest shot of the film (56:34–58:13) records Dolan proposing to Helen. Beginning with the two-shot in which Helen prepares sugar for the next day's service, the camera tracks to the corner of the counter where Dolan declares (under a sign for Boston Clam Chowder), "Come on, be a good fellow and marry me, will yah?" The shot tracks back to the jar on which Helen sets her arms—to mark her affinity with a glazed doughnut—where she accepts the proposal, *not* with spoken words but with a quick nod. She adds, as if indicating how sign language, the lingua franca of the silent tradition, prevails in this film: continuing to chew, she pauses and continues, drawing attention to the sound track, "consider it said" (57:54).

Figure 6.6. Danny proposes to Helen over a doughnut jar.

Because her establishment is "closing up" the only option she has is to open herself to his vows. With delightful innuendo Dolan adds, "well, I'm closin' in before you're closin' up" (58:10).[16]

Another Writing Scene

The fifth and final sequence (1:09:43–1:11:40) stages passage of visually coded oral messages from the tradition of intertitles crafted to nestle into narrative. As if the robbery were a model for the daring but aborted theft in Jules Dassin's *Rififi* (1955), Castaneda and his crew have just entered the bank vault by cutting their way through the floor of an apartment (occupied by an anxious family of Italian immigrants) in the area above. Using an acetylene torch that scatters sparks as it cuts into the metallic joists and beams, the thieves (wearing goggles) cut through the metal panel. The film dissolves from night to the following day, only hours after Helen and Danny have used sign language to transcribe Sarge's (Henry Walthall's) blinks, in Morse code, warning them that the evil Duke is hiding in the attic immediately above Pop's apartment (59:00–1:01:30). In a suave sequence shot establishing the scene (1:09–55–1:10:30), the camera dollies back from a close-up of Helen, seated at her corner of the counter, behind the telephone and cash register (icons of the film) in the center of the frame. She studiously consults a gazetteer to decipher the dots and dashes, while Dolan, now in the shot, wearing his bowler hat, is seated on a stool (at a right angle). His cheeks are full as he chomps his victuals (orality pervades in the chowder house) while stealing a glance at Helen (1:10:00). The camera dollies back, leaving Helen out of frame, to include the short-order cook informing Dolan of the bank robbery. Amidst clatter of cups and saucers, set adjacent to the cash register in the foreground (obliquely reminding us of the exchange value of the words bantered), the shot suavely envelops (or even exceeds) the story line:

> **Cook**, who would be reading a paper: "Here's a hot one."
>
> **Dolan**, pouring cream into his coffee: "Who'd the bank rob this time?"
>
> **Cook** (after reading paper): "No one. This time the bank was robbed."

Dolan: "Ah, this time the bank was double-crossed, uh? Gettin' a little dose of their own medicine." [He stirs his cup, still eating.]

Cook: "Can you imagine? (He reads a newspaper hidden behind the cash register). Six bandits held up a family living over the bank and bore through the floor into the vault" [Paying no heed to the conversation, a client in the back, leaning on the counter, lifts a cup of coffee to his lips.]

Dolan: "Oh, I remember that job. They got away with $87,000, didn't they? That ain't a bad haul, 87 grand!"

Cook [as if having the last word at the end of the shot and predicting the events of January 6, 2021]: "One of these days, they'll steal the White House in Washington!" (1:09:58–1:10:30)

Food, chatter, clatter, and narrative. First, because whatever the cook is reading is *not* shown, the "hot one" would be any number of things: the mise-en-scène, a plate of food, Helen, or the words themselves.[17] How Dolan would have known of the heist is left unexplained. A close-up of Helen (110:30–36), still chewing gum and studiously transcribing the code into alphabetical characters, gives way to a close-up of the process of "writing," a production of icons and "signs" both linked to narrative and intertitles belonging to the "hieroglyphic" character of silent cinema. On the left, seen at an oblique angle, an open book displays an alphabet adjacent to its code. On the right, her left hand pressing on a notebook and her right "translating" the message with a pencil (1:10:36–49) before an extreme close-up, a virtual intertitle, follows the pencil that has written in majuscule (110:50–51), its tip ending at the foot of the last letter, while ambient noise fills the soundtrack,

DUKE CASTENEGA
IN ATTIC

before cutting back to Helen, in profile, adjacent to the cash register, who now reads and understands the words. Behind her (although in most likelihood we attend to the "scene of writing" in the foreground), in soft focus, behind her blonde pate, Dolan looks directly at what she is doing. "87 grand, that's a lotta jack, ain't it!" All the while, keeping in view the cash register that displays a recent sale of forty cents, the camera tilts up, as if it suddenly were hearing what he says. Amidst the clatter, talking with his mouth full, Dolan continues: "If we had 87 grand we could get married this afternoon." His spoken words are countered by the written characters Helen suddenly reads. An oblique two-shot (1:11:00 sets the iconic telephone and register in the middle of the frame between Helen and Danny, speaking as if he were married, who quips, "Hey stupid, have you filled the check yet?" Voices seem to scatter in the space of the diner. Helen, discombobulated, "No, uh, yes. [She gets up with the pad.] I've got to go on an errand." Danny, wryly: "Why don't you do it?" As if responding to Helen, who nervously replies, "I'm going," the camera pano-dollies effortlessly across the interior, stopping momentarily on the couple (Helen: "I'll be right back. Will you wait for me?" Dolan, ironic, talking with his mouth full: "I'll think it over"), setting a scene of everyday life in a workers' restaurant in counterpoint to the urgent turn in the narrative. Following Helen, who exits hurriedly, the camera pans right, catching in the foreground (and recording, -*off*, a voice uttering, "an order of fries, Eddie") a seated couple busily eating their fare.

As in the best tradition of efficient editing, the shot cuts back to Danny exactly when and where Helen closes the door behind her (1:11:20). Relentless in its stress on orality, a medium shot places Danny's mouth on a sightline that joins his lips with the CHOWDER sign on the wall in the background. Having eaten his portion (or the word), he wipes his lips and chin with a white handkerchief, exhales with pleasure ("ahhhh") while the short-order talk continues ("a plate of clams!"). He gets up and, as the camera dollies back, he barks, "How 'bout a check?" Since no one is at the register (there is no one or any machine to record or respond to what he says, while the camera dollies in), "If you're not gonna write out a check I'll write it out myself." Cut (1:11:30) to Dolan (honestly) *writing* his own bill on the top of the register whose last sale was "40 cents." He speaks, chewing and tracing at the same time, taking careful account of the amount of money spent: "one cheese sandwich, 15 cents, one Java, 10 cents ... uhh ... one rice pudding, two bits."

With the next shot, a coyly inserted intertitle in extreme close-up, a Freudian "mystic writing pad" effect comes forward (1:11:43–46). The sheet on which Danny has written his bill (in cursive characters) is torn away, revealing its carbon copy below, that itemizes his meal ("1 Cheese sand / 1 Java / 1 Rice pudding"). Given the correlation of money and mouth, the figures adding up to 55¢ are inscribed above the "memory-trace" of Helen's transcription of Sarge's winks in Morse code. A lynchpin in the narrative, the image of the two scripts—one darker and the other, lighter, pressed through another sheet (fig. 6.7)—sums up all the sign theories of tracing and memory that bring Freud into cinema.[18] The film coyly reflects on its mode of production, and beyond the story line it offers a glimpse of its political economy.

Hat Tricks

In an earlier sequence, following Dolan's comical rescue of the drunk from the East River, upon his promotion Danny awards himself a derby to replace his officer's cap. When he jaws with Helen in the stairwell of Pop's apartment, she takes it, puts it on her head, and sports it with a slight tilt. Mention of the style forces recall of the brief but telling episode in the haberdashery where Dolan absent-mindedly buys the very hat he wears (0:19–24). Accompanied by Mike, his moronic double or dummy, Dolan rushes into the store, removes his derby, and sets it on the counter. Barking to a salesman who had congenially said "hello," he responds, "Never mind the hello, I came here to tell you the hat

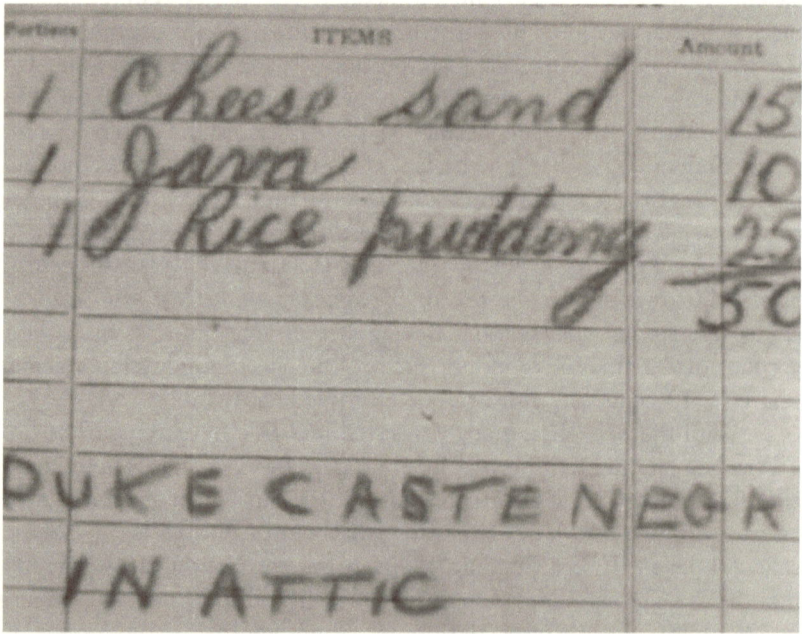

Figure 6.7. A bill, its copy, and a message: an imprint of the film.

I bought is no good!" An assistant in the foreground exits, revealing a sculpted head that rests on the counter. A two-shot puts the bald-headed salesman opposite Dolan, hirsute, who barks, "Hello, no hello, I've come in here to tell you the hat I bought is no good." The salesman, turning and pointing to shelves behind him, replies "What are you kickin' about, I've got hundreds here that are no good. How do you think I feel about it." In full view of the sculpted head, Dolan, voice-off, " 'Yeah, how do you think he . . .' you got me doin' it now! All kidding aside, now, I want another hat. You got a nice one?"

Plopping a hat on the sculpted head, he offers Dolan another, announcing, "There you are, a happy warrior." (He sets it on the table, pointing to it with his index finger.) "Now there's a hat I sold to Al Smith. There's the hat Smith wore when he ran for president." Pan up to Dolan putting it on his head, angrily: "Yeah? Well, he might have worn it when he ran, but he didn't win." Cut to a medium shot (salesman off), as Dolan tries on a couple of hats. "You know, I was disappointed when Smith didn't win." Voice-off: "I couldn't help it. I couldn't run for him. You know, there's enough Smiths in the phone book to elect him."

Once again politics intervene, are quickly elided, but cannot be forgotten. Mention of Smith's defeat (and his derby), in view of Herbert Hoover's program that brought economic collapse, interrupts the comedy. Behind Dolan, in the middle of the frame, curiously, a mirrorlike figure, a sculpted head wears a hat doubling the bust on the counter. Dolan, doffing a gray derby: "Yeah, that's much better! Much better!" Salesman, voice-off: "Too small." He turns toward the counter, "I want the black one anyway!" The camera pans back to the counter, the bald salesman, and sculpted head that wears a black hat. Dolan takes it, palpating its brim: "Hey, that don't look bad! Ya know [camera pans into medium close-up], Smith might not have been a bad president at that!" He puts the hat on his head. Dolan in close-up, salesman, off: "Ahh, ya can't tell. You know, it took two Smiths to make a cough drop." The sequence alludes to the dismal character of Hoover's domestic policy, which perhaps is cause enough for Dolan to purchase his own hat—or perhaps to the condition of viewing cinema circa 1932, when boxes of the bearded Smith Brothers' jet-black cough drops were sold in the lobbies of movie theaters.

If so, the sculpture becomes an icon or double of the viewer (20:27, fig. 6.8). In a last exchange of words in the haberdashery, amused at Dolan's oversight, in close-up next to the sculpture, the salesman looks toward the door while addressing the bust (crafted in the style of sculptor Jo Davidson). He speaks softly in its right ear: "Now there's a fine detective! I sold him his own hat!" The mute speaker—the sculpted

Figure 6.8. In a local haberdashery, a bald salesman comments on the hat Danny will soon purchase.

head—listens. One quip follows another: when Helen enters promptly, Dolan and the detective return. She spars with her suitor and turns to the salesman, informing him (for no good reason) that a marriage sequence will follow: "I just wanted to remind you, there's going to be a wedding tomorrow night." Dolan mimics her, departing, sucking a stogie and looking directly at the contours of her buttocks while egging her on, "There's a wedding tomorrow night," which Mike repeats. Close-up of the salesman who whispers to the dummy who listens: "I just wanted to remind you. There's going to be a wedding tomorrow night." The bust that seems to see and listen but refuses to speak puts stress on the autonomy of the sound and image tracks.

Precode Fancy

In one of the feature's best-remembered sequences midway through the film, pushing the limits of the regulations concerning sexual conduct in cinema prior to 1934 (40:28–40), Helen and Danny, finally alone in Pop's apartment, take time to get acquainted. Helen doffs Danny's bowler and struts around to the tune of a jazz broadcast from a console radio (in the 1930s an icon of an earlier technology, underscoring what cinema is now doing in coordinating and differentiating its sounds and images). A reverse shot establishes Danny staring and smiling at what he beholds. Helen bends over the machine to amplify the music, wiggling and almost thrusting her buttocks before the camera, suggesting that her bottom is where the melody begins (fig. 6.9). Surely aiming to entice Danny, she also challenges cinematic codes. Little surprise that the shot follows her dancing and strutting to the couch where, now seated, holding a box of chocolates in his left hand with his mouth full, he offers a sample to Helen (39:11). The fingers of his right hand that clasp the bonbon are exactly at the eyeline of the nipple of her left breast. "Want another piece?" "Thanks." He lies down, resting his head on her lap. Helen: "Why don't you send for your trunk?" She continues to chew the candy ostentatiously. Danny suddenly raises his legs and thrusts his feet into the foreground of the shot whose background displays a framed print of HOME SWEET HOME. To which, looking forward and not backward,

Figure 6.9. Wearing Danny's bowler hat, Helen adjusts the volume of a radio playing upbeat jazz.

Danny's words draw attention. As the shot fades, sucking his chocolate, he replies, "Well, I did, it looks like I won myself a home." Losilla (2020, 31) remarks that when her ass (*su culo*) is front and center, and when Danny, on the divan, sticks his feet into the foreground, the staging seems intended to push the limits of accepted taste before adding, pertinently, that the shots destabilize or even invert the terms that go with the rules of "classical" cinema. "The ass, the feet: these parts of the body that are not assumed decorative, that a conventional shot tends to occlude [*ocultar*], are situated along a primary sight line." What would be vulgar, he adds, is treated with gracious harmony because the tracking shot that followed Helen from the radio to the couch, in synchrony with the music emanating from the radio engages its "moral" dimension of attraction and distanciation, what later, in the 1950s, Luc Moullet (and after him, Jean-Luc Godard) would contend about its heritage and its ethical virtue. Less direct but in the same spirit, tending more to Walsh the man than to the rhetoric of the film, Moss observes that "the closeups of Tracy's and Bennett's bodies, the mannerisms as these two fall in love with each other, seem to come directly from Walsh's unconscious" (2011, 136). If, as analysts have said over and over again, the unconscious is structured like a language, it follows that its idiom belongs to cinema, and that the aim of cinema, *Me and My Gal* being no exception, is to produce and disseminate the drives and conflicts that define the unconscious. This sequence and others show exactly how and why it does.

Closure in Dialogue

Pop Riley (J. Farrell MacDonald) bears the task of ending the film. Long beforehand, in three close-ups, he breaks the implicit barrier a conventional film would set between itself and its spectators. In the first, to which the last will allude in buckling the narrative, in a short sequence shot (0:21–46), amidst revelry in flagrant defiance of Prohibition, the unabashed Irishman celebrates the first of two marriages, on this occasion his daughter Kate's betrothal to her inept groom. When the rings are exchanged the Irish priest's last words presage the outcome: "I now pronounce you man and wife, and *may the devil take the first one* that goes between ya!" It will be the devil—or Danny—who shoots Duke Castenega. In this sequence Pop pushes the officiant away, walks toward the camera in close-up, grinning, inviting spectators to join the party. "C'mon! Who'd Like a Drink!? C'mon!"[19]

So also, later in a median sequence: early in their courtship, Helen and Danny find a moment of intimacy. Having no space of their own to share, they pay a visit to Pop. Realizing the couple needs time together, Pop leaves on the pretext he must see his other daughter. At the doorway (where Helen and Danny felt attraction amidst the flow of beer and whiskey at Kate's marriage), as if spoofing a future signature-sequence of *The 39 Steps*, Pop turns around, addresses the camera with salty words:

> Here's one for you, Jack. The first time Pat ever saw a train enterin' a tunnel at 60 miles an hour, he said, awwwh, if that thing ever missed the hole, hahaha! (39:42–43)

In its flagrant obscenity the parting shot anticipates Pop's last words capping Helen and Danny's send-off that goes with the film at its ebullient end. The bride and groom board the boat that will take them to Bermuda. Helen asks Danny to wear his hat tilted (as she had done when flirting on the couch at the midpoint of the film). They kiss, and Pop suddenly appears in extreme close-up, addressing and reminding the viewer that it is *a film*: "Well! It's all over!" *He winks his right eye*: "Tomorrow, let's have another drink! Ha ha ha! Ho ho ho!" (1:19:47–50, fig. 6.10). Would

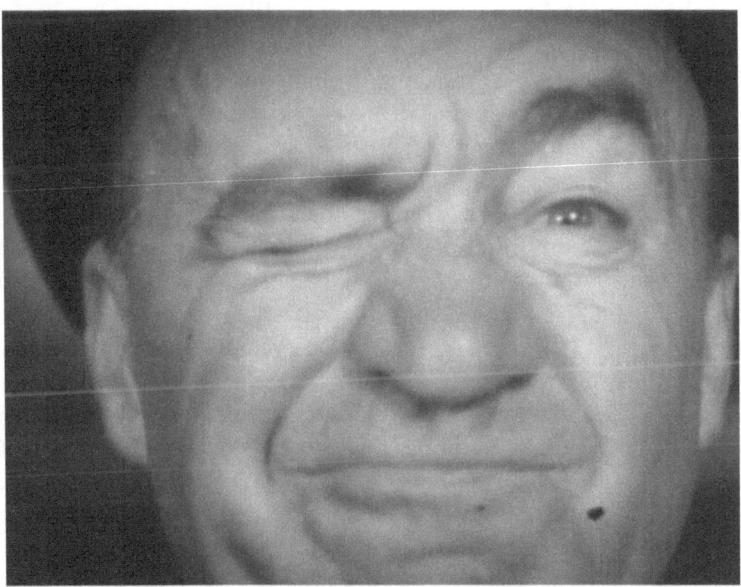

Figure 6.10. Ending the film, Pop winks at the viewer.

the wink be to Walsh at the threshold of the end credits? In view of so many allusions to the ocular traits of the film—who sees what and from what point of view—it might be a nod to the one-eyed director. And moreover, just as the beginning of the comedy featured the unsettling episode of the old man and his dog, signaling the "inconvenient truth" of the Depression Danny prefers not to acknowledge when looking at a newspaper, the arrival of Sarge in the back seat of a limousine forces recall of the history the film had bracketed. Invalid, immobile, communicating only by *winking* his eyes, victim of World War I, he reminds revelers and viewers of a discomfiting, even traumatizing past and present that hilarity can assuage but not entirely wipe away.

The success of *Me and My Gal* could not have been lost on 20th Century Fox. In 1940 the studio launched *Pier 13*, a remake aimed perhaps at turning attention away from the imminent onslaught of World War II. In the beginning shots the longshoreman's (Moran's) words about economic collapsing are gone. The new cop-on-the-block (Lloyd Nolan, lifelong member of the Republican Party) snickers where Dolan had spoken with committed wit. Mention of "puss" and "kisser" are gone. Absent is the destitute man attempting to drown his hungry dog. Nary a drunken stooge intervenes to offer comic diversion. Lynn Bari's sappy interpretation of Helen shows what makes Bennett so special: streetwise, plebian, a Shakespearean lady par excellence, as noted, a Beatrice or a Rosalind reminiscent of *As You Like It*, she carries aristocratic wit and style. Pausing before launching carefully uttered ripostes, she draws attention to elegance of timing and crisp elocution. Close-ups celebrate the synching of the movement of painted lips with the words that pass between them. Eddie (George Chandler), Kate's hilariously nerdy, bespectacled Navy recruit husband is replaced by a svelte and masculine refugee from a western (Louis Jean Heyt) who would be a handsome rival of the principal thug. Contrary to *Pier 13*, Walsh's film teems with movement, background and foreground, with figures bustling about, taken with and performing their labors. Seen in deep focus, interiors are speckled with objects, having everything and nothing do with the narrative, that lead the eye all over and about the field of view. In the remake Walsh's diagonal and ever-skewed views in the diners or apartments, so telling in the feature of 1932, become flat and monochrome. But not *The Bowery*, a virtual sequel to *Me and My Gal*, another feature set in New York, that reaches back to the time and space of *Regeneration*. Realized in the spirit of the film of 1932, another comedy born of the Depression, *The Bowery* stays true to the play of tradition, technology, and (however inferred it may be), like the brother act in *Me and My Gal*, in its crass joviality it carries a political aesthetic of consequence. Such the topic of the chapter to follow.

7

The Good, the Bad, *The Bowery* (1933)

IN A SEQUENCE OF *In Old Arizona* (1928), the first western talkie shot outdoors and on location in Zion National Park, Utah, roguish cavalry sergeant Micky Dunn (Edmund Lowe) romances lovely Tonia Maria (Dorothy Burgess). In the shade under a grove of desert palms he teaches her how to sing "The Bowery."[1] Accompanied by the notes a nearby noncom plays on a harmonica, his accent definitely out of Brooklyn, Lowe intones, "The Bowery, the Bowery . . ." Holding her in his arms, he croons, "They say such things, they do such things, on the Bowery, the Bowery, I never go there anymore." Lowe could have been recalling his pranks in *The Cock-Eyed World*, when he baited Flagg, his beloved enemy brother, into trashing the restaurant where he had been romancing a floozie named Fanny (Jean Laverty). Shortly after the mayhem is over Flagg receives a bill. Amounting to $16.75 ($2.00 for the room and $14.75 for damage to furniture), the numbers and addition were penned under the emblem of the "Bowery Plaza Hotel" at the corner of Spring Street and Third Avenue, not far from where, fifteen years earlier in *Regeneration*, Owen Kildare learned how to survive among warring gangs of thugs and impoverished Irish locals.

In Walsh's early cinema Manhattan's Lower East Side is identified with the world his forebears might have known long before the turn of the century: one of pauperism, squalor, and misery. No wonder that in the front credits of *The Bowery* (1933) Walsh reprises the song Dunn had sung to his lady. The tune calls forth a rollicking, fin-de-siècle Bowery, perhaps as a panacea to the Depression, the condition the film briefly acknowledges but no sooner leaves unspoken. The wide-open spaces of the western frontiers, the settings of recent features include not only the rocky desert spotted with Joshua trees where the Cisco Kid rides in *In Old Arizona*, not far from the mountainscapes of *High Sierra*, but also the magnificent sequoia forest (near Big Trees, California) in *The Big Trail* and *Wild Girl*. They find an apt foil in Walsh's city movie that romanticizes the destitution Jacob Riis had made known in *How the Other Half Lives* or the director himself in the early sequences of *Regeneration*.[2]

The history of *The Bowery* suggests that after absorbing four failures at the box office, which include *The Man Who Came Back* (1931), *Women of All Nations* (1931), and *The Yellow Ticket* (1931), plus the all-but-forgotten *Hello, Sister!* (1933), Walsh needed success. Darryl Zanuck, a "brash and very independent producer," came to the rescue with the offer to have him direct a feature about a location dear to his heart. The romantic treatment of the slum, with the "exuberance, the male bonding, and the thrill of good drinking among men" (Moss 2011, 138–39) would have been a salutary antidote to the condition Franklin D. Roosevelt was inheriting from the aftereffects of the Hoover administration. The biographer adds that based upon a story titled "When the Bowery Was in Bloom," published in the *Saturday Evening Post* (December 19, 1925), the production set into opposition two difficult—obstinate, egotistical, objectionable—characters and their players, Chuck Connors (Wallace Beery) and Steve Brodie (George Raft). The requisite mediatrix and love object whom Brodie wins over Connors—as Quirt (Edmund Lowe) had Charmaine (Dolores del Rio) over rival Flagg (Victor McLaglen) in *What Price Glory?*—is Lucy Calhoun (Fay Wray). At the beginning of *King Kong*, we recall, Lucy is an innocent beauty, an Eve of sorts and a scapegoat of the Depression held guilty for stealing an apple; she's a person whose grace and charm have calmed the wrath of an enchained gorilla. Lucy enters *The Bowery* in the same way. Lost and penniless, she manages to negotiate the hostility two apelike rivals, another pair of enemy brothers, share with each other. Despite her empathy and kindheartedness, Lucy is hardly an exemplar of moral fortitude. Descending from the upper echelons of Midtown Manhattan to the Lower East Side, adrift in its maze of crooked lanes, fearful, she walks timorously into Connors's saloon. Two habitués invite her to make a living in prostitution just before Connors, a rough-cut angel with dirty wings, lifts her out of her misery, offering her sanctuary in his modest apartment. But this is not long before she meets Brodie, whose aggressive advances pull her out of her savior's orbit. Although indebted to her crude benefactor, who cannot muster words adequate enough to convey his nascent affection and empathy, falling for Brodie, she lets desire (and perhaps unspoken ambition) take command. Swipes McGurk (Jackie Cooper), the blond and blue-eyed orphan child, a juvenile delinquent whom Connors had taken under his wing, is hardly cute or endearing. His puerile hate of Lucy, whom he takes to be a rival, makes her life intolerable. A lousy brat, Swipes is the boy who fires stones with a slingshot at the windows of a crowded tenement in Chinatown. One of them cracks the glass, whose shards knock over a kerosene lamp, causing a conflagration that burns alive countless residents.

Logographs

Rife with memories of World War I, the logo emblazoning "20th Century Pictures, Inc" (prior to the more familiar "20th Century Fox") introduces the front credits. A megalith of majuscules, the name is set on a great stylobate, heralded by beacons sending five shafts of light into the cloudy sky above. The logo makes us wonder if the film internalizes or projects memories of international conflict.[3] Like the last shots of the two war films of 1926 and 1929, the conflict and waste of the years 1917–18 are shunted onto Connors's and Brodie's trivial pursuits.

Now, in 1933, push coming to shove, the two men ultimately repatriate, join the army, and march off in glory and fanfare. Taking leave of questionable situations at the moment the Spanish-American War is announced, the couple sets off to defend a nation's policies for which neither has an inkling nor would they ever care. Narrative resolution or reflection on the situation is deferred—or ended catch-as-catch-can—when Connors and Brodie join to fight not against each other, but merely for the sake of fighting (fig. 7.1).[4]

Anchored in the site of its name, *The Bowery* blueprints (and, it can be ventured, inspires) Martin Scorsese's epic *Gangs of New York* (2000), one of whose narrative sequences, in homage to the film of 1933, stages a battle between rival fire departments. (Viewers cannot fail to recall its last bird's-eye shots of Lower Manhattan, anticipating the carnage of 9/11, setting on display the megalithic World Trade Center Towers.) In *Gangs*, where Scorsese envisions a mythic world writ large, *The Bowery* is intimate, local and, to its honor, everywhere self-deprecating and proud of its refined treatment of bad taste. Like the district attorney and his sister

Figure 7.1. Connors and Brodie are off to war.

in the beginning of *Regeneration* who visit the lower depths of Manhattan, viewers are invited to go slumming in a riotous and wacky world.

Along the way, many of the street names of Little Italy and Chinatown—Delancey, Mott, Grand, Forsyth, Rivington, etc.—become familiar landmarks of a carefully plotted topography. Yet, in 1933, in most likelihood viewers were clearly aware that, just as it had been in 1898, the Bowery was a dump, as it would be for those seeing *On the Bowery* (1955). But now the Bowery belongs to the rich and well heeled who have converted the area into a site of luxury, a playground for the rich, much as housing developments in Brooklyn have done in their alignment along the infamously polluted Gowanus Canal. By virtue of the name of its director, indirect acknowledgment of (or a curtsey to) *Regeneration* accounts for the gap between the Bowery then and as it is in different times. Here, in 1933, in the nostalgic tenor at the beginning of *The Bowery*, we are told to suspend disbelief and take pleasure in slumming for a duration of 132 minutes. The brash, boorish, unstintingly obnoxious manner of the two protagonists, both unabashed racists, perhaps tells us why, before Amazon dared to stream it for rental or purchase, DVDs or videotapes of the film were hard to find. Only when seen and shown in retrospectives, so it appears, had the feature found a critical context capable of bracketing its often slovenly banter and bawdy comedy.[5] Yet, notes Walsh's biographer: "From the two main lugs [Wallace Beery and George Raft] to young Jackie Cooper's tragic [?] little street-urchin, to the homeless waif (Fay Wray) whom Berry [sic] takes under his wing, the picture teams [sic] with exaggerated street-smarts that render it nothing less than authentic" (Moss 2011, 140).

Authentic? In view of lithographs and photographic documents of the Bowery in the last quarter of the nineteenth century, or even the opening shots of *Regeneration*, authentic *The Bowery* is not. The origin of the screenplay in a popular weekly aside, the film is much like a "novel without a hero," or a work of "*contredictz*" crafted to disallow any sustained identification with a single object or character, beckoning us to see it as an arena of *contradiction*.[6] Evidence of a proto-Brechtian composition cannot be dismissed. The ostensive "nostalgia" of its time and place that would foreshadow *The Strawberry Blonde* (1941), another feature about two rivals seeking a same love object, skips over memories of Lower Manhattan in the feature of 1915 while holding to the disquietingly jovial depictions of fraternal enmity in *What Price Glory?*, *The Cock-Eyed World*, and *Women of All Nations*. Loose enough to allow inclusion of George Walsh in a deftly drawn cameo in the role of John L. Sullivan, in a ringside sequence the camera delights in displaying muscle and sweat for which the director's brother had been known in his many silent films; and further, "John L.," as Brodie calls him, seems to pre-empt another cameo, in *Gentleman Jim* (1942), in which the same rugged boxer (played by Ward Bond), defeated at the hands of an effeminate and gracious adversary, breaks into tears when, movingly (to the tune of "Auld Lang Syne"), he avows that his glory days are over.

From the outset the film establishes a tempo as fast as *Me and My Gal*. Shot with dispatch, fisticuffs, nasty wit, boorish sentimentality, pizzazz, and raunchy choreography are flawlessly meshed. Fast-paced montage offsets deliberative sequences, conferring upon the film an uncommon rhythm, alternating action and release, expenditure, and occasional pause for reflection. Signatory elements include, per usual, stress on ocular attraction (fitting for pre-code cinema), emphasis on "perspective" (surface effects, depth of field in the views of streets and of the East River), heavy emphasis on closed spaces (taverns, apartments, thresholds), staging of illusion (dancing and boxing), doubling (one personage mirroring the other), and the contrast of an inert or dead form, a dummy or simulacrum (analogous to the film itself) with its living other—a regime suggestive of ventriloquism, in which personages visibly mime the very personages they are slated to be.[7] The play on the myth and history of Lower Manhattan pervades, and so also an oscillation of style and mimetic levels, in view of which the implied viewer would be "above," superior to, or outside of the antics, but also by way of attraction or under the force of guilty pleasure, within or indulgently close to them.

The front credits say much about the film's affective hierarchies. "Joseph M. Schenck presents a Darryl F. Zanuck production" (0:14–20) is printed in shadowed characters on stucco-like stone over wafting folds (surely signaling the sight of water from the Brooklyn Bridge at a turning point in the movie (1:00–01) before Beery, Raft, and Cooper, three "men" (in sans serif majuscule) constitutive of the "man's world," the formula Connors coins in conversation with Swipsie (0:21–27), before a wiperlike beam—recalling the 20th Century logo just above (0:03–10)—brings the title forward (0:28–35). The hierarchy could not be clearer. It is a "man's world" where the names of three leads, two lugs and a boy, are spelled out in uppercase (sans serif) letters over the female counterparts, in lower-point majuscule:

WALLACE BEERY...................	Chuck Connors
GEORGE RAFT.....................	Steve Brodie
JACKIE COOPER...................	Swipes McGurk
FAY WRAY	Lucy Calhoun
PERT KELTON	Trixie Odbray

They are poised above five others (including George Walsh and the well-named Lillian Harmer, who plays "Carrie A. Nation," the famously brazen tea toddler at the head of the (famously vicious) women's temperance league that in the film will trash Connors's saloon). The director's card (0:36–42), followed by the first narrative credit, in recall of silent cinema, gives the lie to what the music suggests is a jovial *genius loci* in the late 1890s. Against the same stucco background, to the *boom-bah* of trombone and tuba, the card marks its distance from *Regeneration*:

> In the gay Nineties, New York
> had grown up into bustles and
> balloon sleeves . . . but the Bowery
> had grown younger, louder and
> more rowdy, until it was known as

the "Liveliest mile on the face of
the globe" . . . the cradle of men who
were later to be world famous (1:12–28)

Would a "cradle of men" be men being boys? Males fiercely proud of their impudence, puerility, heterophobia, or fear and distrust of females?[8] The song chanted in voice-over, in staccato, notches a time *then* (the turn of the century) implied not *now* (the Great Depression). Just as the song was crooned in *In Old Arizona*, "They say / such things / They do / such things/on the Bowery / the Bowery / [the card fades into black], *I never go there any more*" (01:15–30, stress added), the Bowery is dead and done. When the film fades into the front window of a tavern on which is printed NIGGER JOE'S, a distasteful emblem both then and now (perhaps the reason why DVDs of the feature are unavailable), the foot of the letter R aims at a white bouncer in the foreground, an intermediate figure, a viewer of the film within the film. Like a screen on which shadows of the bodies of clients in the establishment are moving, the window is a sign of the film itself, especially with the bouncer who would be a hawker inviting spectators to enter. Yet, sporting a bowler hat, he looks away indolently, holding a cigarette in his left hand (1:30–34), whose tip points to the glass window—a reflector of the movie itself—when a diagonal wipe inaugurates a montage: (1) a waiter in a white apron, singing out of tune, knocks an intruding drunk onto the floor, who continues to chant. Passersby come and go unimpressed, before (2) a second diagonal wipe (2:18–19) gives way to a band and a tuba (indicating the origin of the music heard since the front credits) on which a drunk strikes a match against the brass. Another wipe (3) (02:26–37) opens onto a lateral pan, moving left and right, following a prostitute who drops a handkerchief. When she realizes that her bait fails to attract a customer, she bends over to pick it up, exposing a derriere a hawker slaps with a cane. The fourth wipe (02:51–52) catches two Italian tailors taking measurements of a baffled young man, unaware of the ways of the Bowery, whom they knock silly. Another (5) (3:15–16) reveals a salesman, promising gold buttons and an inflammable celluloid collar that a stray match ignites (as if referring to nitrate film stock) in a cloud of smoke. Then (6) (3:33) a comely prostitute allures a passerby into the doorway of "Suicide Hall" before (7) a crane shot records helmeted police herding prostitutes into a paddy wagon. There follows a closeup (8) (3:48) of a pair of patent leather shoes under spats being shined: the film cuts to a copy of the *Police Gazette* whose front page displays a lithographic portrait of John

L. Sullivan—George Walsh—who will subsequently enter the film on two occasions. Seen from below, frontally, while a crooner (off) chants an Irish song, upon hearing "Hello, Chuck!" the reader lowers his paper, revealing who he is. Taking a drag on a cigarette, he proudly looks about and spits with pride (figs. 7.2–7.3). An undersized bowler atop his pate, for viewers he happens to be the then-famous "Wallace Beery" *before* he is identified in the name of Chuck Connors.

So ends the exposition. Chased by a pack of angry Chinamen, a blond-haired boy enters the frame. A ruffian and a rascal, he takes refuge under Connors, who quickly shoos them away. So begins the studied crudeness of the film, and so also (counterintuitively, but no less perversely) the caring aspect of Connors, despite himself, an Irish lout of both paternal and maternal inclination, who beneath the braggadocio is a character who cares and is caring. The boy and Connors meet (in medium close-up) in front of a placard advertising a STAG PARTY, a sign implicitly referring to the film as such: Connors cites the name of the character noted in the front credits: "Now listen to me, Swipsie, you gotta

Figure 7.2. The *Police Gazette* that masks its reader (Chuck Connors) and displays John L. Sullivan (for whom George Walsh will have a cameo) (3:53).

Figure 7.3. And its reader, Chuck Connors, while getting his shoes shined (3:54).

stop throwin' them rocks at them Chinamen's windows, or I'm gonna have to throw you out" (05:16–18–21). Cut to a diagonal two-shot (05:21–43): "You can go right back to the gutter where I picked you up at, eatin' out of them garbage cans, and sleepin' in them gutters, and hidin' in the cellars from them orphan asylum coppers." Swipsie: "But Chuck, it was only a chink's winder." Connors: "Oh, I know, but a winder's a winder. You know, when I picked you up, you told me you'd be the right kinda' guy with me. I've got a reputation down here. Me friends don't want to see me followed by a little punk that's throwin' rocks through winders! It ain't refined. [He wipes his nose with his left hand.] Now stop it, and be a good boy. C'mon." Cut to diagonal of a mustached man wiping clean an egg splattered against the front window of Connor's establishment, that reads, "Chuck Connor/Largest Schooner of Beer" (05:58).

A first indication of the Connors-Brody rivalry is given, which is immediately left aside for a suggestive musical number that Trixie Odbray (Pert Kelton), leads with a team of chubby chorus girls, kicking and baring their bottoms, who sing "Rah, rah, boom bay" for the crowd below the footlights (who would be, as the staging insists over and again, the implied viewers of a film within the film).⁹ The girls exit, and with a ninth wipe (8:33) Connors lifts a stein of suds to his lips, posing for a sort of rebus that identifies *Beery* with his beer (fig. 7.4). In proud display Connors chomps on a cob of corn, dribbling its flecks and his own spittle when Swipes comes to the table (08:41). Proudly describing the trading cards he has obtained, the brat—stupid as he is obnoxious—boasts with a racial slur: "Look, Chuck, I traded cigarette pictures with the guinea kids. I gave 'em Maggie Kline and P. T. Barnum for Frankie Bailey and Lillian Russell. Ain't they pips!"¹⁰ Conners, staring at him over his goblet of ale, would prefer that the rascal collect images of strong men. Connors: "Yeah? You're too young to be lookin' at those things, why don't you get pictures of Buffalo Bill and Jake Kilrain and [he wipes his mouth with a cloth napkin] and Bill Muldoon and those boys, uh?"¹¹ Swipes: "They ain't good lookin' like the skoits." Connors: "Yeah? Get your mind off the skoits [as he points at his mug of beer]. There's where the booze is. They're fulla' hot air and all they want is the spon-doo-licks. Remember what I first tell'ed ya? [He hits the table

Figure 7.4. Connors (Beery) sipping his beer (8:34).

with his index finger]. This is a man's woild." [He wipes his mouth.] Never believe the women. There's none of 'em on the up-and-up. *This is a man's woild*." He looks away, at what the next shot will display of three fawning drunks showering accolades on the blowhard. Almost echoing the words of Sergeant Flagg (Victor McLaglen) in *The Cock-Eyed World*, "Am I right?" Cut to the drunks, in unison: "Right!" An inebriated hussy comes to the table to offer her services. She slobbers over Connors, and he knocks her silly, surely affirming that he is a man in a man's world; but then with maternal affection, he wipes clean Swipes's face before the camera follows a waiter dragging the woman out of the establishment.

Now manifest, the "man's world" avers to be an Irish oligarchy sharing little or nothing with others, no matter what the race or religious conviction may be. Connors continues to take pride in being an Irish supremacist, a self-styled King of the Bowery. To Swipes, as he continues to munch on his corncob (0:10:24–11:17), Connors growls (in objectionable but historically veracious words): "See, what did I tell ya' about them crows. They're all just the same, nutty as fruitcakes! Yah get me?" [He chews on his corn.] Swipes: "Sure, thing Chuck!" Connors: "Now go on home, your time's up, and don't go rovin' around, do yah understand?" He continues to masticate, blabbering with his mouth full. Swipes: "Oh Chuck, but I promised to stop by Nigger Joe's!" Connors, rolling his head and his eyes, all the more disgustingly: "Now what had I told yah about that 'coon?" Cut to diagonal two-shot in close-up of the would-be father and son (10:37): "And no more throwing any rocks at that Chinese laundry! Them Chinks are your friends! 23 Skiddoo!" Swipes: "Oh, I won't stop at Joe's, Chuck, but just one, let me throw just one little rock at the Chinks!" Connors, smiling: "All right, one, but just one, heave just one, but that's all." Swipes: "Awh, come on, please, just one, just one little one!" Swipes kisses Connors on the cheek, annoyed, who has conceded. Swipes: "Gee, Chuck, you're all that I mustered!" Slobbering, kernels of corn dropping from his mouth, Connors pushes the rascal away, obliquely describing the person he would never admit wishing to be: "Awh, stop that! *People'll think I'm your mother!* Now go on home and straighten up the joint. It looked *crummy* this morning. [Swipes runs off left]. And throw them cats outta' there, too!" (stress added). A framed picture in the background portrays a team of firemen running down a street, a still photograph shown as if in anticipation of the following sequence, that identifies Connors's brigade and serves as a visual model for the battle the two fire departments will soon engage during a blaze on Mott Street, which (by implication) leaves the Chinese residents, trapped in their apartments, to burn and die (16:16–19:48). The grotesque sequence cuts with a harder edge after Brody, Connor's arch enemy, had entered the establishment with so much flourish and fanfare that the camera is obliged to dolly back as he dances his way into the space (14:14–26), reminding spectators of the early 1930s that in 1925 Raft had been known as the best Charleston dancer in New York, forecasting a later sequence in which, figuratively, he dances over what he hopes will be his rival's grave.

The rampage and pandemonium of the battling fire brigades that leave the tenement and its inhabitants in ashes, which make Connors the victor and Brodie the defeated, become grist for a rematch—in other words, sufficient reason for the narrative to move ahead. The plot thickens (or sickens), first, when Brodie consults a scheming Irish scoundrel, a witch doctor in a back room, who can furnish him with a poison, when mixed with Connors's cup of morning coffee, in Brodie's words, that will "put him under the daisies" (0:21:05). Enraged at thought of murder (at least so it appears in the framing of the sequence), rather than paying $500 for the elixir, suddenly and unexpectedly, Brody slugs the thug on the nose. Knocking him unconscious, he bends over his victim's body, uttering the parting shot that comes with the exploding cigars he gives to Connors on three occasions: "Don't tell me I never gave you nothin'" (the double negative suggesting that he is always "givin' him somethin'"). Early in the exposition, Brody's nasty words indicate that the narrative will be a matter of difference and repetition, not of development and resolution.

Caricature and Cameo

Just as winners depend on losers, Brody cannot live without a rival or an opponent to kick around. Loser of the first battle, in a sequence that seems to be a throw-in of little structural consequence, Brodie stages a rehearsal of the rivalry will be played out when the pair will duke it out on a barge docked near "Grogan's" tavern (beyond the east end of Delancey Street). In this iteration Connors and Brodie hire two pugilists to fight for the cause of their fire departments and for braggers' rights on the Lower East Side. A boxing match (23:00–25:00) opposes an Irish thug to a handsome figure, a magnificent specimen of the male body. The battle is about to begin: standing opposite Connors and Swipsie (now in formal attire, wearing a sport coat and a bowler) and in front of the fighter seated at a corner of the ring, a marvelously grotesque referee inaugurates the event. Proud of a paunch that makes him wide as he is tall (recalling the fat man in *Regeneration*), he introduces the match in a thick Irish drawl, proclaiming, "In this corner we have the well-known fourth ward boy, Chuck Connors!" Applause and shouts explode while Connors plays fisticuffs in anticipation of victory. "Here the un-de-feat-ed pro-té-gé, Bloody Butch!" Cut to a close-up of the fighter, in proud display of his chest and its nipples (23:24–26). In a close-up of the fighter's pocked face, a hand—identified as Connors's—intercedes, nudging him to look at and acknowledge his opponent. Cut to the opposite corner (in a medium shot tilting up) where Brodie stands between the referee and his seated contestant who wears a black mask. His hair waxed with brilliantine, his body, a sight to behold, captures the gaze of men drinking goblets of beer who press from the right. "And in this corner, another well-known the fourth ward boy, Steve Brodie!" Wearing a bright carnation in the lapel of his snugly fitting jacket, Brodie dances a couple of steps (23:27–39).

Pointing at Bloody Butch's opponent, the obese referee continues: "Presentin' the man we know nuttin' 'bout, but who looks like a woithy contestant . . . known as the Masked Marvel" (23:40–59). Standing and bowing to the rowdy audience, his chest huge and strapping (his erect nipples conferring a feminine effect on the bulging muscle), wearing a mask covering his entire face, he turns about and around to ingratiate himself to the crowd.[12] Facing each other, Butch and the Masked Marvel stand on either side of the obese referee who reviews the rules of the game. "I warn youse pugs. There's no hittin' below da belt. No bitin' or kickin' in da clinches. Butch, if you so much as sink a tooth . . . [he waves a billy jack] I'll lay ya' out meself!" (24:20–24). The fight begins. Their arms and bare fists raised, the two men shuffle around the rink in sculpted pose before the Masked Marvel decks Bloody Butch with one punch. Connors stumbles haplessly into the ring (eliciting laughter), yelling (in what would be a description of himself), "Get up, you big lummocks!" Standing and staring (with difficulty) over his big belly, the ref watches over the Masked Marvel's supine victim, counts to seven, and proclaims, "There's no use countin' no more, he's out fer da night!" The Lower East Side now belongs to Brodie. In a two-shot—a preferred composition in this film—the Masked Marvel is placed between the angry adversaries. Flexing his fists, Connors yells, "Who is this guy!? Pull off his mask and I'll fight'im meself!" Brodie lifts his fighter's mask, laughing boisterously, announcing, "Allow me to introduce the Boston Strong Boy, John L. Sullivan!" (25:10–16).

With or without memory of the front credits, seasoned viewers of cinema prior to 1927 would have identified George Walsh in place of John L. Sullivan. Famous for a body so developed and so Grecian that it became a model for sculpture, George Walsh fits the role as a fetish object, a figure recalling fame from the silent era, and, in a sort of wink (at least in the eyes of alert spectators and readers of the contemporary *Photoplay* and other illustrated film journals) to a family romance, and all the better at the end of the sequence when the winner exits the boxing palace (25:28–32) (fig. 7.5).[13] Now shown from the back, Walsh's broad shoulders are the envy and contempt of Swipsie, standing aside the exit, who kicks him in the rear (25:28–36). Pivoting, turning around, displaying a great handlebar mustache, fists clenched, Walsh-as-Sullivan lets the boy be a boy. Although unspoken, the "brother-act" that had been part of a sequence in *Me and My Gal* is reprised here.

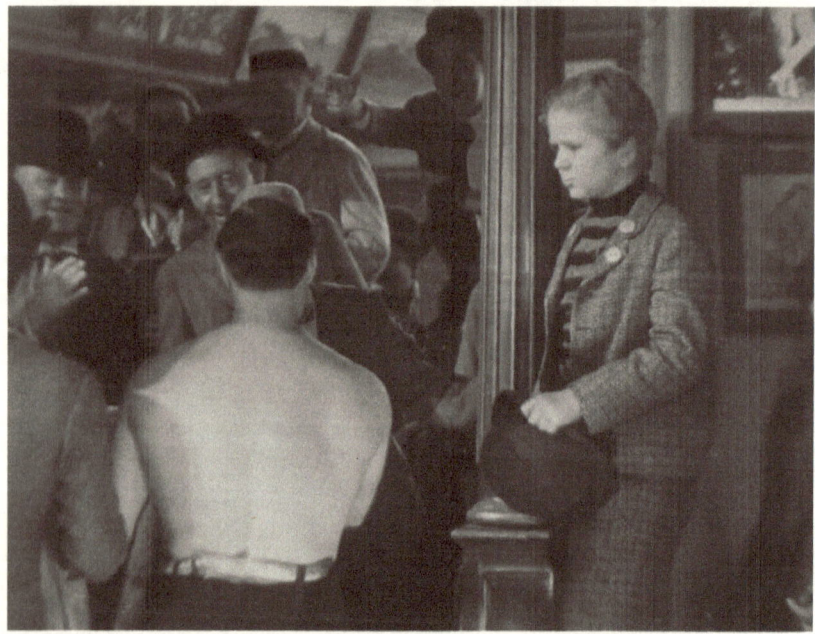

Figure 7.5. John L. Sullivan (George Walsh) exits the boxing palace (25:29).

Perspective and Prospection

In memoirs and interviews Roberto Rossellini had said that when obliged to direct movies of little interest to him, he invested his creative energies around a single shot or in the construction of a brief sequence, often marginal to the narrative material, that for indiscernible reasons stand strong in his memory and, as fate would have it, ours as well.[14] If any sequences are of similar force and facture in Walsh's feature, some of them may belong to the visual rhetoric of the director's silent cinema. Both within and apart from the plotline that binds them, two shots in *The Bowery* prompt reflection on the film's condition of possibility in 1933 and on the relation it holds with past and future history—in other words, on its balance of politics and aesthetics. In view of the depressive condition of current reality, the producers would offer something a viewing public might welcome with wonder and relief. One such shot would be a counter-tilt, implied taken from the arc at the middle of the Brooklyn Bridge, that watches Brodie plummet into the East River before a cutaway, a documentary view of the bridge taken from the bay, records a minuscule body (or marionette) falling into the water (fig. 7.6).[15] The sequence in which they are embedded begins with oblique reference to cinema of earlier vintage. Two German beer barons, wishing to advertise their product, concoct a publicity stunt. If he survives a jump from the Brooklyn Bridge, Brodie will acquire Connors's saloon and become an icon of the Lower East Side. In preparation Brodie and his cohort fabricate a dummy, a life-size replica of Brodie, that he will carry in a horse-drawn wagon and quickly toss from the center of the bridge. Heralded by music of fanfare, an intertitle reproduces a newspaper article (58:15–26): "Today is the day a crowd of 100,000 will gather in the vicinity of the Brooklyn Bridge to see if Steve Brodie will make good his publicised [sic] boast to leap from Brooklyn Bridge. Police dragnets will be placed at each end of the bridge to prevent Steve from going through with his herculean feat." The writing dissolves into a two-shot in crepuscule, seen in diagonal, from the shore of Manhattan below the bridge (a tugboat chugging upstream establishes the illusion of a greater depth of field). Brodie faces Swipsie (58:26–33). Pointing his right index finger as if it were a revolver, Brodie tells the boy about the plan to deceive the populace: "Now don't take any chances! I'll be waitin' under the first pillar. Stay in the bottom of the cab until you get to the place I show'ed ya." Cut to a closer view of the pair (58:33–50)]: "Then throw

Figure 7.6. A body plummets from the Brooklyn Bridge (1:03:03).

the dummy with all your might! The coppers are watchin' at both ends of the bridge. And if anyone asks ya' where you're goin', tell'em your grandmother is sick in Canarsie" (in Brooklyn, beyond the other side of the bridge). Apprehensive, Brodie turns and looks left and right, then removes his hat, spitting on it for good luck: "Here, take my derby." They shake hands. "Good luck, Steve!" "All right, Swipes!"

When Swipes runs off, the film cuts to the point on the bridge from where Brodie will make his leap. A crowd anxiously awaits, but suddenly Swipes returns, telling Brodie that the dummy is missing. A deaf-mute (a living double of the marionette), a figure who had been in the margins of the scheme, appears in front of the warehouse where the replica had been stored. Brodie takes him by the neck, threatening to strangle him before Swipes tells him the man was not the culprit. A crowd appears to wish Brodie good luck (or good riddance). After looking directly at the camera, he yells to the deaf mute who had been assigned take the reins and drive the carriage over the bridge. "Get in your cab, *dummy*, we're on our way!" (59:45). Who or what is the dummy? The driver? The mannequin? The viewer? Brodie makes good on his enemy brother's dare and challenge, whose success, no matter how unlikely it may be, will wipe Connors clean of all his belongings. He refers to his double, a real dummy, that calls the plot in question, and to those *in* the film who would be two others—the doll and the mute driver, but possibly three, if Brodie/Raft is counted among them. They cue the artifice of the scheme and, from a broader angle, stress the gap between the narrative and its force of illusion.

The deaf-mute guides the horse-driven hearse to the bridge where the police who have roped off entry. Feigning a person crying over the death of a beloved one, Brodie buries his face in a handkerchief. He wins them over and has the driver put his whip to the horses. Soon aware of their mistake, three corpulent Irish cops hustle as best they can (reverse tracking shot oblige) in hot pursuit of the carriage: stopping the vehicle at the center of the bridge, do or die, Brodie must make the jump or be the laughingstock of Manhattan. A volley of cutaway shots locates Swipsie who looks upward from the shoreline, his eyes focused on the bridge, who cries (to have the viewer take note of the deep perspective and behold the scene in the counterpoint of the near and the far), "There he is now!" (but where? He cannot be seen in the image). So also Lucy, in close-up, searches with her eyes, before a medium shot registers the crowd looking at the bridge. As for the jump itself, a matte shot (in rearview projection the river and a tugboat are visible below the ironwork balustrade) has Brodie grasping a guardrail and pausing for an instant (1:03:00–01). He climbs over the barrier and leaps. Cut to an ichnographic shot of the waters in which an inert body drops into view from above and plummets downward.[16] Suddenly the film cuts to two real-life shots, first, a minuscule figure dropping from the bridge, the second a cityscape east of Manhattan, *the only documentary take of Brooklyn in the entire film*, a scenography of the structure seen from the water, a site entirely unrelated to any of the points of view in the film as such. Its arms uplifted, falling feet first, in the space of an instant it splashes into the East River (1:03–04). The sudden shift in perspective could not be more surreal.

The Dummy

As Brodie rises to the surface amidst the din of applause, fanfare, and music, the film cuts to Connors and his crew swaggering out of his tavern. Exiting the swinging flap-doors, Connors asks, "What's all the whistles?" A friend exclaims, referring both to Al Jolson's prediction in

The Jazz Singer (1927), heralding the beginning of sound cinema and to what will happen next, "You ain't heard nothin' yet! Here comes Carrie Nation!" On a warpath, Carrie A. Nation (played by the aptly named Lillian Harmer), the stalwart enemy of alcohol, leading her cohort in lockstep, confronts Connors: "Stand aside, you son of Satan!" "Listen," he retorts, "this place is on the level! It's a woiking man's club, it ain't no salooon!" "Out of my way, you viper!!" Cut to Brodie, carried toward the camera on his admirers' shoulders. Back to Connors, conceding: "Ladies, youse absolutely right! I'm convoited." Gesticulating, "I'm a hypocrite! Down with demon rum! Down with likker!" The establishment is trashed so violently that the men must take refuge in the "Gents" room. The pandemonium subsides, and the film fades into a new (and equally tacky) setting, a clean bar in front of a mural over which "Steve Brodie" (not "Brody," occasionally spelled as such) is written in grandiose majuscule. Armed with brush and a maulstick, standing in front of his handiwork, an Italian painter puts the finishing touches on the mural depicting Brodie's leap. Stretching across the frame, the stately (and in the time frame of the film, utterly modern) suspension structure extends over the East River. Below its gently arched platform a small stick figure—Brodie—is shown suspended in the air. The painter turns to Brodie who casts his eye on the image: "Hey, you like, eh, Steve?" In other words is the depiction faithful and "true-to-life?" Does it do justice to the personage and the story? Smug and glib, holding a cigar, Swipsie admires the hero of the day who will be immortalized on a mural. Brodie, squeezing a fat stogie between his teeth, squawks: "The Bridge is all right. But how about me? Make me bigger! Make me bigger!" (1:05:38–42). And the painter, responding, wide-eyed, "But what about all zee pro-spec-tive?" Brodie: "Awh, yeah, who made the job? Me or the pros-pector?" (1:05:48–53). And the brat, answering a gentleman who asks his name: "Buster Brown!"—the words no doubt reminding viewers of the jingle that went with the brand of children's footwear since the beginning of the twentieth century (and not the 1890s), "My name is Buster Brown! I live in a shoe! Here's my dog Tige: he lives in there too!" The making of the mural and the banter about its perspective indirectly addresses the issue, given that the film is conceived in contradiction, in the distance spectator might wish to assume in relation to what it says and what it does.

His ego indomitable, his admirers fawning about him, Brodie struts forward, as if obliging the camera to pull back, much as he had when entering Conners's saloon earlier in the film. Brodie leaves the bar, the painter, and Swipsie, who has opportunistically changed paternal allegiance.

Pushing his way through the cheering clientele, the champ happens upon an old buddy. "Well, if it ain't John L.!" In the thick of the throng, sporting a handlebar mustache, the great John L. Sullivan (clearly George Walsh in his cameo), turns toward the camera, raises a schooner, announcing, "Wait a minute, everybody! To Steve Brodie, the King of the Bowery!" (1:06:8–10). It is clearly George Walsh in the cameo in which, in the boxing match at the beginning of the film, he was the "Masked Marvel," then revealed to be "the great John L. Sullivan" (22:51–25:36). At the very moment reference to the director's brother is tacitly acknowledged, like a messenger in a classical play, "history" intervenes to interrupt the merriment: in close-up, an intertitle (in a coy reference to the silent style) displays a headline of the *New York Herald* (February 14, 1898), MAINE SUNK! (1:06:38). A *deus ex machina* but also a reminder both of the time of the story and news from the world at large, promises the sense of an inconclusive ending, akin to those capping the ventures of Flagg and Quirt, that send the couple off to war.

The transition is practically seamless. Indigent, pauperized, and disheveled (no longer under a derby, now wearing a cheap woolen cap), Connors says goodbye to Lucy (whose expression of sympathy betrays an affective opportunism the film prefers not to stress). He packs into a small suitcase his few belongings and leaves the apartment where, thanks to him, she had found refuge. To the sound of "Auld Lang Syne," the camera tracks him looking for his bearings, searching left and right, his eyes watching his feet where they lead him, "thinking" as best he can about life and fate on what would be the corner of Mott Street and Third Avenue, the area he had commanded. An efficient dissolve intervenes: a poster on an easel guarded by two indolent street urchins (one of whom indolently scratches a match on the sole of his shoe and lights a cigarette, signaling that an outer world or world-historical issues are of no interest), announces "Go to Cuba! Join the Army." An implicit intertitle in the silent tradition, the poster gives way to the sight of an enlistment paper in close-up. Unidentified, an index finger enters from the top of the screen, accompanied by the voice (-off) of an agent: "Sign your name under that line, in full" (1:09:38–52).[17] On the sheet that bears his home address as "the Bowery," Connors's hand scrawls a stylized "X" (voice-off, he adds, "that's me mark"). Cut to his face, addressing the agent, now seen from behind while seated, as an anonymous authority of the kind seen in the officers' quarters in *The Cock-Eyed World*), looking at the signature: "My name's Chuck Connors . . . But [he points his finger at the paper] everybody knows me by that mark." The camera pulls back.

In voice-off: "You want to go to Cuba?" Connors, voice-in: "Awh, any place but the Bowery." Cut to the agent, now facing the camera, who has just stamped the paper. "You're in the army now. Report tomorrow morning at 10:00 a.m. for your uniform and equipment" (1:10:00–08). He leaves, philosophizing while walking, maybe wondering why his brawny hands have crumpled the enlistment papers. He encounters a diminutive passerby (Chester Conklin, soon a regular in Preston Sturges features), excited at having also joined the effort, who gleefully tells Connors, "Boy! We'll clean 'em up. They can't get away with sinkin' the *Maine*! We'll teach 'em a lesson they'll never forget! Won't we?" To which, either in ignorance or, unbeknownst to himself, in prescient awareness of the stupidity of armed conflict, Connors responds, no doubt mirroring the fading memory of spectators of 1933: "Whose we fighten'?" Ambling down the street, to the tune of "Auld Lang Syne," Connors watches Brodie and Lucy pass by in a horse-drawn carriage, happily waving at their admirers. Chagrin could not be greater: a long close-up (11:45–57) records Connors at odds with his situation. Rubbing his neck and face), looking left and right, he can hardly to cope with his destiny. A dissolve and long take (1:11:58–1:12:03) of a streetlamp illuminating "Mott Street," a point of reference along a line of divide demarcating Chinatown and Little Italy, fails to offer consolation.

Two Dummies

At this moment, in a first viewing, it is difficult to predict how the film can (or should) end. Connors meets up with hooligan Swipsie, whom he finds distraught for having split his sympathies, leaving him, a loser, and leaning toward Brodie, a winner: even the child, the delinquent who would be his son, has betrayed him. What to do? Where to go? Like the repressed, the return of the dummy extends and complicates the storyline. The two crooks who had solicited Lucy for a career in prostitution, and who had offered Brodie a vial of arsenic to put Connors, as Brodie had put it, "under the daisies," now bait Connors with the idea that a doctored double in paper and cloth, and not Brodie, plummeted from the bridge (1:14:56–62). After Connors reacts defiantly ("You got rats in your belfry"), the schemers unveil the life-size doll. Bringing into the narrative the idea of a fake speaker (viewers recall that Edgar Bergen and his doll, "Charlie McCarthy," famous for their display of ventriloquism, who rose to fame in the 1920s), the simulacrum makes Connors bristle with anger, while it also refers to the "constructed" nature of the film, to its inherent ventriloquism, which effectively "theorizes" the narrative describing Brodie's return to power. Listening to the two scoundrels, speechless and perplexed, Connors leaves the scene. At its middle, an extraordinary diagonal wipe momentarily aligns Connors's new world with Brodie's. In their back room, gleefully watching Connors depart, one of the two announces to the other, "And that, my friend, is the end of Mr. Steve Brodie" (1:16:16).

But it is hardly the end of the film: the scene that arouses Connors's ire elides with its opposite, Brodie dancing triumphantly (and marketing talents for which Raft was known outside of *The Bowery*) before the line of chorus girls (whom Connors had employed in his saloon) wiggling their rumps for the camera. Entering the cabaret, Connors gazes on the mural behind the bar. He squints (1:16:42–44) (fig. 7.7), looking at the stick figure caught in its fall from the bridge, calling in question its representation (and by implication, that of the film). Picking up and tossing a cuspidor at the image, he shatters the mirror on which it was painted.

Figure 7.7. Connors squints at the mural in Brodie's new saloon (1:16:42).

What to make of Connors's squint when, in close-up, he confronts Brodie amidst the ruckus (1:17:11 and 1:17:32–33)? Does he wish to gain a better (or flatter) focus on the mural's "perspective"? On the "truth" of what the documentary shot (1:03–04) had shown from a point of view available to no one in the narrative?[18] Can the image fleetingly recall the director's enucleated (right) eye at the same time it signals how the film manages its points of view and asks viewers to see it in both depth of field (in cognizance of its illusion) and a two-dimensional fiction (a piece of writing or an image in the depth of its surface)? If so, it ties into a network of authorial references brought forward through staging of the Bowery itself (*Regeneration* versus *The Bowery*) and the cameo of George Walsh (recently, as we have seen, Duke Castenega of *Me and My Gal*) in the person of John L. Sullivan (whom Ward Bond will portray seven years later in *Gentleman Jim*). Even more in the play of truth-and-lie taking place when Connors alleges that (like the movie here and now) the event was staged. In heated words directed at his enemy, the fallen idol growls,

> You didn't jump off the Brooklyn Bridge! You didn't jump off of nothin'! [He raises the dummy for everyone to see.]. This is what jumped off the Brooklyn Bridge!"

Brodie looks forward, as if also asking the viewer: "Don't believe him, boys, it's a lie! You know I jumped off the Brooklyn Bridge [now turning to the clientele all around], *you seen me, didn't ya?*" (1:17:26, stress added). Did or didn't ya? Was it "me" whom "you" saw? Was it the dummy? Or were we watching three dummies (Connors, Brody, and the marionette)? Beyond Connors and Brody's ongoing rivalry, when *film* is factored into the matter, as it was in *Regeneration*, authority of ocular testimony, or authority *tout court*, becomes a bone of contention.[19] Assigned to put an end to things, a wrestling match is slated to determine the truth of the matter. Following a dissolve and a cutaway shot to a clock set at 12:29 a.m., it begins (1:18:03) with a throng pushing into a space from where everyone can behold the pugilistic spectacle. Odds are made, and bets are taken. Curiously framed from an oblique angle, the spectators wearing bowler hats crowd aside a frame of sorts (what seems to be a curtain rod hangs from its upper-right corner) angled into the background. The gray cast of the inner space suggests that Connors and Swipsie are standing in front of a process shot of the greater crowd: thus, seen from

behind, Connors and Swipsie seem to be looking at the movie (1:18:47–53).
Assigned to take place on a river barge announced moored next to Grogan's Bar ("Grogan's," also the name of the cabaret in *Regeneration*, either in praise of the Irish haunts of the Bowery, or in sly reference to the feature of 1915), the struggle (1:19–23–1:21:22) leads to an outcome no less questionable than Brodie's great leap. After appearing beaten, his face bruised and bloodied, Connors emerges from the fog victorious and is soon feted at a party celebrating his affiliation with the Ace Brewing Company. Trixie rises to sing "I'm the Belle, they say, of Avenue A," dancing and parading her gartered thighs and buttocks around the dinner table before, again, like a messenger in a Senecan play, history intercedes. News arrives with the police (of Irish lineage, it goes without saying) who transmit an indictment on the part of Brodie accusing Connors of criminal behavior, including assault and battery. Bedridden in the Delancey Street Receiving Hospital, Brodie is visited by Lucy, by now entirely supernumerary, who soon leaves before officers arrive to have him identify his assailant, Connors, in their company, next to Swipsie, who wears a military uniform.[20] Alleging that he lost the battle only because he "slipped," Brodie informs the police that he has never known this "big bag of baloney" who stands by the bed with Swipsie at his side. As soon as the officers leave the room the enemy brothers, picking up where they had left off, resume their fisticuffs. Swipsie intervenes and adjudicates. Befriending his wounded adversary, Connors convinces Brodie to join the army and be off with him to Cuba. A convenient *deus ex machina* signals the end of the film.

No End in Sight

The finale rehearses those of *What Price, Glory?* and *The Cock-Eyed World*. In the former, like the Marines dispatched to continue fighting the war to end all wars, or in the latter, the same pair, somewhere in the Philippines, who march by a sparse crowd bidding them goodbye, Connors and Brody (the rifles they shoulder are aimed backward, as if at their homeland) parade off and away. In accordance with the template of practically every departure for "the front," from King Vidor (*The Big Parade*) to John Ford (*Rio Grande* and a host of other features), a woman standing in the street assigned to bid adieu, like Charmaine, like Mariana, and now Lucy, must wave, blow kisses, and disappear. In *The Bowery*, however, Brodie marches forward before Connors bustles his way from behind to join him. He looks back to catch sight of his lover while his elder mate, smiling broadly, only looks ahead. Now that the female is out of the picture, in a last gasp the narrative has to account for Swipsie. The story cannot leave him in the lurch. Thus, concealed in a wagon of ordnance that goes with the parade, the rascal raises the lid of a box in which he has been hiding. He smiles, cheers, and seals himself away.

The final shots confirm that the film cannot conclude. Herein the political latency. A film "without a hero," like a novel "without an ending," *The Bowery* is less story than serial.[21] Refusing to identify with any of the star players, the camera follows the lines of the signature traced at the terminus of the two war movies that would have little to do with the space and place of *The Bowery*. If an ending is there, it is located less in the parade and flourish of brass than in the design of the final card, on which, against the mottled background seen in the front credits, in bold letters "The End" stands above (in lower point size) "A 20th Century Picture released thru United Artists" (1:22:26–34). In superscription, below "NRA/MEMBER," its wings spread wide, adjacent to "U.S." (that could be "US"), an emblematic American Eagle clasps in its right claws a cogwheel and, in its left, three thunderbolts. Below is written: "We Do Our Part." In the flow and drift from the parade to the card it is inferred that after all their foibles, fun, and games—and like viewers who take time to read the notice before exiting the theater—the protagonists are finally called to "do their part" in a world *hic et nunc*. The "Bowery" of the good old days, the place the singer of the tune in the exposition told us he never visits anymore, is squarely set in the Depression. Subscribing to the recently organized National Recovery Administration (not the National Rifle Association), the film affiliates itself with newly elected Franklin D. Roosevelt and the first New Deal. If, at its end, *The Bowery* is a slice of contemporary life, or a "writing of history" constructing a past to deal with what cannot be said in the present, its comedy depends on the depressive condition it indirectly addresses. Yet given how it repeats the ending of the war movies of 1926 and 1929, displaced onto the state of the world in 1933—a light year's distance from the state of things in 1898, 1926, and 1929—the conclusion signals an uncertain future. The Nazis had burned the Reichstag on February 27. A way out of the Depression was unsure, and its impact could only further the cause either for isolation or collective action. Self-centered, caring little about where they are going, Connors and Brody are fodder for war and conflict soon to come.

Conclusion

What Became of *The Wrath of the Just?*

THE PAGES ABOVE HAVE dealt with early features in the long career (1912–1964) of a director, in the eyes of many historians, who was a founding figure in Hollywood in its studio era. They contend, too, that the director might be an author, an *auteur*, whose style and manner emerge from six features, two in the silent mode, one on the cusp of the divide between the silent and the talkie, three others in the early years of sound cinema and, for heuristic ends, one possible remake of a later period. I have sought to show that the traits of the signature become visible in how the films give themselves to *action*; how they draw attention to their ocular character, and thus bring forward issues concerning the stakes of "seeing" and "reading" images; in what ways they belong to Hollywood's ideological machinery in its formative years, on either side of the line of divide between silent and sound cinemas, be it in the context of the First World War or the Great Depression. Using frame-by-frame analysis, thinking of the shots taken in the shadows of the great sequoias at the end of *The Big Trail*, I wonder, nonetheless, if the forest has been lost from its trees. To wit: having directed over 160 films of vastly different stamp and genre, in periods of different technology, concern, and urgency, is the director an *auteur* or, as he projected in many interviews, is he simply a craftsman who knows how to get films done on time and under budget? A first and safely formulated response would be that surely he is both. When certain films are juxtaposed, a unique and inimitable style prevails.[1] When others are brought forward, their direction could be attributed to any number of directors. In all events, relying on the tradition of textual explication and painfully close reading, I have sought to lay stress, it is hoped, on how the director's films address or internalize social, ideological, and aesthetic *contradictions*.

The work has been in concert, so it seems, with a resurgence of interest in the director's oeuvre. Retrospectives have been many: the greatest of all in 1974, when the Museum of Modern Art included among its featured guests Walsh himself, his brother George, and numerous actors and actresses he had known throughout the silent and sound eras. Others have followed. After the turn of the new millennium, the Cinemateca in Lisbon featured an important review of the films, and in 2005 the Cinémathèque in Paris organized a quasi-complete program. In 2011, when publication of Marilyn Ann Moss's groundbreaking biography of the director's "true adventures" called attention to a life and times unlike others in the history of American cinema, Hollywood's Egyptian Theater ran a brief program of renowned titles. In early winter of 2013 the Harvard Film Archive ran a major retrospective, the success of which led to a sequel several months later. The Pacific Film Archive followed suit in the summer of 2013, calling on Dave Kehr, an unmitigated enthusiast and discerning reader of Walsh's films, to serve as plenary speaker. In 2014 the Brooklyn Arts Museum's Cinématek presented *Under the Influence*, a series of twelve films that proved how the aesthetics and politics of Walsh's films strongly influence the work of Martin Scorsese.

Despite the attention Walsh has gathered, whether in the cinema, in the mythic texture of *Each Man in His Time* (his rollicking memoir), or in his reputedly selfless contributions to the film industry, as far as I know, scant attention has been paid to his novel, *La Colère des justes* [The wrath of the just] (Paris: Belfond, 1972), which appeared solely in French, in Jacques Lourcelles's translation.[2] Upon cursory view, *La Colère des justes* would have qualified for inclusion in "L'Ouest, le vrai" (The west, the true), a series of American pulp westerns Bertrand Tavernier had translated and issued in 2013 at Actes Sud, a visible and active publisher in Arles. Unlike the higher order of Zane Grey's many novels, such his *Riders of the Purple Sage*, or Karl May's famous fictions about the adventures of "Old Shatterhand" in the Wild West, Tavernier brought to French cinephiles authors Ernest Haycox, Charles O. Locke, Niven Busch, W. R. Burnett, Alan Le May, Luke Short, Walter Van Tilberg Clark, A. B. Guthrie, Tom Lea, and Harry Brown.

La Colère des justes does not figure in the collection, perhaps because it is in French, or else, in view of its ideal readers, its heady mix of righteous violence, brutality, and embrace of prostitution is unsettling.

Less romantic than much of the western pulp, and more like Walsh's films that make no bones about brutality (e.g., *Blackbeard the Pirate*, *White Heat*, or *Band of Angels*), *La Colère des justes* recounts the adventures of three veterans of the Confederate army, devastated by what the postwar economy has wrought under unbridled capitalism and racism, who resort to corrective violence in a world of manifest destiny and expansion. In light of the cinematic style in the silent films, the pace and tempo of features realized in the early sound years and others in the 1940s that pose just criminals against loathsome agents of the law, in guise of a projective conclusion, the novel merits a brief overview.

Departing from war-torn Tennessee where three bedraggled soldiers meet, following a horizontal axis, the story *goes west* and ultimately turns *south*. Of Aristotelian facture, it refuses concession to psychic complexity. A terse and limpid prose conveys relentless action in what seem to be storyboarded tableaus (or, in the idiolect of Gilles Deleuze, "action-images") bearing resemblance to the framed units of comic strips. Descriptions of the just, who are pursued, in juxtaposition with those of their corrupt and ruthless pursuers, are crosscut so efficiently that *editing* becomes a signal trait. The novel begins in the ruts of Sherman's March. In matter-of-fact prose:

> Le 9 avril 1865, la guerre de Sécession avait pris fin. Le Nord fêtait sa victoire par des défilés, des banquets et des feux d'artifice ; on allumait de gigantesques feux de joie pour célébrer le retour des héros. Dans le Sud, l'industrie avait été anéantie, les maisons n'étaient plus que des ruines carbonisées. Là où autrefois s'étendaient de vastes champs de coton, il n'y avait plus aujourd'hui qu'un désert calciné ; la pauvreté et la désolation s'étaient répandues à travers tout le pays. (5)

> (On April 9, 1865, the Civil War had ended. The North celebrated its victory with parades, banquets, and fireworks; huge fires of joy were lit to celebrate the heroes' return. In the South, industry had been destroyed, houses were little more than charred ruins. Vast fields of cotton had become a desert of ash; poverty and desolation were widespread all across the country.)

Enter three young soldiers who fought in defeat under the banner of the Twelfth Cavalry. They meet in Berryville, "a little city in the

South" (perhaps near Nashville, Tennessee). First, Johnny McGraw, "un robuste garçon de vingt-quatre ans, né à San Francisco dans une famille de la classe moyenne" (a robust young man, twenty-four years old, born in San Francisco from a middle-class family) (6). A talented boxer whom his father coaxed into joining the family's stable and transport business with a gift of $900 to purchase twenty mules, Johnny is a prodigal son. In 1861, not far from home, hearing fanfare and the song of Dixie, he gets drunk, joins the army, and wastes the money on "drinks, women and song" (6). Throughout the war, remorseful for failing to heed his father's demands, he wonders how he can repatriate himself with the family. Then comes Jebnah Carter, "un grand gars efflanqué, natif du Kentucky" (7) (a strapping specimen of a man, native of Kentucky), whose parents raised horses in the vicinity of Lexington. Despondent when his fairly well-to-do parents sell their farm and the horses he loves, Jeb joins the cavalry. Stinging over defeat, Jeb and Johnny meet, as if anticipating the future orations of Frederic Jackson Turner, deciding to go west, over the Rockies, and make amends with Johnny's father. While in Berryville they hear of a young man, surrounded by admiring lady friends, also a veteran of the Twelfth Cavalry, who longs to go to Kansas

> voir son oncle qui possédait pas mal de terre là-bas et chez qui il se trouvait justement en visite quand la guerre s'était déclarée . . . un beau garçon, en effet, avec les caractéristiques classiques d'un dieu grec: plus d'un mètre quatre-vingts, une musculature puissante, des cheveux bouclés et un profil élégant. Pretty Boy était le surnom que lui avaient donné ses compagnons. En réalité, il appartenait à la noblesse anglaise et s'appelait Lord Wesley Connaght Saint George. (8–9)

> (to see his uncle who owned a lot of land, whom he was visiting when war was declared. [. . .] A handsome guy, he had the classic traits of a Greek god: over six-feet tall, powerful muscles, curly hair and an elegant profile. "Pretty Boy" was the name his companions conferred upon him. In reality, he belonged to English nobility and was known as Lord Wesley Connaght Saint George.)

Facing hardship, just as had the three circus players in *The Monkey Talks*, Jeb, Johnny, and Pretty Boy call themselves "three musketeers: all for one and one for all" (10). Chapter 1 (5–22) ends when Brooksie Nell, a roguish prostitute worthy of her name, eagerly befriends and serves the boys. They meet Olga (whose name recalls the Russian prostitute in *The Cock-Eyed World*, and that of a "dark lady," an unknown lover in Walsh's memoir) and Greta Hansen, with whom they head off for Pretty Boy's uncle's estate in Kansas, which he announces he might soon inherit.[3]

Chapter 2 (23–41) describes the men's character and constitution. En route, wary of carpetbaggers, they stop at a bar in a small town where they witness three sinister-looking dudes, proud men of sorts, who ostracize local Blacks. One of them takes notice of their dusty gray uniforms. "Look at these Southern bums!" (27). Johnny strikes the first in the stomach, then knocks the teeth out of the second. When the third, an olive-skinned companion, reaches for his gun, Johnny shoots him in the head. "Le lascar chancela un moment comme une danseuse espagnole, puis s'effondra" (31) (the rascal teeter-tottered for a moment like a flamenco dancer, then fell to the ground). The musketeers move on. Unwilling to return to a farm of the kind where they had toiled in their earlier lives, Olga and Greta envisage a sorry and ultimately boring fate that might await them in Kansas. Tears flowing, the women take leave of the three men, whose remorse is shared as they sadly mount their horses and cross the Mississippi. Destiny remains to be determined. Chapter 3 begins with the men crossing the Great Plains. Fatigued, stopping to gather themselves after a rainfall, Pretty Boy buoys Jeb and Johnny in anticipating the pleasures they will find at Uncle Desmond's estate. As if referring to the author's formative years in Hollywood, recalling the words of an "old colonel Griffith" (45) who had admired Johnny's pugilistic talents, the English nobleman thinks fondly of Desmond's literary predilections, quoting at length scene seven of the second act of *As You Like It*—a sly reference to the director's taste for Shakespeare (set forward in *Each Man in His Time*) while establishing for the reader a critical distance from the narrative: "All the world's a stage . . ." (II, vii).

Upon arrival at Carnnarvon, the estate in Kansas, they meet a Black maid, Magnolia, who laments the devastation wrought upon Desmond and his belongings. She reports that a "M'sieur Harrington," a representative of the railroad, accompanied by Charles Pike—owner of the Rockville Bank—extorted the property before their henchman, "Big Jake Doremus," brutally murdered Desmond and burned the buildings. Consoling Pretty Boy, who is utterly devastated by what he sees, Jeb concludes, "La justice et le chemin de fer sont deux choses bien différentes! (. . .) C'est un pays neuf ici. Les Blancs dépouillent les Indiens de leurs terres et les gens de chemin de fer dépouillent à leur tour les Blancs" (51–52) (Justice and the railroad are two different things. [. . .] Here, it's a new country. The Whites rob the Indians of their lands, and in turn the men of the railroad rob the Whites"). Angered and aroused, the threesome decides to rob Pike's bank in Rockville (north and west of Wichita) and blow up a locomotive in the railyard. They capture a bank clerk, abscond with $25,000, detonate a load of dynamite they have placed under the locomotive, and gallop away. Hot on their heels (and rehearsing the finale of the novel), in vertically disposed scenes reminiscent of the cinema (from *The Big Trail* to *High Sierra* and *Colorado Territory*, and even *The Sheriff of Fractured Jaw*), Harrington and his patrol arrive at a cliffside where they see the three men riding off in the distance far below. Because no reward awaits, they turn around and return to Rockville.

Chapter 4 marks the beginning of *pursuit* and being *pursued*, as it happens in so many of the director's films. The motif propels the novel forward:

> Ainsi, lorsque le célèbre détective Robert Pinkerton fut convoqué par Spencer Harrington, que devait commencer l'une des plus grandes chasses à l'homme de toute l'histoire de l'Ouest. Ce fin limier avait capturé de nombreux voleurs et bandits de grands chemins et en avait envoyé une quantité à la potence. (65)

> (And so, it was when Spencer Harrington called on Robert Pinkerton, the famous detective, one of the greatest manhunts in the history of the West began. This sneaky bloodhound had captured many thieves and robbers, and he sent a good lot of them to the gallows.)

Mention of Pinkerton invokes the ocular emblem of the notorious Pinkerton Agency. Known in the late nineteenth century for intimidation tactics and having workers killed, busting unions, and ruthlessly breaking strikes, it worked in the service of corporate America. Its name goes with an image of a watchful eye set over the motto, "We Never Sleep," in the frame of the pupil of a larger eye outlined by "Pinkerton's National/Detective Agency" (fig. C. 1). What allusion could be more apt for a cinema that plays on binocular and monocular vision?[4] The bulk of the chapter crosscuts scenes of Pinkerton and his men smelling reward while Pretty Boy and his companions scramble to elude them. Time for reflection is brief. The Pinkerton men follow the tracks of their prey, the

Figure C.1. The emblem of the Pinkerton Agency, circa 1850.

three musketeers keep moving ahead, sometimes pausing to open their eyes onto the great vistas:

> Pretty Boy chevauchait en tête sur un chemin de montagne très escarpé. De temps en temps, les trois hommes s'arrêtaient pour admirer la beauté de l'immense paysage. Au sud il y avait de larges et fertiles vallées avec des cours d'eau et des troupeaux en train de paître. Au nord, on apercevait des montagnes aux sommets enneigés et, dans la direction où ils allaient s'étendaient d'immenses forêts d'arbres géants. (68)

> (Pretty Boy rode forward on a path along the steep mountain slope. Now and again the three men stopped to admire the beauty of the immense landscape. To the south, wide and fertile valleys with waterways and packs of grazing animals. In the north, snow-capped mountains while, in the direction they were headed, stood immense forests of gigantic trees).

Begging us to think of the finale of *The Big Trail* or the setting of *Wild Girl*, "gigantic trees" displace the men into an area that would be anywhere between the Rockies and the Sierras. The renegades of good will meet an imposing mountain man and his hospitable Indian companion. Rehearsing the last paragraphs of *Each Man in His Time* that defend Native Americans, speaking to his guests while clearly addressing readers, the mountain man declares, "Cette terre appartient aux Indiens mais ces salopards de Washington voudraient la leur faucher" (71) (This land belongs to Indians, but these bastards from Washington want to steal it for themselves). The threesome enjoy the company that has no affinity for the agents of the law. While the mountain man and the guests walk off to spend a moment in view of the landscape, two whites enter the host's home and rape and then murder the young Indian woman. The mountain man returns, lassoes one of the culprits, and hangs him upside down. He takes the other by the neck and thrusts his face into a campfire that burns him alive.

Chapter 5 (81–102) relates the men's journey to Denver. They meet a man named Pedro, in his words, "'de Guadalahara, là où le soleil brille toute l'année, où les fleurs sont épanouies toute l'année, où on entend partout de la musique, où on chante et où les señoritas sont les plus jolies du monde" (88) (from Guadalajara, where the sun shines all year, where flowers are in bloom all year, where music is played everywhere, where people dance and sing, and where the señoritas are the prettiest in the whole world. Reiterated over and again in the following pages, the words clearly designate the novel's vanishing point and the three men's site of "projective" identification. In chapter 6 (103–74), Pretty Boy, playing the role of the English nobleman he is, impresses the local population—but only after Pedro has unguardedly revealed his nickname to Pinkerton and his crew. Wearing the moniker "Lord Wesley" in a spectacle at the Grand Palace in Denver, Pretty Boy meets Pinkerton. Quoting verbatim the text of Abraham Lincoln's Gettysburg Address, impressing one and all, Pretty Boy becomes a man of envy and honor. In a moment of flirtatious inebriation, he proposes to marry the horrible daughter of Spencer Harrington, a rich railroad magnate, in whose company his vice-president, Tom Murphy, had just declared, "le seul Indien recommendable, c'est l'Indien mort" (111) (the only worthy Indian is a dead Indian). Pretty Boy meets Mark Twain, who declares that his real name is Samuel Clemens, and before the American satirist and novelist's eyes he recites the great soliloquies from *Macbeth* (II, i) (157–58), *Hamlet* (III, i) (158–59) and *Romeo and Juliet* (II, ii) (163). Failing to appear at a lavish ceremony Harrington had prepared for the marriage with Barbara, Pretty Boy pays the hotel bill in $50 gold pieces and hurriedly rides off with Jeb and Johnny.

Chapter 7 (175–207) begins "[j]uste après le lever du soleil" (just after sunrise), when "les trois amis chevauchèrent jusqu'au Saloon de la Dernière Chance" (175) (the three friends rode as far as the Last Chance Saloon).[5] They meet a generous Black domestic who serves them a plate of ham, string beans, corn, and bread. Restored, now heading west, they briefly contemplate the beauty of the spaces they encounter. Johnny dilates at the sublimity of "l'étrange paysage qui s'offrait à sa vue. Il se demandait comment ces énormes rochers pouvaient se trouver là, dans cette terre abandonnée des dieux" (178) (the strange landscape extending before his eyes. He wondered how these enormous rocks ever happened to be there in this land the gods had left behind). Quietude and visual splendor are brief: the heroes witness a stagecoach hold-up that leaves two men dead and another wounded, whom they rescue and take to "the Nest," the hideaway of the victim's father, "Bull Evans," another enemy of the law, who welcomes them with open arms. They set the victim to rest and extract a bullet from his shoulder. They meet Joanne Marie, a daughter of the good owner's friend, Sam, who had been killed in the Mexican-American War. Joanne, a beauty who communes with nature, captures Pretty Boy's admiration. Exchanging impressions of their lives, they fall in love. Pretty Boy tells her of Europe, its cities, and the great museums that display the paintings of Velasquez and Goya. Listening intently, Joanne exudes tenderness, responding by nurturing the flora and fauna in their midst. Forced to continue southward, the men depart after Pretty Boy, distraught, reveals his name in leaving his legacy for Joanne Marie.

Chapter 8 (209–37) relates the men's departure for Junction City. Noticing a train destined for Yucca that is passing through Rio Puerco, they catch sight of Jake Doremus. Much in the manner of the train robberies in *Colorado Territory* and *White Heat*, they detach the locomotive, instruct the passengers in the other wagons to leave the train, and then dynamite the mail car. Looking over the debris, they discover their enemy's body stretched out on the ground, blood streaming from his head (215). Johnny throttles the locomotive at full tilt. Approaching a freight train coming from the opposite direction, they jump off and watch a spectacular collision: "Parmi les flammes et la fumée, des morceaux de métal furent projetés à plus de cinquante mètres dans les airs. Le métal enflammé retomba sur les wagons du train de marchandises qui contenaient des barriques de goudron, d'essence et des sacs de charbon et de coton : quand tout se mit à brûler, on vit des nuages de feu et de fumée à vingt kilomètres de la ronde" (216). (In the conflagration and smoke pieces of metal flew over 150 feet into the air, the flaming bits of metal falling onto the freight cars that contained barrels of tar, gasoline, bags of coal, and cotton: when everything began to burn, fire and smoke were visible from fifteen miles away.) Arriving on the outskirts of Hondo, caring for Pretty Boy who has fallen ill, they meet a young Black woman who leads them into a house where, unexpectedly, they happen upon Olga, with whom they recount their adventures since their departure in Kansas. A newspaper tells them that Harrington (and on his heels, Pinkerton) will soon arrive to lead an inquest concerning the destruction of the trains. As in the final sequences of *They Drive by Night*, the courtroom becomes the stage of farce. Olga belittles the lawmen to allow time for the men to head off for Mexico.

Thus begins chapter 9, the longest of the novel (239–318): "It was an exciting pursuit. The horses the three men were riding and those of the patrol following them left in their tracks thick clouds of dust" (240). Desperate, evading Pinkerton and his phalanx, the heroes ride their horses down a steep slope, cross a valley, and climb another where they stop to catch their breath while the lawmen camp far below. Finding food and solace in a Spanish hamlet beyond the crest, they regroup and stand guard over the range here as they watch the enemy, where allusion to the end of *The Big Trail* could not be clearer. "A mesure que l'obscurité gagnait, une pléiade d'étoiles apparaît dans le ciel. Pretty Boy, qui n'était plus qu'une silhouette solitaire dans la nuit, se demandait s'il reverrait un jour le Nid, s'il prendrait par la main sa jolie petite montagnarde pour la conduire à travers la forêt où les arbres géants s'élèvent jusqu'au ciel" (246). (As night fell, a cluster of stars appeared in the sky. Pretty Boy, who was little more than a solitary silhouette in the night, wondered if he would ever again see the Nest, if he would take by the hand his lovely mountain girl and lead her through the forest where the giant trees rose up to the heavens.) Suspecting the enemy of its devious devices ("There's something rotten in the kingdom of Denmark," quips Pretty Boy [256]), they open fire on the phalanx, killing several, but not before Gomez (one of Pinkerton's men) cuts a rope that holds Jeb on the slope, who plummets to his death. Rapidly crosscut, the narrative follows the two survivors who ride off, following the meanders of a river that cuts deeply into the arid landscape.

The law is never far behind. The sheriff pays local Apaches for information to help them negotiate their itinerary. One Indian responds: "Sunda—a. Ah-Pilo. Ugahate. Tuhe, Dogata, Arbute, Shinta—Shinka Iga Iga, Kuk-si, Shon Ka Ka" (266). First transcribed as such, and later translated, the words inform Pinkerton's men where they must go while, from another angle, outside of the narrative and if the last paragraphs of *Each Man in His Time* are recalled, the exchange exudes sympathy with an idiom and a culture we fail to understand. Yet, as the novel has it, the Native Americans are not entirely blameless. Black Cloud (*Nuage Noir*), an appropriately named Apache interpreter (a *truchement*, also a betrayer) helps the posse guide its way through the rugged landscape. Pretty Boy and Johnny ride to the upper edge of the Grand Canyon then hastily descend the steep slope while the lawmen bicker with each other over how they will distribute the spoils of the award. Spurring their horses, Johnny and Pretty Boy men arrive at a ranch where they meet Reverend Simpson, a libidinous preacher who strikes the fear of God into the women he has corralled and locked in chastity belts. Befriending two of the females, Pretty Boy and Johnny free them from their shackles before, together, the foursome shares unexpected pleasure in the sanctuary of a barn. Meanwhile—in accelerated oppositional montage moving between pursuers and pursued—the lawmen draw near. With Simpson's help, the two men and Wilbur, a young guide, repair a rickety boat; with cords, courage, and muscle, they believe they can guide the craft over impossible rapids on route to the Mexican border. On the eve of their departure, resting under the stars, exclaims Pretty Boy, "Je suis impatient de voir ces imposantes falaises se découper dans le ciel bleu et le soleil mettre en valeur toutes les nuances du paysage" (293). (I really want to see these great cliffs as they cut below the blue sky where the sun brings out all the nuances of the landscape.) And then adds: "J'ai hâte de passer ces rapides en furie et surtout d'arriver au Mexique." (I really want to get through the furious rapids and especially arrive in Mexico.) To which Johnny replies with sarcasm: "Surtout ça, comme tu dis . . . Enfin on va voir Guadalajara où le soleil brille toute l'année, où les fleurs sont épanouies sur le versant des collines, où on chante et on danse et où les señoritas sont les plus jolies du monde" (293). (Yeah, for sure, as you say . . . we'll finally see Guadalajara where the sun shines all year, where the flowers bloom on the hillsides, where they sing and dance and where the señoritas are the prettiest in all the world.)

Learning from the sheriff that Pretty Boy and Johnny are bandits, Simpson tells the posse how best to cross the landscape and reach the river. After almost unsurmountable difficulty, the heroes and their guide manage to get through the rapids. When they see the posse on the shoreline, "[q]uatre coups de feu retentirent. Trois adjoints vinrent frapper le sol et le quatrième tomba à la renverse. Son pied se prit dans l'étrier et il fut traîné par son cheval; sa tête heurta plusieurs fois de gros rochers qui se trouvaient sur la piste" (308). (Four gunshots rang out. Three of the posse struck the ground and the fourth fell topsy-turvy. His foot caught in his stirrup, dragged by his horse, his head banged into rocks strewn along the path.) The men arrive at a hamlet where Wilbur, smelling reward, betrays his friends, informing the posse of their whereabouts. Passing by a church in its Sunday service, noticing the law hot on their heels, Johnny and Pretty Boy jump in a fountain, take aim at their enemy, and shoot three men before running out of ammunition. In a last effort they carry their money-laden saddlebags to a bridge, leap, and fall eighty feet into the water to the sound of tolling church bells. When they come to the surface (we recall *The Bowery* when Steve Brodie emerged from the depths of the East River after his jump from the Brooklyn Bridge) the lawmen riddle them with bullets. "Many bystanders ran to the railing to see what was happening. A splotch of blood came to the top of the waters. It became larger and larger, floating toward Mexico" (317).

> Au loin, tel un mirage, la petite ville de Guadalajara baignait dans le soleil. Les collines étaient recouvertes d'un tapis de fleurs sauvages. Dans un patio, sous une tonnelle recouverte de bougainvillées odoriférantes, des musiciens, coiffés de sombreros colorés, jouaient des airs folkloriques mexicains, Près de la place, des danseurs, dans leurs costumes chamarrés, jouaient des castagnettes et dansaient avec le flamenco. Dans les jardins de Notre-Dame-de-Guadalupe, de jeunes et jolies filles de Guadalajara chantaient d'agréables mélodies de la vieille Espagne. Le soleil commença à décroître et alla se cacher derrière un bouquet de pins. Dans la vieille cathédrale, la cloche sonnait et les fidèles adressaient leurs prières au Sauveur de l'humanité, au Prince de la Paix. (318)

(Far away, like a mirage, the little town of Guadalajara was in sunshine. The hills were carpeted with wildflowers. In a patio, a barrel was covered with odorous bougainvillea. Wearing brightly colored sombreros, musicians played folkloric Mexican songs. Near the square, dancers in brocaded costumes played castanets and danced the flamenco with elegance. In the Garden of Notre-Dame-de-Guadalupe, the pretty young women of Guadalajara were singing lovely melodies from old

Spain. The setting sun hid behind a clump of pines. In the old cathedral, the bell tolled, and the brethren addressed their prayers to the Savior of Humanity, to the Prince of Peace.)

The novel bears the traits of many films, not only the landscapes of *The Big Trail* and *Wild Girl* (such as the passages where Pretty Boy marvels over high trees) but also, in vertical and cavalier shots, recalling the arid vistas of *High Sierra*, *Cheyenne*, *Colorado Territory*, and other westerns Walsh directed at Warner Bros. The narrative of pursuit and passage is blueprinted in those films, and also in *Desperate Journey*, *Northern Pursuit*, *Objective, Burma!*, *Distant Drums*, and other features, reminding us that displacement and voyage—and *motion* rather than affective emotion—are at the crux of the author's narrative.[6]

Among the virtues of *La Colère des justes* are its concision, its mix of rough and soft edges, and its refusal to indulge in sentimentality. Its crosscut montage describing evasion and pursuit is as lean and clear as the cinema. An adventure that moves across the Americas, from Tennessee to Kansas, from Kansas to San Francisco, from San Francisco to Arizona, and from Arizona to Guadalajara, with and without either the righteous cause for which they break the law (or the females who drive their desires), the heroes are wedded to the spaces they discover and to the environment they defend. *La Colère des justes* belongs rightfully in the greater body of the director's work.[7]

Notes

Preface and Acknowledgments

1. Few or none can be found in university libraries. In *Air France Magazine* (December 2013), Bertrand Tavernier, fervent admirer of Walsh's cinema, took up the pulp genre for which Field was well known. Wishing to turn ephemera into art, he launched a series of French translations later published at Éditions Actes Sud. See "Fortunes of the Western," catalogue of a retrospective at the Harvard Film Archive (February 14 to March 22, 2014), in which Tavernier's project and vision play a role: https://harvardfilmarchive.org/programs/fortunes-of-the-western.

2. Walsh dwells significant pages of "Cyclops," the aptly titled chapter of his memoir, *Each Man in his Time* (New York: Farrar, Straus & Giroux, 1974) on the event and its immediate aftermath. See also Moss (2011: 116).

3. Tavernier makes explicit the "diagonal" view that marks Walsh's sense of perspective in commentary on a fifty-second film of one take depicting a team of horses drawing a wagonload of stone. He links the Lumière Brothers and Walsh, in a DVD, *The Lumière Brothers' First Films* (Chatsworth, CA, 1998).

4. Some shots have been recovered from *The Life of General Villa* (1914), a graphically violent film of a complicated history, in which Walsh played Pancho Villa in his youth, took part in the cinematography, and was a codirector. In *Raoul Walsh: The True Adventures of Hollywood's Legendary Director* (Lexington: University Press of Kentucky, 2011), 35–40, Marilyn Ann Moss recounts in detail the making of a film that for Walsh might have been the lynchpin to his career, which in fact Walsh stresses in "Viva Villa!," a significant chapter in his memoir (1974), bearing the subtitle, *The Life Story of a Director*, 85–104. Some of its unsettling shots are available. See https://lostmediawiki.com/The_Life_of_General_Villa_(partially_found_silent_film;_1914).

5. An exception is *Sailor's Luck*, a feature Amazon includes in its collection of films available for rental or purchase. So also, and famously, *The Thief of Baghdad* (1924), a feature affiliated more with Douglas Fairbanks, star and author of the story, and to its lavish art direction and costume design, than the director.

Loving the Classics has distributed (forcibly) poor copies of *The Man Who Came Back* (1931) and *Wild Girl* (1932).

    6. Michel de Certeau, "Récits d'espace," in *L'Invention du quotidien, 1: Arts de faire*, ed. Luce Giard (Paris: Gallimard, 1990), in English as "Spatial Stories," in *The Practice of Everyday Life*, trans. Steven Rendall (Berkeley: University of California Press, 1984); Lefebvre, *La Production de l'espace* (Paris: Anthropos, 1974), in English as *The Production of Space*, trans. Donald Nicholson-Smith (New York: Blackwell, 1991).

    7. Jacques Rancière, *La Fable cinématographique* (Paris Éditions du Seuil, 2001), in English as *Film Fables* (New York: Berg, 2004).

    8. Marie-Claire Ropars-Wuilleumier, *Le Texte divisé: Essai sur l'écriture filmique* (Paris: PUF, 1981); *Écrire l'espace* (Saint-Denis: PUV, 2002); *Le Temps d'une pensée: Du montage à l'esthétique plurielle* (Saint-Denis: PUV, 2009); Jacques Rancière, *Les Écarts du cinéma* (Paris: La Fabrique, 2011), in English as *The Intervals of Cinema*, translated by John Howe (London and New York: Verso, 2014).

    9. https://harvardfilmarchive.org/programs/action-action-action-a-raoul-walsh-retrospective. And an announcement in the *Harvard Political Review*: https://harvardpolitics.com/wonders-of-walsh-action-action-action-a-raoul-walsh-retrospective-at-harvard-film-archive/.

Chapter 1

    1. *My Mamie Rose: The Story of My Regeneration* (New York: Taylor and Baker, 1903). Available online at https://babel.hathitrust.org/cgi/pt?id=wu.89040960049;view=1up;seq=12. Marilyn Ann Moss notes that the book sold well enough to merit a theatrical adaptation that premiered in New York on September 1, 1908 (48). In the *New York Sun*, September 6, 1908, the play is advertised under the name of Arnold Daly adjacent to William A. Pinkerton's blurb, "Plays like 'The Regeneration' will do much to Depopulate the Penitentiaries," a remark that would seem to inspire the idea for Walsh's *The Honor System* (1917).

    2. His remembrance of time past is not lost in later cinema. In *The Public Enemy* (1932, d. William Wellman), in his youth, delinquent James Cagney is shown taking stock of his life in the same fashion.

    3. By chance, gazing at the face of an infant he sees in a window of the settlement house Owen begins to turn away from his coequals in crime (41:58–43:32).

    4. Arresting and graphic, the shot recording the maze of clotheslines appears inspired by a sentence in Kildare's memoir: "Located on the top floor of an old-style tenement house on Catherine Street, our home was lighted and ventilated by one small window, which looked out into a network of wash-lines running from the windows to tall poles in the corners of the yard" (14). A cutaway (or nondiegetic) shot of a rat exiting from a hole matches the iris that frames Skinny making his getaway. As noted below, it is implied is that the camera assumes a rat's view of the criminal.

5. Indication of the film's mode of production and "condition of possibility" within the narrative is found in other features. *Objective, Burma!* (1945), begins with photographs taken from a reconnaissance plane and delivered to a darkroom. When the soldier assigned to process the pictures closes the door, a panel on its outside reads, *film developing* (studied in Conley 1991, chap. 4).

6. See Gilles Deleuze, on Pier Paolo Pasolini's concept of "free indirect subjectivity" in *Cinéma 1: L'Image-mouvement* (Paris: Éditions de Minuit), 110–12; or on point of view, in *Le Pli: Leibniz et le baroque* (Paris: Éditions de Minuit, 1988), 25–26, which is likened to narration in the novels and stories of Henry James.

7. Deleuze (1988, 25–26) notes how close-ups of faces or of faciality tend to be emotive, hence what he calls affect-images are distinguished from action-images (medium shots of narrative import) and perception-images (generally long shots that lay stress on the birth of visibility). In *Raoul Walsh*, Carlos Losilla (2020, 50–52) remarks that between the close-ups of child Owen and the eyeline takes of the hearse, narrative effects are missing, leaving us with "an impossible mosaic, a chaos of reflections and of time," an interval in which a vision of the "world in its integrity" is out of the question in the space and time of this film, implying that in contrast to *A Birth of a Nation* and its tightly knit montage in the editing of Walsh's film, a feeling of the unknown and of unpredictable destiny is given.

8. It becomes a virtual "shifter" in visual, social, and moral registers. It leans against the Conways' door in the stairwell (3:49) or in the boy's new setting picked up now and again (4:26–29), and it is even behind him when the drunken foster father tosses him through the doorway (4:36–39, 4:44–50, etc.). In an exterior shot of the entry to the tenement (resembling that of the settlement house) where unkempt children are amassed (5:51:6:00), a girl uses a truncated broom to sweep the stairs at the entry. In a later intertitle a new city official and his mission will be compared to the object itself: "Like all proverbial brooms, the recently elected district attorney resolves to sweep the city clean" (12:39–44). Walsh returns to the formula in *Manpower* (1942). Sipping a cup of coffee in a diner, Eddie Adams (Ward Bond), a wry and cynical member of the cohort of highwire workers, learns of the unlikely marriage of the tragic hero, Hank "Gimpy" McHenry (Edward G. Robinson) to a vamp, Fay Duval (Marlene Dietrich), riposting, "a new groom always sweeps clean."

9. The same effect is given in the opening shots of *The Big Trail* (1930), in which women who are preparing for the westward voyage wash their hair in a fashion recalling paintings by Degas. See below, chap. 5, fig. 3.4.

10. At this point the film qualifies as a "spatial story" for which the camera establishes a visual dialogue with its milieu, thus turning the "place" into an area where a practice or a discourse is enabled: see Michel de Certeau, "Récits d'espace" (cited 204n6). Walsh's films, from *Regeneration to A Distant Trumpet* (1964), qualify as such, and surely merit close study from this point of view, as Natacha Pfeiffer has done in published work on Anthony Mann and a forthcoming study of milieus in Walsh.

11. The play of reflection and of spaces inside and outside recurs later when, on the heels of his rescue of the Flaherty baby, Owen returns to a tavern.

Marie sends the hunchback to fetch him; in its filming of the boy approaching the swinging doors (38:15–22), in an inordinately long shot—perhaps to allow spectators to discern the inside/outside opposition and to see the film mirroring itself—the camera records a reflection on the left panel of a person leaning on a railing and overlooking the scene.

12. Personages looking at windows or glass panels tend to cue reflective pause. In a study of *M* Jacques Rancière takes note of a moment of calm and reprieve when the child killer (Peter Lorre), standing before a shop window with a child—a possible victim—who remains beside him, is suddenly calm and contained, in a state of possible self-reflection [in "From One Manhunt to Another: Fritz Lang Between Two Ages," chapter 4 of *Film Fables*, Emilio Battista's translation (New York: Oxford and Berg, 2006) of *La Fable cinématographique* (Paris: Éditions du Seuil, 2001). It can be asked whether, on a broader plane, topical and conventional as they are, reflective scenes that juxtapose adult and child designate the effect in which cinema bears on childhood memories as they are revised in the course of a lifetime.

13. See also Moss (2011: 49–50).

14. Reference is made indirectly to Kildare's account. In the memoir Owen grew into the world with his fists. And in Walsh's novel, *La Colère des justes* (1972), a sequence in San Francisco has two men nearly kill each other, one whose ear is torn off and puts his arms around the other, the winner, before they "head off together toward the bar, the best friends in the world" (85).

15. Jacques Derrida, "Freud et la scène de l'écriture," in *L'Écriture et la différence* (Paris: Éditions du Seuil, 1967), 318–27, on the "mystic writing pad" (which could be cinema) is pertinent: *Regeneration* could be a point of reference for Derrida's landmark essay that can be read in conjunction with film theory: *espacement* or spacing, "a becoming-space of time," a "silent spacing" in which "concatenations are possible that do not follow the linearity of logical time, of conscious or preconscious time, or of 'verbal representation.' It is difficult to distinguish between the non-phonetic space of writing (and even in 'phonetic' writing) and the scenic space of the dream" (321): hence a hieroglyphic mode of the kind that Walsh's mentor and master, D. W. Griffith, had inaugurated.

16. Jean-François Lyotard, *Discours, figure* (Paris: Klincksieck, 1968), studies desire and repression in Freud's writing, notably in the rebuses and in what the founder of psychoanalysis had called *Bilderschriften* or "picture-writing." In this shot we witness the beginnings of what (in the front-credits of *Sans toi/Ni loi* (*Vagabond*) Agnès Varda called *ciné-écriture*, film that "writes" itself, in variation on Alexandre Astruc's famous formula of the *camera-stylo*, a sort of *crayon-caméra*, a pencil-camera that develops its matter through sketches and writing.

17. "Thoughts for the Time on War and Death," in Vol. 14 of *The Standard Edition of the Complete Psychological Works of Sigmund Freud*, ed. James Strachey (London: The Hogarth Press, 1957/1986), 273–300, an essay written in close affiliation with a first study of the unconscious (159–215).

18. Jean-Louis Comolli, *Corps et cadre: Cinéma, éthique, politique* (Paris: Verdier, 2013) 85.

19. Karel Reisz and Gavin Miller, *The Technique of Film Editing* (New York: Hastings House, 1953/1975), 21, a propos the sequence of *The Birth of a Nation* in which Walsh, first shown in an iris, plays John Wilkes Booth.

20. Guy Rosolato, "L'Objet de perspective dans ses assises visuelles" [The object of perspective on its visual field], reprinted in *Pour une psychanalyse exploratrice dans la culture* (Paris: PUF, 1993) 29–52.

21. In a first oneiric insert (1:07:48–51) having nothing to do with the narrative, a shot that would qualify (in the idiolect of Gilles Deleuze) as a "mental image," or an anticipation of what will befall him, Skinny, fantasizing his fate, shrieks in front of the shadow of a gallows on the wall behind. In subsequent shots it is visible from a slant, in anamorphic perspective, after Owen jumps down from the skylight to confront his nemesis (1:07:59–1:08:06).

Chapter 2

1. *Raoul Walsh* (Madrid: Cátedra, 2020), 15–16.

2. The only extant copy is in the George Eastman House. Writes John T. Soister in *Up from the Vault: Rare Thrillers of the 1920 and 1930s* (Jefferson, NC, and London: McFarland, 2004), "Preprint material shows extensive image deterioration, with fully half of the footage barely visible, even when run on a flatbed viewer" (65).

3. A success in Paris and London, Fauchois's play was performed one hundred times on Broadway. Contrary to the film, whose violence is immediate and unsettling, the malfeasants are apprised that Jocko was not a real monkey. Soister (2004: 60) writes pithily of Olivette, "[w]ith her physical assets . . . it's little wonder that the 'real' monkey who attacks her late in the proceedings very obviously has romance on his mind" (60).

4. In a famous photo-op on the cover of the 1962 issue of *Présence du Cinéma*, Walsh and a lion read the script of a screenplay. A tamer of sorts, Walsh had directed *A Lion is in the Streets* (1953). Where the lion mauls the tamer in *The Monkey Talks*, many of his actors and actresses have recalled Walsh as being famous for charming or putting the whip to difficult or recalcitrant players.

5. Moss (2011, 101–104).

6. "Rain," in *The Trembling of a Leaf: Little Stories of the South Pacific* (New York, George H. Doran, 1921), 301. See also: https://books.google.com/books?vid=HARVARD:32044050960715&printsec=titlepage#v=onepage&q&f=false.

7. Other films of the era include Chaplin's *Shoulder Arms* (1918), which would inspire Jean Renoir's *Tire-au-flanc* (1928) (The sad sack), a feature said to play on *le comique troupier*, on farce and foibles of idle soldiers who find ingenious ways to amuse and gratify themselves. As *The Monkey Talks* had shown, grisly aftereffects of the war and, in another vein, the success of King Vidor's *The Big Parade* (1925) were surely on the minds of the producers and directors.

8. In *Le Corps du cinéma: Hypnoses, émotions, animalités* (Paris: POL, 2009),

implicitly paying attention to Griffith, Raymond Bellour argues that emotion, mobilizing much of silent cinema, is tied to a convergence of hypnosis and bestiality. An ideal case study, *Sadie Thompson* would support Bellour's observation.

9. The film asks the question concerning the origin of authority that Flagg and Quirt pose to each other in *What Price Glory?* and *The Cock-Eyed World*: "Sez who?" (see chapter 3).

10. In *Each Man in His Time* (New York: Farrar, Straus & Giroux, 1974) Walsh recalls that in directing the film in which he was a player, "I found myself coming on with something approaching stage fright. I could tell *them* [the cast] what to do and how they were doing it, but who was to tell *me*?" (208). Who or what was the authority? Extended to include the history of the occupation, the question indicates that the industry "would prefer not to" provide a reasoned answer.

11. Victor Hugo, *William Shakespeare* (Paris: Éditions Hetzel-Quantin, 1866), 212.

12. Historians have remarked that the success of some of Walsh's best-known films can be attributed less to him than to certain others. Surely *The Thief of Baghdad* (1924) centers on Douglas Fairbanks, whose erotic presence takes control, and on Cameron Menzies's art design that enhances the feature's outstanding choreography. *East of Suez* (1925) may be remembered for what Walsh did with Edmund Lowe and how it evinces the director's difficult relationship with censors (Moss 2011, 88). Features of the years 1933–35, such as *Baby Face Harrington*, are what the biographer (147) rightly qualifies as second features or perhaps, potboilers.

13. Reference is made to Dennis Doros's impeccable restoration of the sole copy of the film, available in DVD format (New York: Kino International, 2001).

14. Playing the role of a drunk in many movies of the 1930s, Stanton figures thus in several Walsh films, most famously in the café sequences in *Me and My Gal* (1933), taken up in chapter 6. He is the riotous bartender in *Wild Girl* (1932), plays the comic role of (the well-named) J. Felix Hemingway in *Sailor's Luck* (1933), and is a drunken prisoner in *Baby Face Harrington* (1935).

15. Here and elsewhere I have reproduced the lineation of the intertitles to stress that they are crafted to draw attention to tonic words or phrases at their conclusion. The graphic design is anything but haphazard. Among other studies on the importance of the framing and spacing of front matter in classical cinema, there is Alexander Böhnke, Rembert Hüser, and Georg Stanizek, eds., *Das Buch zum Vorspann: 'The Title is a Shot'* (Berlin: Vorwerk 8, 2006), especially André Gardies's contribution, "Am Anfang war der Vorspann," 21–33.

16. Cast as a dream (or a nightmare), it is important to recall the beginning of "Miss Thompson": "It was nearly bed-time and when they awoke next morning land would be in sight." The sentence following the incipit denotes that Macphail, who will be both within and outside of Davidson's orbit of attraction, is the principal "reflector" or conveyor of the narrative, and that the "pipe," as Michel Foucault made famous, is at once an emblem of oral pleasure and an

instrument that allows its smoker to "think" or take distance from the situation while sucking on its lip: "Dr. Macphail lit his pipe and, leaning over the rail, searched the heavens for the Southern Cross": 'Rain," in *The Trembling of a Leaf and Other Stories* (New York: George H. Doran and Company, 1921), 241. For Foucault see *Ceci n'est pas une pipe. Deux lettres et quatre dessins de René Magritte* (Montpellier: Fata Morgana, 1973), in English as *This is Not a Pipe*, trans. James Harkness (Berkeley: University of California Press, 2008).

17. The duration of the otherwise sparse intertitles suggests that they "hold" long enough to allow the viewer to get the double entendres. Duration of the shots and their intertitles is parenthetically noted to suggest that the relation of moving images and written material has much to do with the way (in contrast to earlier films such as *Regeneration* where accelerated montage is keynote, or *The Lucky Lady*, in which intertitles are effusive and offsetting) the formatting of the late silent film indicates how it can be "read" as an object held at a distance, hence a critical agent in dialogue with the viewer.

18. The shot recalls the barracks-style humor (recently called "locker room talk") filling much of *What Price Glory?* Aimed against strictures of the Hays Code, its obscenity would riddle the silence of erotic attraction. The point is stressed in Susan Sontag's "Fascinating Fascism," a watershed essay on Leni Riefenstahl. The German director's embrace of "the primitive" in *Nuba* could be a foil to the situation of exile in *Sadie Thompson*. The aesthetics of fascism "flow from (and justify) a preoccupation with situations of control, submissive behavior and extravagant effort; they exalt two seemingly opposite states, egomania and servitude," in the *New York Review of Books*, first published February 6, 1975: http://www.nybooks.com/articles/1975/02/0. The remarks are close in spirit to Henry Miller, in *Obscenity and the Law of Reflection* (Yonkers, NY: O Baradinsky,1945) who argues that outrageousness, especially wit and humor, break the spell that fascist aesthetics seek to impose.

19. In the commentary accompanying his presentation of *The Lumière Brothers' First Films* (New York: Kino on Video, 1998), Tavernier notes that *cinématographe* means *film writing*. Commenting on a fifty-second film of a team of horses pulling a cart laden with stone, he watches the pioneers deploying a diagonal perspective, he says, that becomes a signature in Walsh's cinema (31:07–48). The same idea can be found here, in the work of Marsh and company, who lay stress on an angular treatment of the confines of the hotel.

20. *Sadie Thompson* appears at a moment when Freud's writings on war and on the unconscious had ostensibly taken hold, especially with the publication of "Notes on the Mystic Writing Pad" (1926), a brief essay on a child's writing toy, the *Wunderbloc*, which Freud compares to the mind and memory. A reader today would compare it to the effects of memory and movies. The point is not lost on Jacques Derrida in "Freud et la scène de l'écriture," in *L'Écriture et la différence* (Paris: Éditions du Seuil, 1967), chap. 7 [in English as "Freud and the Scene of Writing," in *Writing and Difference*, trans. Alan Bass (Chicago: University of Chicago Press)]. See also n21.

21. Famously studied in "Leçon d'écriture" (punning on "writing lesson" and "the sound of writing" [*le son d'ecriture*]), a pivotal chapter in Claude Lévi-Strauss, *Tristes Tropiques* (Paris: Plon, 1955) that affiliates writing (and by extension cinema) with orders of control and subjection. Along a similar axis, see also Michael Gaudio, *Engraving the Savage* (Minneapolis: University of Minnesota Press, 2008), on Theodor de Bry's depictions of tattooed Amerindians.

22. Free indirect subjectivity would be the equivalent in cinema to free indirect discourse in literature. Gilles Deleuze remarks how Pasolini articulates the concept and turns it into a practice in *Cinéma 1: L'Image-mouvement* (Paris: Éditions de Minuit, 1983), 108–12.

23. In *Rabelais and His World* (Bloomington: Indiana University Press, 1984), Bakhtin proposes that the "lower body" is matter for communal pleasure and laughter. Fitting Walsh's challenge of the codes of censorship, it becomes something of a chronotope in the oeuvre. Losilla (2020, 31–32) takes note of it in *Me and My Gal* (1932), when the camera focuses on Helen Riley (Joan Bennett), who wiggles her buttocks in medium close-up, but here and elsewhere it goes with Sadie's defiantly jovial—Rabelaisian—character.

24. Moss suggests that Marcus had been an associate producer and, in the 1920s, a long-standing friend and colleague of the director (2011, 74 and 80).

25. "Jim Marcus," recalls Walsh, "with body padding and some artful makeup, was a typical boozer trader. When he entered yawning from the bedroom, I could fairly smell the gin" (1974, 206). Walsh seems to remember James A. Marcus both in his film of 1915 and in *Sadie*. Moss notes that Jim Marcus, one of Walsh's assistant directors (2011, 75), was part of a group that went on a two-week trip to Tahiti in 1923, which in fact included Carl Harbaugh (2011, 80), another lifelong friend, we remember as the district attorney in *Regeneration*, who played a role in *Lost and Found on a South Sea Island* (1923). Of generous corpulence and demeanor, Horn's body belongs to satire and carnivalesque caricature, already seen in *Regeneration* and other films, such as Eugene Pallette in the role of "Yuba Bill," the stage driver and postman in *Wild Girl* (shot only four years later), who delivers to the community (and puns on) the "mails and the males."

26. The reference to the Victrola and "his master's voice" could be taken as a "silent-sound cue," a sign of the recording apparatus that will come with the talkie, notably in *In Old Arizona* (1928), where, in the shape of an ample megaphone (like the one the director uses), it appears again, perhaps in oblique reference to Walsh's comments in his memoir about the difficulties he faced when having to wield a megaphone in directing sound films (1974, 222).

27. In her detailed and informative account of the production, remarking that cinematographer Robert Kurrle had worked on *Regeneration*, Moss surmises that perhaps because of Walsh's attraction to Swanson and the "chemistry" they share he "looks uncomfortable in many of the scenes, especially in long shots where the most striking thing about him is his relentless habit of hitching up his trousers" (104). Discomfort or perhaps a hilarious visual cue? Is the character

who has fallen in love with Sadie adjusting his pants in order to keep an erection under control? Is he is drawing attention to the animal region of the body?

28. The moment begs recall of Baroque "point of view" that is not a general relativity but a point from which all possible points of view can be ascertained: in Gilles Deleuze, *Le Pli: Leibniz et le baroque* (Paris: Éditions de Minuit, 1988), 25, in English as *The Fold: Leibniz and the Baroque*, trans. Tom Conley (Minneapolis: University of Minnesota Press, 1993), 17.

29. See below, in *Me and My Gal* (chapter 6), how Helen Riley (Joan Bennett) chews gum obsessively, as if at once to flirt, to signal an erotic potential, and to sell the novelty that perhaps was used to obviate the desire for alcohol during Prohibition.

30. Walsh suggests that to avoid gossip and keep his trousers buckled, duty required him to temper his fondness, a sentiment production stills and advertisements otherwise promoted to sell the film. His remarks about his uncertainty in playing roles of both director and actor flow into his recollections of his fondness for Swanson, who was then married to the well-named Marquis de la Falaise (Marquis of the Cliff). He recalls or invents a conversation they shared at the beginning of the shoot. Responding to his uncertainty, "Gloria . . . came to the rescue with her customary tact. 'Remember you are O'Hara [not Walsh], the battle-tested marine. You are in love with me, and I am beginning to fall for you.' That was as near a director being directed as I had so far heard, and it worked" (1974, 208). Freudian transference could not be more obvious.

31. Her anger over the question concerning who and what constitute authority responds to a leitmotif of political implication. *What Price Glory?* builds its narrative upon the tension between two rivals, enemy brothers of sorts, who effectively admire and are in love with each other. Whenever one of the two utters an order (a "catch-word"), the other rejects it. Lieutenant Flagg (Victor McLaglen), an older and wizened brother, negates whatever the master sergeant Quirt (Edmund Lowe, as if a younger sibling), ventures to say. In the same spirit Quirt jabs at Flagg: Who sez? Sez-me! Sez-you?!, Sez-me!, and so on. In his memoir, recalling getting tired of the characters—forever fighting for the same love object, endlessly jawing at each other—Walsh leaves aside the broader (or political) implications of the exchanges that question authority (taken up in chapters 3 and 7).

32. Which is not the effect of footage the editors add in the remastered copy: reprising close-ups of the Victrola and its record that spins at 78 rpm, the lens then closing in on Sadie when she was dressed in full plumage, without a hint of irony, an intertitle reads (without following the lineation of the original subtitles), "Behold me in all my/*glorified glory*—I'm/radiant, I'm beautiful!" (1:29:01–06, emphasis added).

33. In *The American Cinema: Directors and Directions* (New York: Da Capo, 1996), Andrew Sarris noted that as early as 1935 (in *Every Night at Eight*, with George Raft, seen tossing and turning in bed) the director tends to lay stress on

masculine frailty and even trauma in depictions of nightmare. The remark holds here and pertains to other films that include *High Sierra* (1941), when Marie (Ida Lupino) witnesses Roy Earle (Humphrey Bogart) in the dark and gesticulating in his sleep, murmuring, "Don't hold me back! I'll crash out, I'll tell ya, Ma, yes, you can't take it [the farm in Indiana] away" (44:05–45:18). So too in *Colorado Territory* (1949), in darkness, when Colorado (Virginia Mayo) listens to bandit-lover Wes McQueen (Joel McCrea), who talks in his sleep: "Martha . . . Martha . . . Martha . . . wait, don't go, don't go" (45:54–46:13).

34. Published in 1922, a stunning piece of writing, the sonnet captures much of what escapes the narrative frame of the movie while complicating what goes in the name of the male gaze:

> Quels secrets dans mon cœur brûle ma jeune amie,
> Âme par le doux masque aspirant une fleur ?
> De quels vains aliments sa naïve chaleur
> Fait ce rayonnement d'une femme endormie ?
>
> Souffle, songes, silence, invincible accalmie,
> Tu triomphes, ô paix plus puissante qu'un pleur,
> Quand de ce plein sommeil l'onde grave et l'ampleur
> Conspirent sur le sein d'une telle ennemie.
>
> Dormeuse, amas doré d'ombres et d'abandons,
> Ton repos redoutable est chargé de tels dons,
> O biche avec langueur longue auprès d'une grappe,
>
> Que malgré l'âme absente, occupée aux enfers,
> Ta forme au ventre pur qu'un bras fluide drape,
> Veille; ta forme veille, et mes yeux sont ouverts.

[What secrets in my heart burns my young love, / A soul who breathes through a mask of flowers?/ With what food does its fresh warmth make a sleeping woman radiate? / Breath, dreams, silence, invincible calm, / You triumph, o peace of power greater than a tear, / When from this full sleep the ample fullness / Deep waters conspire upon the breast of such an enemy. / Sleeping woman, golden mass of shadows and repose, / Your formidable sleep is filled with such gifts, / O doe with long languor seeking a cluster, / Despite the absent soul, soon taken in the nether depths, / Your form with a pure belly draped by a fluid arm, / Overlooks; your form overlooks, and my eyes are open.] (This is a very rough translation.) In *Œuvres complètes de Paul Valéry* (Paris: Éditions de la NRF, 1933), 110, available via BNF Gallica, https://gallica.bnf.fr/ark:/12148/bpt6k15102930/f11.item#. Although the context is far from the film, the staging of the gaze in Valéry's poem indicates that the scene in the feature reaches beyond its narrative frame.

35. *Sadie Thompson* cannot be dissociated from the concurrent impact of Margaret Mead's controversial *Coming of Age in Samoa: A Psychological Study of Primitive Youth for Western Civilization*. A dissertation written under Franz Boas and published in 1928 on the heels of her extensive fieldwork on the island, *Coming of Age* contrasts pubescence and sexual mores of Samoan women to what she had observed to be neurosis and conflict in North American society. The controversy the book fomented finds parallels in the style and form of *Sadie Thompson*. Mead's conclusions about the casual sexuality of teenage life and deferred marriage would have been a foil to the cultural conditions the film represents.

36. In his memoir Walsh recounts having driven to Swanson's "lavish party" celebrating what the actress called her finest picture. Stopping his car at the driveway, he looked up to the mansion that seemed illuminated as if it were a set. Avowing that he was strongly drawn to her, he wonders if he had fallen head over heels for the prostitute in the guise of the Marquise de la Falaise. Letting discretion take the better part of valor, he departs. "'Adíos, Gloria.' I waved at her front door and drove away. At home, I packed a bag in a hurry and took off for Mexico" (1974, 174). Moss (2011, 106) adds that after spending time with her at the MOMA retrospective of 1974, Walsh wrote a letter to Swanson replete with words of care and undying love. "Your lips, your eyes, your hair have been with me for these many years. To me, I can see my lovely Gloria." The romance was still kindling.

Chapter 3

1. Thus Dave Rickard (Basil Ruysdael) in *Colorado Territory* (1949) (35:28–35), a gentle scoundrel in the last days of his life, tells bandit Wes McQueen (Joel McCrea) that whiskey is the best prescription for his condition. Rickard looks directly at the viewer as he utters the words in conversation with McQueen.

2. *Women of All Nations* makes direct reference to Walsh's enucleation. At one point, wearing an eye patch in the shape of a five-sided star, El Brendel faces McLaglen (Flagg) and Lowe (Harry Quirt), the odd couple who are the leading players. They ask why he wears it: the comedian states that in (amorous) conflict he was punched in the eye.

3. Satirical literary works that make the case for anamorphosis are Béroalde de Verville, *L'Histoire veritable, ou le voyage des princes fortunez* (1610) and its obscene counterpart, *Le Moyen de parvenir* (1616). A graphic manifestation is Erhard Schön's *Was Siest du?*, a satirical woodcut of 1538. When seen from an oblique angle, an image of a harbor and a landscape displays a man defecating at the origin of the angle. The wit of Schön's woodcut ("here's lookin' at you") seems to be the antipode of what psychoanalysts make of the death's head that Holbein sliced into the lower area and foreground of the *Ambassadors*, the painting that hangs in the National Gallery of London. See Jurgis Baltrušaitis, *Anamorphic Art* (New York: Harry N. Abrams. 1977). For Schön, see Larry Silver, ed., *Grand*

Scale: Monumental Prints in the Age of Dürer and Titien (New Haven, CT: Yale University Press, 2008). For the fabliau, Per Nykrog's work is definitive: *Les Fabliaux* (Geneva: Librairie Droz, 1973).

4. For the heritage of the Macrobian (zonal or thermal) map, see Rodney Shirley, *The Mapping of the World: Early Printed Maps, 1472–1700*, 4th ed. (Riverside, CT: Early Worldly, 2001), or the world map in Ambrosius Macrobius, *In somnium scipionis* (1485), illustrated in my *Self-Made Map* (Minneapolis: University of Minnesota Press, [1996] 2007), 177, fig. 5.4. The itinerary of *The Cock-Eyed World* goes from north to south, from a frigid zone, then to a temperate area, and finally ends in a "torrid zone" (the title of William Keighley's feature of 1940) close to the Equator.

5. The opening shots of arrival at the Brooklyn Navy Yard were taken in San Diego (35:55–36:56), which would have been a logical site of arrival.

6. It is difficult to tell whether the captain's name is "Griffith" or "Griffin." In either instance there is recall of Walsh's own "superior officer," D. W. Griffith, whose montage and mastery of the silent mode initially shapes the form and style of Walsh's early silent films.

7. "Illegalism" is a key concept in Michel Foucault's *Surveiller et punir* (Paris: Éditions Gallimard, 1975) that applies to proscribed activities a given society legitimizes or even advocates, as in *The Cock-Eyed World*, where wanton skirt chasing is encouraged, much in the way early screwball comedy revels in the joyous traffic and consumption of alcohol, effectively setting viewers at odds with the general order of things. (See also n11 below.)

8. The words are rife with issues of policy and politics: gamboling with others (Russians) of the (implied) other sex begins in so-called primitive society where forces of attraction and uncertainty are mixed when two parties meet. When an encounter of two groups ends with regulated exchange, the possibility of war or violence gives way to give-and-take: in Claude Lévi-Strauss, *Tristes Tropiques* (Paris: Plon, 1955), in a parabolic account of the meeting of two Nambikawa tribes where "*le conflit fait place au marché*" (conflict gives way to exchange) (p. 363), and recently, in *Œuvres*, ed. Vincent de Baene et al. (Paris: Éditions Gallimard/Pléiade, 2008), 304. See Pierre Clastres's critique of Lévi-Strauss's "exchangist model" in *Archéologie de la violence: la guerre dans les sociétés primitives* (La Tour d'Aigues: Éditions Aube, 1999) and *La Société contre l'état: recherches d'anthropologie politique* (Paris: Éditions de Minuit, 1974), in English as *Society Against the State* (Cambridge, MA: MIT Press, 1987).

9. In *La Fable cinématographique* (Paris: Éditions du Seuil, 2001), in English as *Film Fables*, trans. Emilio Battista (Oxford and New York: Berg, 2005), and subsequent essays, Jacques Rancière studies cinema as a medium that moves between narrative, of verbal character, and its optical counterpart. In its extensive history a fable is an economic equation whose wit (or performance at the most fitting moment) becomes its worth. Randle Cotgrave translates *fable* into English as, "Fable: f. *A fable, fib, lie, leasing, false tale, unlikelie thing reported; also, a Comedie,*

or Enterlude," in *A Dictionarie of the French & English Tongues* (London: Adam Inslip, 1611).

10. See 10:50–52, after Quirt announces he will leave the military service.

11. See *Surveiller et punir: Naissance de la prison* (1975) on illegalism, reprinted in *Œuvres*, v. 2, ed. Frédéric Gros et al (Paris: Éditions Gallimard/Pléiade, 2015), 343–44.

12. See Henry Miller, *Obscenity and the Law of Reflection* (New York: O. Baradinsky, 1945), who opposes healthy obscenity, that he associates with Rabelais and Louis-Ferdinand Céline, to the affected and pretentious prurience of the Marquis de Sade, which in fact is treated quite differently in Luis Buñuel's *L'Âge d'or* (1932) and Pier Paolo Pasolini's *120 Days of Sodom* (1976).

13. Olga is a familiar name in Walsh's world. In *La Colère des justes*, the western novel of 1972 (*The Wrath of the Just*) published exclusively in French, translated by Jacques Lourcelles, a hefty, no-nonsense manager of a whorehouse who keeps her ladies in tow (except for the vivacious and mean-spirited "Brooksie Nell"), Olga and her girls first ride west with the three heroes (who have robbed a bank and demolished a locomotive) before going on her own way with her bevy. Well into the novel, the three heroes meet her in the town of Hondo, where she covers for them at an inquest under the orders of Pinkerton, the agent pursuing the fortune the three men had robbed from a bank. In this feature she is a Russian prostitute who seduces Flagg before Quirt steals her away for immediate pleasure. Moss (2011, 45) notes that in his autobiography Walsh never mentions his first wife, Miriam Cooper (who obtained a divorce in 1927), but replaces her with a certain "Olga," whom Kevin Brownlow surmises had been Olga Grey, a player in *Pillars of Society* (1916). Whoever she is, in Walsh's fictions Olga is a "love at last sight," a person whose force of attraction is felt at a moment of departure or separation, a "rupture of contact." The *topos* is fitting for any romantic novel or film. Walsh reported taking Olga to the Los Angeles railroad station before boarding a sleeper bound for New York from Los Angeles. "'I kissed her pretty mouth and walked sadly to the train'" (*Each Man in His Time*, cited by Moss 2011, 46).

14. See Paul Radin, *The Trickster: A Study in American Indian Mythology* (London: Routledge, 1955).

15. The play of cat-and-mouse with the code is at the crux of the film narrative. *The Cock-Eyed World* is a far cry from what Nora Gilbert documents in her informative monograph, *Better Left Unsaid: Hays Code Films, Novels, and the Benefits of Censorship* (Stanford, CA: Stanford Law Books/Stanford University Press, 2013).

16. Among a host of films: Jean Renoir, *La Chienne* (The bitch) (1931), when Legrand (Michel Simon), who witnesses Dédé (Georges Flamand) in bed with the woman to whom he has given his life, is reprised in Fritz Lang's *Scarlet Street* (1945), taken up again in *The Big Heat* (1952), and with parallels in Edgar Ulmer's *Strange Illusion* (1947).

17. In fact, this had been actively debated as of 1925, when Billy Mitchell (like Flagg) made a strong (but losing) case for development of an air force. Both here and in the battle sequence the film illustrates and defends Paul Virilio's studies of the correlations of cinema and air power (in *Guerre et cinéma: Logistique de la perception* [Paris: Cahiers du Cinéma/Éditions de l'Étoile, 1984], in English as *War and Cinema: Logistics of Perception*, trans. Patrick Camiller [London: Verso, 1989]).

18. Hardly by chance William Fox, producer of the film, would be part of 20th Century Fox, the logo of which, designed in 1933, is tied to air war. Its beacons, as shown by Virilio and, later, Jean-Luc Godard, in the first section of *Histoire(s) du cinéma* (1988–2002), correlate cinema with the advent of antiaircraft technology and aerial photography. The lessons learned from World War I were not lost on Nazi strategists in their design and implementation of the *Blitzkrieg* in 1939 and 1940.

19. Guy Rosolato, "L'Objet de perspective dans ses assises visuelles," in *Pour une psychanalyse exploratrice dans la culture* (Paris, PUF, 1993), 29.

20. When Flagg and Fanny take a table in a nightclub (50:15–37) they sit between a panel on which is drawn a lover's heart that resembles a death's head, and below it are two lines, variants of crossed bones, in the shape of an X, all of which seem to signal the fate to befall Flagg when he angrily trashes the club and lands in jail. It is hard to tell if the signboard is of decorative or allegorical design.

21. Mikhail Bakhtin, *The Dialogic Imagination: Four Essays*, trans. Michael Holquist (Austin: University of Texas Press, [1981] 2004).

22. The film scripts the style of combat that American armed forces would face in Vietnam. After reporting for duty Flagg exits headquarters where he meets a corporal packing his bags. Stating that the men will be off to Santiago (surely not in Galicia!), he describes new ways of war unlike what the soldier had known in the earlier film. "These mugs don't fight out in the open. The hills are full of snipers. You can't look at a rock, a bush, or a tree. And the way they throw a knife in your back is nobody's business . . . what we need is aeroplanes to bomb'em and drag'em out in the open" (57:05'-58:00).

23. See Michel de Certeau on the *logique de perruque* ["wig logic"], a practice of overwrought conformism and mimicry required for survival in repressive societies, in *L'Invention du quotidien, 1: Arts de faire*, ed. Luce Giard (Paris: Éditions Gallimard, 1990), in English as *The Practice of Everyday Life*, translated by Steven Rendall (Berkeley: University of California Press, 1984).

24. The scene is a first iteration of a similar sequence in the exposition of *Objective, Burma!* (1945) that has men looking over maps and a model or *maquette* of the jump site where the paratroopers will land. It rehearses what follows, suggesting that the film "develops" itself as it goes.

25. Set at the onset of the Depression, the economy of the film hints at laughter and farce as waste and excess. It could be tied to the potlatch, a willful destruction of goods that Marcel Mauss takes up at the end of his landmark *Essai sur le don* (Essay on the gift) (1929), which Georges Bataille pushes to its limit

in his *Part maudite* of 1932, now as *La Part maudite de Georges Bataille: La dépense et l'excès*, ed. Christian Limousin and Jacques Poirier (Paris: Classiques Garnier, 2015). In English as *The Accursed Share: An Essay on General Economy*, translated by Robert Hurley (New York: Zone Books, 1988–1991).

26. The shots bear resemblance to those tracking along Schumacher and his beaters in the famous hunt-sequence of *La Règle du jeu* (1939) [*The Rules of the Game*], calling to mind what adepts of the New Wave (Michel Mourlet and Jean-Luc Godard) stated about the *moral drama* of the parallel tracking shot: recording the event, the track implicitly asks the viewer to account for its distance from what it records and thus acknowledge its critical virtue. See Antoine de Baecque, *La cinéphilie: Invention d'un regard, histoire d'une culture, 1944–1968* (Paris: Fayard, 2003).

27. Lewis Milestone soon exploits its effect in a series of unsettling shots in *All Quiet on the Western Front*, from a machine gun's point of view, killing advancing troops while the effects of exploding hand grenades are a pair of forearms and detached hands grasping a barbed wire fence). See Elisabeth Bronfen, *Specters of War* (New Brunswick, NJ: Rutgers University Press, 2013), whose introduction and conclusion implicitly address this film.

28. In these shots the scream of sirens is heard as the bombs are dropped. No wonder that during the Blitzkrieg Nazis sent slow-moving Stuka dive bombers to drop their payloads in advance of the oncoming *Wehrmacht*. The scream of whistles accompanying the bombs was intended to strike fear and dread *before* their explosion. From this angle the film may be prescient in its representation of aerial strategy.

29. In the classical tradition, a Parthian arrow (or *flèche de Parthes*). See Louise Labé, Sonnet 16, in *Œuvres complètes*, ed. Mireille Huchon (Paris: Éditions Gallimard/Pléiade, 2021): "Quand quelque tems le Parthe ha combatu,/Il pren[d] la fuite et son arc il desserre" (ll.7–8) (At a time when the Parthian has fought/ He retreats and lets an arrow fly).

Chapter 4

1. For a history and a balanced assessment of its theory and practice, see Codruta Morari, "Properties of Film Authorship," in *The Anthem Handbook of Screen Theory*, ed. Hunter Vaughan and Tom Conley (London: Anthem, 2018), 157–72.

2. "Adolescence" is understood here in its early modern inflection, as a formative period in the life of an individual, that extends between the age of twelve and twenty-eight or even beyond. It is famously the topic of poet Clément Marot's *Adolescence clémentine* (1534), a collection of poems the author, greatly influenced by the Corinthian Letters of Saint Paul, assembled from the time when he felt he had seen the world "through a glass darkly." As Walsh moved forward, Moss notes well (2011: 352–53), prefacing her pages on *The Revolt of Mamie Stover*, the director "believed more strongly in the love between man and

woman" and, a propos *Mamie Stover*, that "an alternate Walshian woman would be the woman traveling alone, meeting a man to love, but finding in the end that she must light out for the rest of her life without him."

3. Losilla is keen to note how, from the very beginning, the tracking shots portray Sadie (Jane Russell) walking with resolve, vertical pride, and self-containment (2020: 324–26).

4. *The Revolt of Mamie Stover* became a cult film in the early 1970s, when Pam Cook and Claire Johnston contributed an essay to a collection (based on Phil Hardy's conference held in Edinburgh in 1974 on Walsh) on Mamie and money. Writing from a British-Lacanian perspective, the authors argued adroitly how, despite a scenario in which subjects are at odds with themselves (or in a condition of lack), in this feature both financially and psychically needy, Mamie knows how to be and to live where she is without the crutch of an "other." A point of reference in feminist criticism, the essay was republished in the second volume of *Movies and Methods*, v. 2, ed. Bill Nichols (Berkeley: University of California Press, 1985).

5. Allusion is made to *crible*, a "screen" that for Gilles Deleuze (1988–1993, chap. 6) gives rise to an *event*, an encounter where the world and perceiver converge upon one another. Deleuze notes how a "something" (call it here the film coming into view) gets sifted (or screened) through a dark, brown-black background, what Leibniz called a *fuscum subnigrum* of chaos, sensed and perceived in an interactive process of "chaosmosis." The beginning of *The Revolt of Mamie Stover*, a Baroque film par excellence, qualifies as that kind of event.

6. It is licit to wonder if the placement of the name of the director at the end of the front credits in classical cinema, a last word or sign seen and read before the image track takes hold, had been a condition of possibility for auteur theory. The blending of the final piece of writing into the field of the image would have been the area where the author and film disappear and meld in unconscious memory. See, for example, the *contractual* yet ambiguous relation of a text or a movie with what its title and credits name and identify, that Jacques Derrida spells out in readings of Francis Ponge and Maurice Blanchot, in "Le Titrier: titre à préciser," in *Parages* (Paris: Galilée, 1986), translated as "The Titleer," in *Parages* (Stanford: Stanford University Press, 2010), chap. 1.

7. In *War and Cinema: Logistics of Perception*, Paul Virilio (1984–89) noted that the 20th Century Fox logo reproduces antiaircraft apparatus that had been deployed since World War I to spot and assist gunners to destroy enemy aircraft. In concert with Virilio, in the prewar sequence of *Histoire(s) du cinéma* (1988) Jean-Luc Godard inserts the logo to signal how air power and cinema correlate in the 1930s. See also chapter three, n18.

8. In the film "Mamie" becomes more than a name: she will be the sign of a song, an angry and sultry voice, and even the shorthand designating a pinup girl.

9. At the risk of overinterpretation we can wonder if, as it has been noted in so many of Walsh's films, both before and after the enucleation of his right

eye in 1929 (but most directly shown in *High Sierra*), reference is made to the event that blindsided him.

10. As if rehearsing Jean Genet's *Chant d'amour* (1950) (Song of love), they tap messages to each other across the walls of their compartments. Although unlikely, the connection between the two can be countenanced if erotic pleasure blends distance (absence of an other spurring the imagination) and narcissism (in regard to self-interest, attention to or care of the other felt to be a waste of time).

11. How can a viewer not recall how Flagg and Quirt stood in front of eyelike portholes in the sequences of *The Cock-Eyed World*? Or later, in several shots in *Me and My Gal*, when Joan Bennett stands alluringly in front of an eyelike window? Although belonging to the "realistic effects" of a shipboard setting, the portholes are associated with the agency of sight and perception that pervade this feature and others.

12. The historical context of *Mamie Stover* seems coordinated to promote or anticipate the publication of Walter Lord's bestselling *Day of Infamy* (New York: Holt, 1957) that met eager readers at the apex of the Cold War.

13. See Bronfen (2013, 92–93).

14. For what concerns the trauma of World War II, in *Histoire(s) du cinéma* (1988), Jean-Luc Godard juxtaposes footage from George Stevens's color film of the liberation of Ravensbrück to Montgomery Clift lifting Elizabeth Taylor out of bathwater in *A Place in the Sun*. In Godard's opinion, Hollywood betrayed itself in repressing or eliding images that needed to be made or shown, and all the more after poet Paul Celan had wondered how images could be made in the wake of the Holocaust. Jacques Rancière develops the point in *La Fable cinématographique* (Paris: Éditions du Seuil, 2001), for which *fable* is taken to be a fiction whose affirmations are written *against* or contrary to themselves as they are developed.

15. *L'Écriture de l'histoire* (Paris: Éditions Gallimard, 1975), chap. 9. In English as *The Writing of History*, translated by Tom Conley, 2nd ed. (New York: Columbia University Press, 1992).

16. On the cinematic latency of these formations see Gilles Deleuze on the Baroque, a style (1988: 44–51), in which archives (that could be history films) are contrasted with diagrams (intermediate creations, contemporary films, or else films that take as their task the "invention" of the spectator who is shown different ways of perceiving film and the world at large).

17. Walsh threads references to his life and films throughout the oeuvre: *The Cock-Eyed World* is cited in *Colorado Territory* (see the epigraph to chapter three) which remakes *High Sierra*, in which the event of his enucleation of 1929 is rehearsed.

18. "En marge de l'érotisme au cinéma," in *Cahiers du cinéma* (April 1957), gathered in *Qu'est-ce que le cinéma?* (Paris: Éditions du Cerf, 1998), an essay marked by the presence of Howard Hawks's *Gentlemen Prefer Blondes* (1953).

19. Losilla (2020: 30–31, n4) reminds readers that Dave Kehr, in his "Crisis, Creation, Compulsion: The Great Genre Director Raoul Walsh and his Cinema

of the Individual" (http://www.movingimagesourse.us/articls/crisis-creation-compulsion-20110322) is right to reproach André Bazin, known for his praise of depth of field (and the long take) in Wyler and Welles, for failing to acknowledge or even mention Walsh. Losilla notes the effectiveness of his camera work in *Me and My Gal* (1932), the film studied in chapter 6. Why Bazin, great admirer and specialist of American cinema, pays little attention to Walsh is anyone's guess. And why also Deleuze, who refers only to *The Enforcer* (1951), for which the well-named Bretaigne Windust is credited as director.

20. It is exactly what Bazin theorizes and in *The 400 Blows* (1959), three years after *Mamie Stover* (in implicit homage to Bazin), what François Truffaut mobilizes in the sequence where René and Antoine snatch pinups of scantily clad beauties from billboards outside of a Parisian movie theater.

21. Without casting aspersions on French theory devoted to the "real," taken here to be what cannot be semiotized or visualized and that unsettles and whets desire and fear, it can be said that the sequence offers a genial and terse enactment of what the "real" is (really) about.

22. In *Cahiers du cinéma* (April 1957), gathered in *Qu'est-ce que le cinéma?* (Paris: Éditions du Cerf, 1999).

Chapter 5

1. Such is Moss's view, for whom the film is missing the alacrity and efficiency defining the majority of Walsh's films (2011: 129–30).

2. "Le silence éternel de ces espaces infinis m'effraie." A fragment from "Misère" (Misery), Pascal's remark is fitting for the sense of infinite wonder a member of the Donner party, crossing the plains in 1846, registered in one of its diaries, cited in *The Donner Party* (1992, d. Ric Burns), a documentary reconstruction of the passage: a cloudless sky reaching to infinity, an endless horizon and, at night, a silence that would seem eternal. The winter sequence of *The Big Trail* taps into the history that numerous films have since turned into myth: *One More Mountain* (1994), *The Donner Party* (2009), *Donner Pass* (2011), *Dead of Winter* (2015), etc., and books that include Daniel James Brown, *The Indifferent Stars Above, History of the Donner Party: A Tragedy of the Sierra* (New York: William Morrow, 2009).

3. Moss relates the visual grandeur of *The Big Trail* to Walsh's enucleation not long before the film was conceived and realized. For the biographer Walsh had to relearn how to see the world, and *The Big Trail* shows viewers how he did so. When the storyline is left aside, because space and "human geography" are the province of the film, it taps into a tradition, reaching back to Pierre Vidal de la Blache, Elisée Reclus, and Jean Brunhès, without being specifically mentioned, that Luis Buñuel invokes at the beginning of *Las Hurdes* (1932). In pages that could apply to *The Big Trail* Paula Amad studies the cinematic virtues of human geography in *Counter-Archive: Film, the Everyday, and Albert Kahn's 'Archives de la Planète* (New York: Columbia University Press, 2010); and from another angle, so

also Sam Rohdie in *Promised Lands: Cinema, Geography, Modernism* (London: BFI, 2001). Also pertinent is Yves Lacoste, coiner of the concept of geopolitics, in his seminal *La Géographie, ça sert, d'abord, à faire la guerre* (Geography: It's used, first of all, to wage war) (Paris: Maspéro, 1976; rev. ed., Paris: La Découverte, 2012), surely because *The Big Trail* concerns both geography and war.

4. Author of *The Frontier in American History* (New York: Holt, 1920), Turner's panegyric of the frontier stands behind *The Big Trail*. On the relation of Turner to the history of the western and its variant manifestations in pulp fiction, see Jean-Louis Leutrat, *Le Western: Archéologie d'un genre* (Lyon: Presses Universitaires de Lyon, 1987); *Le Western: Quand la légende devient réalité* (Paris: Éditions Gallimard, 1995); *Westerns* (Paris: Klincksieck, 2007).

5. Among his other studies, see James Akerman, "Twentieth Century American Road Maps and the Making of a National Motorized Space," in *Cartographies of Travel and Navigation*, ed. James Akerman (Chicago: University of Chicago Press, 2006), 151–206.

6. How Wölfflin became a building block in the curriculum of art history in North America could be tied to its pertinence for study of cinematic composition. Its fortunes went with the development of the seventh art: Wölfflin's *Kunstgeschictliche Grundbegriffe* first appeared in 1915 (Munich: Bruckmann), was revised in 1933, and its seventh edition translated by Mary Hottinger into English (as *Principles of Art History*) in 1932 (London: G. Bell). Surely its approach fit well for readings of Frederic Remington's paintings and, given Walsh's sympathy and admiration for the Native American, the legacy of George Catlin in both America and Europe (to which the writings of Charles Baudelaire attest): see Benita Eisler, *The Red Man's Bones: George Catlin, Artist & Showman*, a brilliant study of the persisting myths of the Wild West (New York: Norton, 2013).

7. See Frederick Lewis Allen, *Only Yesterday: An Informal History of the 1920s* (New York: Harper & Brothers, 1931), appearing a year after the premiere of *The Big Trail*, whose reflections can explain how and why the western was fitting for its moment.

8. Moss (2011: 120–30).

9. Apart from the excruciating pain and brush with death he describes at length in *Each Man in His Time*, the production of *In Old Arizona* demanded—*illico*—that Warner Baxter (famously the sheriff riding shotgun with Andy Devine in *Stagecoach*) play the role of the trickster and ladies' man for which Walsh had been cast.

10. "Walsh's vision for *The Big Trail*," Moss writes, "is layered with personal meaning for him. The connection between the loss of his eye and the way of compensating for it, or the way of creating a new cinema from his altered vision, shows the profound psychological investment he made in the film as a way to achieve" what she calls Walsh's "striving for a pure vision of his subject, the natural view that had to be as massive as its subject if it was to be authentic" (2011: 129).

11. Francis Parkman Jr., *The California and Oregon Trail: Being Sketches of Prairie and Rocky Mountain Life* (New York: George P. Putnam, 1849), 9. The preface challenges what *The Big Trail* would set out to do: "The journey which

the following narrative describes was undertaken on the writer's part with a view of studying the manners and character of Indians in their primitive state. Although in the chapters which relate to them, he has only attempted to sketch those features of their wild and picturesque life which fell, in the present instance, under his own eye, yet in doing so he has constantly aimed to leave an impression of their character correct as far as it goes. In justifying this claim to accuracy on this point, it is hardly necessary to advert to the representations given by poets and novelists, which, for the most part, are mere creations of fancy" (iii). He could have added the representations of cinematographers. Quoted from Google Books: https://babel.hathitrust.org/cgi/pt?id=chi.14070312&view=1up&seq=6.

12. And with such resonance that they bring Homer's world in coincidence with the Bible, in styles that Erich Auerbach famously contrasted in the first two chapters of *Mimesis: Dargestellte Wirklichkeit in der abendländischen Literatur* (Bern: A. Francke, 1946), in English, *Mimesis: The Representation of Reality in Western Literature* (Princeton, NJ: Princeton University Press, 2003). The book was first published in German in 1946 (in the wake of World War II) and soon after in English in 1953. The lavish landscapes and shots of moving vehicles bring the film in line with Jacques Rancière's *Aisthesis: Scenes from the Aesthetic Regime of Art*, translated by Zakir Paul (New York: Verso, 2013), arguing with and against Auerbach in proposing that an "esthetic" regime—which would be that of *The Big Trail*—reigns over a "hierarchical" counterpart that would champion myth and history.

13. See Bernard of Clairvaux, *L'Amour de Dieu: La grâce et le libre arbitre/ De diligendo Deo*, ed. Françoise Callerot (Paris: Éditions du Cerf, 1993).

14. In *Qu'est-ce que la philosophie?* (Paris: Éditions de Minuit, 1991), in English as *What is Philosophy?*, trans. Hugh Tomlinson and Graham Burchell (New York: Columbia University Press, 1994), Gilles Deleuze takes up the idea of a paradoxically open totality, a condition of a whole that intransitively "becomes." Concept and calligram, *Tout ouvert*, a formula Deleuze uses time and again, is at once closed and open: T*ou* t *ou* ver t : within the space between the two t's (one voiced and the other mute), are *ou* (or) where (où) and *vers* (a troping toward, almost a cognate of *where*). The condition of spatial possibility inhering the graphic character of the formula is translated aurally and visually throughout *The Big Trail*.

15. Suffused with reflections on cinema, following the publication of *Cinéma 1* (1983) and *Cinéma 2* (1985) in *Le Pli: Leibniz et le baroque* (Paris: Editions de Minuit, 1988), 25, in English as *The Fold: Leibniz and the Baroque*, trans. Tom Conley (Minneapolis: University of Minnesota Press, 1993). Deleuze notes that point of view is "not the variation of truth according to the subject, but the condition in which the truth of a variation appears to be the subject," in other words, the "truth of variation" of this decisive shot that determines how the film is to be looked at.

16. See, for example, the remarks on Rossellini's art of an "all over" effect where every detail in the shot is of equal charge, what he calls the random

"image-fact" (*image*-fait) a propos the last sequence of *Paisà*, in *Qu'est-ce que le cinéma* (Paris: Éditions du Cerf, 1998), 288.

17. Like Bazin on Rossellini, in respect to juxtaposition, so also Maurice Blanchot on poet René Char: in *La Parole en archipel* or other collections, argues Blanchot, Char's words work not where they "compose" an implied progression but where they *juxtapose* quanta of poetic intensity: in *L'Entretien infini* (Paris: Éditions Gallimard, 1969) 212–20.

18. *Plastic* in reference to Elie Faure's stress on visual form in films in the years 1921–37, *De la cinéplastique* and *Le Cinéma, langue universelle*, now available in *Cinéma* (Houilles: Manucius, 2010).

19. *The Big Trail* would be a pilot study for what Jacques Rancière says about how, in viewing and in memory, we fix on details that seem to convey more than what they represent, in *Les Écarts du cinéma* (Paris: La Fabrique, 2011), 13–14, in English as *The Deviations of Cinema* (2013).

20. See above, chapter 4, note 14.

21. Michael Fried's conclusions about the autonomy of the subject in relation to the viewer pertain to this shot. See *Absorption and Theatricality: Painting and Beholder in the Age of Diderot* (Chicago: University of Chicago Press, 1988).

22. What Gilles Deleuze calls the *image-perception* (perception image) is an image defined by the attention it calls to its visibility. The western, he notes, tends to be the genre that best fits the concept because its better directors make the landscapes sites of the consciousness of perception, notably à propos Anthony Mann's western cycle, which ranges from *Winchester 73* to *The Far Country*, in *Cinéma 1: L'Image-mouvement* (1983: 100–103).

23. The scenes in question cannot be qualified as "originary" or primal because the child-intermediary, although outside of what it sees, does not feel excluded or in deficit as it might in a "mirror-stage" scenario. It is here where the title of Skorecki's *Raoul Walsh et moi, suivi de Contre la nouvelle cinéphilie* (2001) tells us that the director is appreciated for refusing to yield to the castration scenarios that come with psychoanalytical readings of cinema.

24. The effects of an oscillation of action and repose, a trait pertinent to many or most westerns in the studio eras, are taken up in Natacha Pfeiffer, *Anthony Mann: Arpenter l'image* (Villeneuve d'Ascq: Presses Universitaires du Septentrion, 2019) and, fleetingly, in Jacques Rancière's study of *Winchester 73*, in *La Fable cinématographique* (Paris: Éditions du Seuil, 2001) (in English, *Film Fables*).

25. Although not referring to this film, the alphabetical register of topoi (taken from a review of six hundred films) under the collectively authored title, *Le Western: Acteurs, auteurs, mythologies* (Paris: Union Générale d'Éditions, 1966) includes "Indian Attack." Written during the heyday of auteur theory by critics including Raymond Bellour, Bernard Dort, Bertrand Tavernier, and others, the volume remains a viable, if not invaluable, critical and historical resource for any work on the American western.

26. Fittingly, in the last paragraphs of *Each Man in His Time* (1974), Walsh pleads for the Native Americans, whom he describes having been mistreated,

brutalized, and decimated by white Americans. Although the plot of *The Big Trail* requires victory over the autochtones, from *They Died with Their Boots On* (1941) to *Saskatchewan* (1954) and other westerns, Walsh's films empathize with Native Americans. So also in the novel, *La Colère des justes* (1972), with the exception of one personage, a turncoat named "Black Cloud," Walsh cares for Native Americans and settlers who enjoy mixed marriages (taken up in the Conclusion).

27. Recalling films he made under compromising conditions, Roberto Rossellini once said that to redeem features he otherwise would not have made, he composed his films around a carefully designed shot or brief sequence—for example, the child's view of the rubble of Berlin from a gutted apartment building in *Germany, Year Zero* (1948), Ingrid Bergman's sight of the plaster mold of two entwined lovers lifted from an excavation of Pompeii in *Voyage to Italy* (1951), or others. Were Walsh to have denominated similar shots in his features, in *The Big Trail* it would be either in the departure of the wagons from the makeshift graveyard or, by the director's own admission, the counter-tilts recording the troupe's descent by rope from a cliffside to a valley, taken up in the paragraphs to follow.

28. Here we have evidence of a style and signature. The vertiginous counter-tilt that makes famous the murder of Roy Earle (Humphrey Bogart) in *High Sierra* (1941) may have its origins here. On its prevalence in the oeuvre see Losilla (2020, 151).

29. As usual, in a long two-shot that sets Flack opposite the priestly Grandpa, the intermediary is a blond-haired child, standing to the left of the latter, who observes the beast who swills and grunts while Lopez, in the center and the background, smiles at the viewer. Following a discernible blocking pattern fitting the aspect ratio, rife with irony and bristling with action, the scene casts some characters in shadows and others in a throng of faces.

30. The sequence rehearses what Claude Lévi-Strauss had called the "culinary triangle," which opposes a woman's cuisine and uses recipients for economy and measure in cooking, and the masculine counterpart, which roasts with less mediation (because the meat is eaten raw or singed on a fire) and stresses prodigality: in *Mythologiques 3: L'Origine des manières de table* (Paris: Plon, 1964), conclusion. In the sequence the animals are of a higher order than Flack and the company with whom he eats his meat. For sake of pleasure (and cultural contrast), see also Anthelme Brillat-Savarin (1838) (in English, *Physiology of Taste*).

31. That a knife could not penetrate the layers of Flack's clothing is of little import. The strained verisimilitude calls attention to the setting—the tree—more than to the killing.

Chapter 6

1. In his memoir Walsh recalls the difficulty of directing when sound recording equipment imposed silence on the set. Unable to talk to his actors and

actresses as they played their parts, he had to leave his megaphone at the foot of his chair. Nonetheless sound, be it noise or banter, must have been appealing. Moss remarks how voice takes command in *Me and My Gal*: the director's "fingerprints stray all over the story, most noticeably in the spirited pace and catchy verbal bantering," which recall the "Flagg-Quirt jabbering in *What Price Glory?* and their subsequent outings" (2011, 136). She implies (discreetly, it seems) that in the war movie the two men are an odd or a gay couple. In the heterosexual pairing in *Me and My Gal*, with Bennett and Tracy an almost equally odd couple, allusions to brothers and brotherly love abound. In his cinema forces of attraction tend to be polymorphous.

2. In "Cinema across Fault Lines: Bazin and the French School of Geography," Ludovic Cortade notes well how the French critic's training in the years 1934–41 allowed him to integrate into his vision three modes of cartographic analysis based on as many different temporalities: "topography (style), geology (sociological and moral layers), and geomorphology (the evolution of forms over time under the pressure of erosion)." In Dudley Andrew, ed., *Opening Bazin* (New York: Oxford University Press, 2011), 27, 13–31. In a subsequent essay in the same volume I have tried to use event theory to sort through Bazin's inflections of evolution and revolution ("Evolution and Event in *Qu'est-ce que le cinéma?*," 32–41), which may pertain to given sequences in this feature.

3. See Erich Auerbach, "Figura," in *Scenes from the Drama of European Literature* (Minneapolis: University of Minnesota Press, 1984) and, for typology, Meyer Schapiro, *Words and Pictures: On the Literal and the Symbolic in the Illustration of a Text* (The Hague: Mouton, 1973) and *Script and Picture: Semiotics of Visual Language* (New York: Braziller, 1996).

4. See Jean-Louis Comolli on the virtues of the autonomy of sound and image in classical cinema, which he finds lacking in the majority of contemporary films, in *Cinéma contre spectacle* (Paris: Verdier, 2009), in English in Daniel Fairfax's admirable translation and critical edition, *Cinema against Spectacle* (Amsterdam: University of Amsterdam Press, 2015).

5. In the eyes of Jacques Rancière, with the advent of an aesthetic regime that begins with Romanticism, readers of literature or viewers of cinema (especially in the digital age, outside of the movie theater and in front of a computer screen) are free to "do with" or "make of" their objects what they wish. In *Le Spectateur émancipé* (Paris: La Fabrique, 2003), in English as *The Emancipated Spectator* (London: Verso, 2009).

6. In "Bartleby the Scrivener" Herman Melville's "Wall-Street Story" of lower New York, *to prefer not to* becomes what theorist Gilles Deleuze calls "the formula" par excellence of *negation* that cues a correlative condition of disavowal, a repressive sense of denial, in *Critique et clinique* (Paris: Éditions de Minuit, 1993), in English as *Essays Critical and Clinical*, trans. David W. Smith and Michael A. Greco (Minneapolis: University of Minnesota Press, 1995). It applies admirably to the politics of *Me and My Gal* and a host of Depression comedies of the early 1930s. They would "prefer not to" address the issues they must deal with.

7. George Walsh (1889–1981) played an uncredited role in *The Birth of a Nation* (1915), in which Raoul immortalized John Wilkes Booth. A renowned actor in the silent era, George played significant roles in his brother's *A Bad Man and Others* (1915), *The Fencing Master* (1915), *11:30 P.M.* (1915), and *The Celestial Code* (1915). With Raoul he cowrote and acted in *The Serpent* (1916), starring Theda Bara. In the same year he played a Harvard fop in *Blue Blood and Red* (that Raoul both wrote and directed), and he was the bridegroom of Cana in Griffith's *Intolerance*. He had a major role in *The Honor System* (1917), a lost film, one of the director's most significant silent features. So also in *The Pride of New York* (1917) and *The Conqueror* (1917), in which he plays Sam Houston. He is Billy Drake in *This Is Life* (1917); boxer Jack Bartlett in *On the Jump* (1918); Robert Booth in Carl Harbaugh's *Brave and Bold* (1918), and Bill Durham in Walsh's *I'll Say So* (1918), a movie about World War I. He costars with Miriam Cooper in *Serenade* (1921). He is Don Diego in Lubitsch's *Rosita* (1923), for which his brother was an uncredited codirector. He directed and starred in *The Seventh Person* (1919). He is Jack Spurlock in Carl Harbaugh's *Jack Spurlock, Prodigal* (1918), like the former title, which featured Miriam Cooper, who then was his sister-in-law. He plays Dave Henderson, a prisoner, in *From Now On* (1920). He shares top billing with Cooper in *Serenade* (1921), a full-length feature. A muscular and highly talented star in the silent era (so renowned that sculptures of his manly body were cast in the 1920), his great roles in talkies include *Me and My Gal* and, less obviously but tellingly, a cameo as the "masked" boxer, John L. Sullivan, in *The Bowery* (1933), studied in chapter 7. See Walter Conley, "The Silent Films of George Walsh," in *The Silent Picture* (1972).

8. With refreshing self-deprecation in *Jokes and Their Relation to the Unconscious*, *The Psychopathology of Everyday Life*, and other writings, Freud reminds us that wit is about saving time and money. Appealing to what Freud does with puns in "A Method of Equality: Rancière, Jokes, and their Relation to *They Drive by Night*" (*Understanding Rancière, Understanding Modernism*, ed. Patrick Bray [New York: Bloomsbury, 2017], 127–46), I have tried to equate economy of speech with issues of thrift and spending in the later years of the Depression. In this film, because the year is 1932, the issues are especially pronounced.

9. In a landmark essay titled "Récits d'espace" (Spatial stories) in *L'Invention du quotidien, 1: Arts de faire*, ed. Luce Giard (Paris: Gallimard, 1990) (in English as *The Practice of Everyday Life*, translated by Steven Rendall [1984]), Michel de Certeau contends that discourse or verbal process turns an otherwise pregiven or preoccupied "place" into an existential or lived "space." In this film each of the locales—dock, precinct, apartment, loft, diner, haberdashery—acquires spatial valence through the gamut of verbal exchanges that animate them.

10. Moss remarks that Walsh inserts "autobiographical humor in the picture," at a difficult moment in his life, falls "in love with Tracy and Bennett falling for each other" while, nonetheless—one wonders why—the "popularity surrounding *Me and My Gal* did little to lift Walsh's career in the remaining years before he went to Warner Bros. in 1939" (2011, 136–37).

11. In classical cinema, the convention that has a film begin with a detail in close-up before drawing back to establish a context often summarizes much of what follows. Such is Renoir, who inaugurates *La Grande Illusion* (1937) with an extreme close-up of a spinning record on a Victrola to suggest that the French aviators are human machines in perpetual revolution; or, earlier, in sequences in *La Chienne* (1932), in the clatter of a bistro, the camera fixes on a pair of hands shuffling a deck of cards, suggesting that amidst ambient noise, chance and destiny are in the making.

12. Does Dolan provide a paradigm for the man-dog friendship on which Fritz Lang's *Fury* (1936) turns? Perhaps: In *Fury* Joe Wilson (Tracy) transfers his affection for his absent fiancée (Sylvia Sydney) onto a lost terrier he reclaims and nurtures before it dies in the fire a lynch mob set to the jail in which it held company with the hero.

13. Pendant or taut chains seem to play an unsettling role here and in other features. In *The Cock-Eyed World*, when hung over, Flagg, en route to the Caribbean, asks another Marine about life in the southern climes, a chain hangs near his head, suggesting that it is both a realistic and a decorative effect but also symbolic of uncertain destiny (54:20–55:48). In *The Revolt of Mamie Stover*, while on the deck of the steamer en route to Honolulu, and in a first conversation with Mamie, projecting what he believes her life story has been, Jim Blair (Richard Egan) holds a chain supporting a mast (suggesting that the plot will "concatenate" or that he will be enchained in a relationship with her. In *White Heat* (1949), when Fallon (Edmund O'Brien) confers with Cody Jarrett (James Cagney) about a breakout, the shadow of a chain attached to a bunk bed cuts across the latter's right eye, suggestive of the greater issue of enucleation (54:06–55:13) in a highly "nuclear" film.

14. The scene rehearses the economy of words and wit with which Rabelais, author in spirit with Walsh, inaugurates the third book (*Le Tiers livre*) of *Pantagruel* (1546). Seeing citizens of the nation preparing for war, Diogenes is perplexed. Miming the activity, knowing he is otherwise good for nothing, he rolls a barrel up and down a hill (in François Rabelais, *Œuvres complètes* [1994, 347–48]). Like Diogenes's barrel, the book to follow will be a fictive cask, a *tonneau fictil*, its worth in the expenditure of its wit.

15. The porthole that "stares back," courtesy of James Elkins's telling study (1997) of the way images respond to our gaze) is something of an ocular commonplace in Walsh's cinema. In the sequences of *The Cock-Eyed World* on the ships carrying Flagg and Quirt to Brooklyn or to the Philippines the protagonists are shown sparring before them. In *The Revolt of Mamie Stover*, after a game of shuffleboard, the portholes behind Jim and his love seem to look at them when they embrace.

16. Throughout the shot, in the extreme background, behind the windows, human figures move about, dispersing focus on the lovers' banter. The critical appreciation of the wit is sensed in the staging that accounts for a larger (and, given the Depression, a more ominous) world in which the words are in play.

In this sequence we can wonder if the donut jar is an erotic topos in classical cinema or if it might belong to the director's fancy. See "A Method of Equality: Rancière, Jokes, and their Relation to *They Drive by Night*," note 8 in this chapter.

17. It almost goes without saying that because the "signifier" precedes the "signified," in any instance of speech fantasy and anticipation fill the gap between an utterance and the meaning (or referent): in Jacques Lacan, "L'Instance de la lettre dans l'inconscient," *Écrits* (Paris: Éditions du Seuil, 1966), 496. If theory were further pursued, the gap between sensation and perception of signs and their decoding attests to what Gilles Deleuze calls the "perception-image," an image that by nature calls attention to the birth or presence of vision and visibility where otherwise, especially in classical film, narrative (or the weaker register of seamless representation) takes command. In the opening page of *La Fable cinématographique* (2001, 3), Jacques Rancière notes that a film's story or "fable" is complicated or deviated by what the lens puts in view, and vice versa.

18. See Freud, "Note on the Mystic Writing Pad," in *The Standard Edition*, vol. 26 (1926); Jacques Derrida, "Freud et la scène de l'écriture," in *L'Écriture et la différence* (Paris: Éditions du Seuil, 1967); Guy Rosolato, on screen memory and surface, in *Essais sur le symbolique* (1969, 226).

19. In this instance we are invited to engage the narrative the direct address momentarily suspends, long before Godard has the characters in his New Wave years (among others, in *À bout de souffle*, *Vivre sa vie*, and *Pierrot le fou*) cut the story lines in which they play when turning and directly speaking to the viewer. Where Godard contests the rules of classical cinema *Me and My Gal* lets direct address be part of its pleasure.

Chapter 7

1. *In Old Arizona* (1:11:36–11:46) (Fox Home Entertainment DVD, 2009).

2. *How the Other Half Lives: Studies among the Tenements of New York* (New York: C. Scribner's Sons, 1890), a book of arresting descriptions and images has witnessed reeditions at Scribner's in 1897, 1901, 1902, and 1918 before appearing in 1957 (New York: Sagamore), 1970, then 1971 (Cambridge, MA: Belknap), again in 1996 (Boston and New York: St. Martin's Press), and of late, in 2010 (also Belknap).

3. In *Guerre et cinéma: Logistique de la perception* (Paris: Cahiers du Cinéma, 1984 and 1991), in English as *War and Cinema: Logistics of Perception* (New York: Verso, 1991), Paul Virilio remarked that the beams of light in the famous logo have as origin beacons antiaircraft artillery deployed to spot Zeppelins and airplanes. No doubt taking his cue from Virilio, Jean-Luc Godard makes similar reference to the logo and to the onslaught of war in the first segment of *Histoire(s) du cinéma* (1988).

4. The war of 1898 is reprised and treated with innuendo of trauma in *Pursued* (1948), from which a marked man, Jeb Rand (almost a homonym of Jeb

(B)rand, played by Robert Mitchum), a wounded hero—as if a veteran from the European theater of 1943–45, returns home wounded and mentally troubled. In *The Bowery* the heroes' departure for the Caribbean—if that is where they are going—invokes confusion about American foreign policy and also where a sequel might be going.

5. "Walsh was not racist at heart, but neither did he have a quarrel with a racist joke if it was humorous for the times": thus the biographer's a classic *apologia* intending to redeem the director for what could be mistaken for bad behavior (not an apology, but a post-facto defense and illustration of conduct deemed to have been misguided or wrong). The author of these pages takes issue with the remark that in "the early 1930s, Walsh needed the kind of optimism the picture's success brought with it" (141). Bawdy and boisterous, the film is a *commodity* engaging a depressive world from which, in a quasi-Brechtian manner, it assumes critical distance—a perspective—on the ideology that shapes it. In his treatment of *The Bowery* John M. Smith (2013), who warns readers that anyone quoting his words risks inculpation, like Moss, tends to take a sympathetic view. In a detailed summary, stressing narrative and plot, he notes a mix of lawlessness and sympathy.

6. On multiple and conflicting points of view, see Mikhail Bakhtin, *The Dialogic Imagination: Four Essays* (Austin: University of Texas Press, 1981). Prior to Henry James, a novel without a hero has a model in Thackeray's *Vanity Fair*, taken up in Nora Gilbert, *Better Left Unsaid: Victorian Novels, Hays Code Films, and the Benefits of Censorship* (Stanford, CA: Stanford University Press, 2013). The master of the *contredit* is François Villon in two ballads of the *Testament*, "Les contradictz de Franc Gontier," which asks readers to set urban life against its rural counterpart, and the "Ballade de la Grosse Margot," whose voice is that of a servant to a prostitute who begs his audience to consider his condition in the low life of Paris. In Villon, like Walsh's film, options are undecidable. See François Villon, *Œuvres complètes*, ed. Jacqueline Toulet-Cerquiglini (Paris: Éditions Gallimard/Pléiade, 2014), 137–39.

7. Although the narrative opposes two characters for whom identification is impossible, Walsh's memories of the film in *Each Man in His Time* tilt toward distaste of the Raft character and an ever-so-slight attraction to the Beery counterpart. Established in the silent tradition as of 1913, playing in many films, Beery (1885–1949) portrayed the evil Pharis in Walsh's *The Wanderer* (1926) before the director tapped him for his role in the feature of 1933.

8. Under the subtitle "Boys Being Boys," Moss locates "two cocky, wisecracking Irish characters" between the "smart-alecky bravado of Quirt and Flagg" and "Spencer Tracy's self-assuredness in *Me and My Gal*" (2011, 138). In his memoir Walsh notes that 20th Century "had built a whole street with a replica of McGurk's famous tavern in New York's Bowery," but in fact he recalls how "the real Bowery, where I shot backgrounds for *Regeneration*, helped in its reconstruction" (1974, 250). It is probable that Swipes McGurk (Jackie Coogan), is named in reference to the tavern.

9. We wonder if Trixie's surname, fashioned from the pig-Latin of *broad*, whom Walsh remembers as "Trixie Carter," the leader of "twenty-five hefty dancing girls, who were immediately named the 'Beef Trust,'" for whose dance numbers "a crowd of extras was hired to leer at them" (1974, 250).

10. The names would have been familiar to spectators of the 1930s. Frankie Bailey (1859–1953) was a reputed actress in silent cinema, having a bit role in John Ford's *Thank You* (1925) and in Paul Bern's *The Flower of Night* (1925) and as an actress in Dimitri Buchowetski's *The Crown of Lies* (1926), also featuring Negri, and other films. The burlesque actress had been known as "the girl with the million dollar legs." Maggie Klein worked with Lillian Russell (1861–1922), a famous singer, diva, and stage performer known as "America's Beauty."

11. Bill Muldoon (1852–1933) was a famous Greco-Roman wrestling champion who prepared John L. Sullivan for a 75-round fight against Jake Kilrain (1859–1937) in 1889, a world heavy weight bare-knuckle boxing match whose winner would be world champion. Kilrain lost the bout in the seventy-sixth round. The fight became a topic of many images and playing cards. History reports that Kilrain was a pallbearer at John L. Sullivan's funeral in 1918. See Edward Van Every, *Muldoon—The Solid Man of Sport: His Amazing Story as Related for the First Time by Him to his Friend, Edward Van Every* (New York: Frederick A. Stokes Company, 1928).

12. When the Hays Code had forbidden display of females baring their breasts—with exceptions in a sequence in Vidor's *Big Parade* (1925) and in Walsh's *Wild Girl* (1932), when Salomey Jane (Joan Bennett) goes skinny-dipping—men's breasts took their place. It could be said that much of Walsh's *Thief of Baghdad* (1925) is about Douglas Fairbanks's body, especially in torso shots that make much of his sinew. Later on, in *They Drive by Night* (1940), jovially inebriated during a dance at the party celebrating his new residence and not finding a female to foxtrot with, Ed Carlson (Alan Hale) grabs his friend "Irish" (Roscoe Karnes), exclaiming, "You'll do!" And in *Manpower* (1941), in a sequence in which George Raft revives his partner, Hank (Edward G. Robinson) from a devastating electrical shock, he is shown "barebacking" his partner before the crowd of other workers (studied in Conley 1991, chap. 3). Here and elsewhere the beauty of the body owes to being polymorphous: hence in the sequence of *Objective, Burma!* in which troops are called to order, a quick panoramic (07:11–13) is taken of men in the nude (one aiming his buttocks at the camera) who wash themselves in a pool of water.

13. See the nude sculpture of George Walsh, illustrated in Walter Conley, "The Silent Films of George Walsh," in *The Silent Picture* (1971).

14. Taking his cue from Eric Rohmer on Rossellini's *Voyage to Italy*, comparing sequences to sketches, Christian Keathley notes that it is "in encounters with marginal, even despised details that cinephiliac moments are experienced," in *Cinephilia and History, or The Wind in the Trees* (Bloomington: Indiana University Press, 2006), 80. It can be assumed that Keathley and his readers recall (as noted elsewhere in this monograph) Ingrid Bergman peering over an excavation

site in Pompeii when archeologists extract from their dig a plaster mold of two lovers in embrace. Reduced to ash, their remains having left in the earth a void the team filled with plaster, the resulting sculpture (or "work of art") becomes a deadly incarnation of the protagonist's confused desires. Or of two or three languid tracking shots in Renoir's *Partie de campagne* (*A Day in the Country*), of the shoreline of the Marne River on a hot afternoon that could—or could not—approximate the mix of anxiety and bliss of two lovers (Henri and Henriette [Georges d'Arnoux and Sylvia Bataille]) feel on a sultry afternoon after rowing away from ambient company and friends. Jacques Rancière confirms the point in the introduction to his *Intervals of Cinema*, trans. John Howe (London: Verso, 2014) when "shadows touch our emotions in deep and secret way" (5), as he notes elsewhere in the same volume.

15. In *Level-5* (1997) Chris Marker includes footage of a stunt (ca. 1900) where a man wearing handcrafted wings announced to the public that he would fly off and away from the mezzanine of the recently erected Eiffel Tower. Obliged to perform the feat before a throng of Parisians below, so the voice-over suggests, the flyer had no choice but to kill himself. In Walsh's cinema, defining deep space, free falls are frequent, from *Regeneration* (Skinny dropping from the clothesline in the tenement complex), *Me and My Gal* (when Duke Castenega falls from a window), to *High Sierra* (famously at the moment Roy Earle, shot in the back on the steep slope of Mount Whitney, plummets to the ground). See note 16.

16. The sight of the body falling into a deep and extensive space from an ichnographic perspective is close to what Luis Buñuel had done in the near-contemporary *Las Hurdes/Land without Bread* (1932), in which his camera, situated atop or on the edge of a cliff, records a mountain goat dropping down the steep hillside. In Buñuel's short film, however, a smoking gun, visible at the right side of the frame, has shot the animal, "sacrificing" it to produce the surreal effect, while in *The Bowery* the stunt invites viewers to note that a "dummy" is fashioned to engineer the sequence.

17. The narrative design of two shots betrays a reflection on the nature of "authority," a theme at the core of the Flagg/Quirt rivalry since *What, Price, Glory?* Detached from its body, a hand or an "index" intercedes to signal that it is of an absent or unquestioned cause. Almost concurrently Fritz Lang calls authority in question at the end of *M* (1931), when a hand enters from the frame to mark the character's destiny. Historians of art and architecture cannot fail to recall a Carolingian fresco in the oratory of the church of Saint-Etienne of Auxerre where the hand of God (on a cerulean background), pointing at the victim, intercedes when he is lapidated by infidels. See http://www.bourgogneromane.com/edifices/auxerre/AUXERREcrypteoratoireStE2.jpg.

18. In his *Reconfigured Eye* (Cambridge, MA: MIT Press, 1992), William J. Mitchell notes that artists (or observers of objects) *squint* to get a clearer perspective on what they see. Inversely, they let the eye dilate to obtain a "softer" (or more affective) view of what they see. Connors's gesture relates to how the film asks the spectator to take account of what is being shown.

19. In "A Film-Event: *Objective, Burma!* (2019, ch. 9), in a study honoring Hanjo Berressem, I invoke the concept of the absent cause, set forth in the war films of 1926–31 and *The Bowery*, to determine its presence in the feature of 1945.

20. The resemblance with the final sequences of *The Cock-Eyed World* is obvious. In the film of 1929 Edmund Lowe, who "copped out" of his duties by falling ill, is interned in a hospital before jumping out of bed and running off in his boxer shorts, as he heeds a call to arms when "history" or the orders of an authority come from without.

21. The film touches on what critic Frank Kermode had called the problematic "sense of an ending" in an eponymous monograph, *The Sense of an Ending: Studies in the Theory of Fiction, with a New Epilogue* (2000), especially chapter 2, 66–72.

Conclusion

1. If another autobiographical excursus is permitted, I recall autumn of 1990 during a residency at the University of Wisconsin's Institute for Research in the Humanities. Late one night, slumbering in a Barca Lounger before a television set in an apartment we had rented on Fish Hatchery Road, around 3 a.m. I suddenly awoke to the blare of what could only be the music of Max Steiner. A tracking shot followed three men in uniforms making their way through a forest, coming to a clearing, crouching, and then setting their eyes on a single-engine aircraft under an elaborate canopy in camouflage. In the space of ten seconds, the way the men tip-toed through the underbrush, the caution they took while advancing, their gestures suggesting dissimulation, and the situation an imminence of action told me that it could only be Walsh. And so it was, in the last minutes of *Desperate Journey* (1942), a forgotten feature I was then seeing for the first time.

2. Although listed in its exhaustive bibliography (p. 470), like its translator, *La Colère des justes* is not studied in the definitive biography. First appearing in octavo and quarto format in 1972, four years later the novel met a broader readership when the Livre de poche, a major publisher in Paris, issued a second edition. Lourcelles, contributor to a compendious *Dictionnaire du cinéma* and a major player at the MacMahon theater, known for its "quadrant" or "ace of diamonds" whose four chosen directors were Fritz Lang, Otto Preminger, Joseph Losey, and Walsh, edited much of a special issue of *Présence du cinéma* devoted to the director in 1962, two years before *Cahiers du Cinéma* followed suit. During a fellowship year in Paris in 1999, former student Margaret Flinn, author of *The Social Architecture of French Cinema* (Liverpool: Liverpool University Press, 2014) and professor of film studies at Ohio State University, caught sight of a copy on the racks of a *bouquiniste*. She generously purchased the book for my use. Twenty years later, when I was leading a wine tour in the Bordelais for Harvard alums and their friends, the Hotel Burdigala graciously lent me an octavo copy

in leather that was on shelves in its little library in the main lobby. I thank them for their generosity and encouragement.

3. Drawing on an interview with Kevin Brownlow, Moss notes that "Olga" could be "Olga Grey, who appeared in Walsh's *Pillars of Society*" (201, 449, n23). In *Each Man in His Time* "Olga" is a Russian beauty of passing presence, she adds, who replaces Walsh's first wife, Miriam Cooper, who goes unmentioned (45). Walsh reported that he was seeing "Olga" when he left Los Angeles, en route to New York, ostensibly to work on *Regeneration*: "She told me, 'I have a feeling in my heart that one day we will meet again'" (cited in Moss 2011, 45). And so they do in fiction, hilariously in *The Cock-Eyed World*, and romantically in *La Colère des justes*.

4. It clearly has parallels in the sequence at the alpine lodge in *High Sierra*, in which the Black custodian warns Roy Earle (Humphrey Bogart) of the stray dog, "Pard," who casts an "evil eye" on those whom he befriends, and also in tensions of enucleation and nuclear disaster in *White Heat*. And in evading the law, what about the three pals' "desperate journey"? In correlative features, especially *Colorado Territory*, the truly *evil* parties are representatives of the *law*, white Americans standing for the flag who doggedly and viciously pursue their prey, in contrast to the clearsighted, wronged, and tragic counterparts who are on the run.

5. Is there oblique reference to *High Sierra*? Driving to Palm Springs to engineer a heist, Roy Earle stops at a "last chance" gas station at the Arizona border, exits his coupe, and marvels at the sight of the Sierras and Mount Whitney, where he is destined to die.

6. *Pursued* (1948), whose story takes place before and after the Spanish-American War, is excepted for the reason that in the cloth of a western *noir* a psychoanalysis of trauma is limpidly depicted, an issue fitting for the post-war moment that saw thousands of battle-weary and scarred soldiers return to a world, unless it comprised veterans of World War I, that could not imagine what they had undergone. See Janet Walker, "*The Searchers, Pursued, Once Upon a Time in the West*, and *Lone Star*," in *Westerns Through History*, ed. Janet Walker (New York: Routledge, 2001).

7. In a coda born of the figments of a cinephile's imagination, the *justes* of the title cannot fail to remind us of the similarly existential character of *Les Justes*, Albert Camus's play (1949) concerning a group of socialists, in the year 1905, who assassinate the Grand Duke Sergei Alexandrovich, and who must deal compromisingly with their actions. By way of comparison, we are asked to consider how, in face of the uncompromising economic development and exploitation of space before their eyes, the western heroes' deeds are justified or ethically just, and we conclude that they are. By all means, Jean-Luc Godard's chiastic formula, *une image juste, juste une image* (a just image, just an image), can be heard through the title and the text of Walsh's novel while, of course, pertaining to the films under study.

Bibliography

Marilyn Ann Moss appends to her biography (2011) an exhaustive listing of films and work by and on Walsh. Although lacking reference to a good deal of criticism in languages other than English, her compilation of primary and secondary material remains an invaluable point of reference. Works pertinent to this study, many of which Moss includes in her bibliography, are noted below.

Alciati, Andreas. *Emblematum libellus*. Paris: Christian Wechsel, 1534.
Akerman, James, ed. *Cartographies of Travel and Navigation*. Chicago: University of Chicago Press, 2006.
Allen, Frederick Lewis. *Only Yesterday: An Informal History of the 1920s*. New York: Harper & Brothers, 1931.
Amad, Paula. *Counter-Archive: Film, the Everyday, and Albert Kahn's 'Archives de la Planète.'* New York: Columbia University Press, 2010.
Arnheim, Rudolf. *The Power of the Center: A Study of Composition in the Visual Arts*. Berkeley: University of California Press, 1982.
Auerbach, Erich. *Mimesis: Dargestellte Wirklichkeit in der abendländischen Literatur*. Bern: A. Francke, 1946. In English, translated by Willard R. Trask as *Mimesis: The Representation of Reality in Western Literature*. Princeton, NJ: Princeton University Press, 2003.
Baecque, Antoine de. *La Cinéphilie: Invention d'un regard, histoire d'une culture, 1944–1968*. Paris: Fayard, 2003.
Bakhtin, Mikhail. *The Dialogic Imagination: Four Essays*. Translated by Michael Holquist. Austin: University of Texas Press, 1984.
———. *Rabelais and His World*. Translated by Hélène Iswolsky. Bloomington: Indiana University Press, 1984.
Baltrusaitis, Jurgis. *Anamorphic Art*. New York: Harry N. Abrams, 1977.
Bataille, Georges. *La Part maudite: Essai d'économie générale, la consumation*. Paris: Éditions de Minuit, Coll. L'Usage des richesses 2, 1949. In English as *The Accursed Share: An Essay on General Economy*. Translated by Robert Hurley. New York: Zone, 1991.

Bazin, André. *Qu'est-ce que le cinéma?* Paris: Éditions du Cerf, 1998. In English as *What is Cinema?* Translated by Timothy Barnard. Montreal: Caboose, 2009.

Bellour, Raymond, ed. *Le Western: Acteurs, auteurs, mythologies.* Paris: Union d'Éditions Générales, 1966.

———. *Le Corps du cinéma: Hypnoses, émotions, animalités.* Paris: POL, 2009.

Bernard of Clairvaux. *L'Amour de Dieu: La grâce et le libre arbitre/De diligendo Deo*, ed. Françoise Callerot (Paris: Éditions de Cerf, 1993).

Béroalde de Verville. *L'Histoire veritable, ou le voyage des princes fortunez.* Paris: Chez Pierre Chevalier, 1610. Harvard Houghton Library *FC 5 B4589 610h. Modern edition: Albi: Éditions du Passage du nord-ouest, 2005.

———. *Le Moyen de parvenir* (Paris, 1616). 2 vols. Edited by Hélène Moreau and André Tournon. Aix-en-Provence: Publications de l'Université de Provence, 1984.

Blanchot, Maurice. *L'Entretien infini.* Paris: Éditions Gallimard, 1969. In English as *The Infinite Conversation.* Translated by Susan Hanson. Minneapolis: University of Minnesota Press, 1993.

Böhnke, Alexander, Rembert Hüser and Georg Stanizek, eds. *Das Buch zum Vorspann: 'The Title is a Shot.'* Berlin: Vorwerk 8, 2006.

Brillat-Savarin, Anthelme. *Physiologie du goût: ou, Méditations de gastronomie transcendante; ouvrage théorique, historique, et à l'ordre du jour, dédié aux gastronomes.* Paris: Charpentier, 1838. In English as *The Physiology of Taste, or Meditations on Transcendental Gastronomy.* Translated by M. F. K. Fisher. Washington, DC: Counterpoint, 1999.

Bronfen, Elisabeth. *Specters of War: Hollywood's Engagement with Military Conflict.* New Brunswick, NJ: Rutgers University Press, 2013.

Brown, Daniel James. *The Indifferent Stars Above, History of the Donner Party: A Tragedy of the Sierra.* New York: William Morrow, 2009.

Camus, Albert. *Les Justes.* Paris: Éditions Gallimrd, 1950. In English as *The Just Assassins.* Translated by Stuart Gilbert. New YorK: Alfred A. Knopf, 1958.

Certeau, Michel de. *L'Écriture de l'histoire.* Paris: Éditions Gallimard, 1975. In English as *The Writing of History.* Translated by Tom Conley. New York: Columbia University Press, 1988/1992.

———. *L'Invention du quotidien, 1: Arts de faire.* Edited by Luce Giard. Paris: Éditions Gallimard, 1990. In English as *The Practice of Everyday Life.* Translated by Stephen Rendall. Berkeley: University of California Press, 1984.

Clastres, Pierre. *La Société contre l'état: Recherches d'anthropologie politique.* Paris: Éditions de Minuit, 1974. In English as *Society Against the State.* Translated by Robert Hurley in collaboration with Abe Stein. Cambridge, MA: MIT Press, 1987.

———. *Archéologie de la violence: La guerre dans les sociétés primitives.* La Tour d'Aigues: Éditions Aube, 1999.

Conley, Tom. *Film Hieroglyphs; Ruptures in Classical Cinema.* Minneapolis: University of Minnesota Press, 1991.

———. *Cartographic Cinema.* Minneapolis: University of Minnesota Press, 2007.

———. "Evolution and Event in *Qu'est-ce que le cinéma?*" In *Opening Bazin*, edited by Dudley Andrew, 32–41. New York: Oxford University Press, 2011.
———. "*It Was a Horserace, Sorta.*" In *The Wiley-Blackwell Companion to Fritz Lang*, 242–56. Boston: Wiley-Blackwell, 2014.
———. "Jokes and their Relation to *They Drive by Night*." In *Understanding Rancière, Understanding Modernism*, 127–46. London: Bloomsbury, 2017.
———. "A Film-Event: *Objective, Burma!* In Jasmin Herrmann, ed., *Revisiting Style in Literary and Cultural Studies: Interdisciplinary Articulations*, 365–85. Berlin: Peter Lang, 2019.
Conley, Walter. "Raoul Walsh: His Silent Films." In *The Silent Picture*, edited by Anthony Slide and Paul O'Dell, 4. London: Patrick Montgomery, 1970–71.
———. "The Films of George Walsh." In *The Silent Picture*, edited by Anthony Slide and Paul O'Dell, n. 5. London: Patrick Montgomery, 1971–72.
Comolli, Jean-Louis. "L'Esprit d'aventure," *Cahiers du cinéma*, no. 154 (April 1964): 11–14.
———. *Corps et cadre: Cinéma, éthique, politique*. Paris: Verdier, 2013.
———. *Cinema against Spectacle*. Translated and edited by Daniel Fairfax. Amsterdam: Amsterdam University Press, 2015.
Cortade, Ludovic. "Cinema across Faultlines: Bazin and the French School of Geography." In *Opening Bazin*, edited by Dudley Andrew. New York: Oxford University Press, 2011.
Cotgrave, Randle. *A Dictionarie of the French & English Tongues*. London: Adam Inslip, 1611.
D'Angela, Toni. *Raoul Walsh o dell'avventura singolare*, Rome: Bulzoni, 2008.
Davis, Natalie. Z. *Society and Culture in Early Modern France*. Stanford, CA: Stanford University Press, 1975.
Deleuze, Gilles, *Cinéma 1: L'Image-mouvement*. Paris: Éditions de Minuit, 1983. In English as *Cinema 1: The Movement-Image*. Translated by Hugh Tomlinson and Barbara Habberjam. Minneapolis: University of Minnesota Press, 1986.
———. *Foucault*. Paris: Éditions de Minuit, 1986. In English as *Foucault*. Translated by Séan Hand. Minneapolis: University of Minnesota Press, 1988.
———. *Cinéma 2: L'Image-temps*. Paris: Éditions de Minuit, 1985. In English as *Cinema 2: The Time-Image*. Translated by Hugh Tomlinson and Barbara Habberjam. Minneapolis: University of Minnesota Press, 1989.
———. *Le Pli: Leibniz et le baroque*. Paris: Éditions de Minuit, 1988. In English as *The Fold: Leibniz and the Baroque*. Translated by Tom Conley. Minneapolis: University of Minnesota Press, 1993.
———. *Critique et clinique*. Paris: Éditions de Minuit, Coll. Paradoxe, 1993. In English as *Essays Critical and Clinical*. Translated by Daniel W. Smith and Michael A. Greco. Minneapolis: University of Minnesota Press, 1997.
Deleuze, Gilles, and Félix Guattari. *Qu'est-ce que la philosophie?* Paris: Éditions de Minuit, 1991. In English as *What is Philosophy?* Translated by Hugh Tomlinson and Graham Burchell. New York: Columbia University Press, 1994.

Derrida, Jacques. *L'Écriture et la différence.* Paris: Éditions du Seuil, 1967. In English as *Writing and Difference.* Translated by Alan Bass. Chicago: University of Chicago Press, 2017.

———. *Parages.* Paris: Éditions Galilée, 1986. In English as *Parages*, edited by John P. Leavy. Stanford, CA: Stanford University Press, 2011.

Eisler, Benita. *Red Man's Bones: George Catlin, Artist and Showman.* New York: Norton, 2013.

Elkins, James. *The Object Stares Back: On the Nature of Seeing.* San Diego, CA: Harcourt Brace/Harvest, 1997.

Faure, Élie. *Cinéma.* Houilles: Manucius, 2010. In English as *The Art of Cineplastics.* Translated by Walter Pach. Boston: Four Seas Company, 1923.

Ferreira, Manuel Cintra, ed. *Raoul Walsh.* Lisbon: Cinemateca Portuguesa/Museo do Cinema, 2001.

Foucault, Michel. *Ceci n'est pas une pipe. Deux lettres et quatre dessins de René Magritte.* Montpellier: Fata Morgana, 1973. In English as *This is Not a Pipe.* Translated by James Harkness. Berkeley: University of California Press, 2008.

———. *Surveiller et punir: Naissance de la prison.* Paris: Éditions Gallimard, 1975. In English as *Discipline and Punish: The Birth of the Prison.* Translated by Alan Sheridan. New York: Vintage, 1995.

———. *Œuvres.* 2 v. Ed. Frédérique Gros et al. Paris: Éditions Gallimard/Pléiade, 2015.

Fried, Michael. *Absorption and Theatricality: Painting and Beholder in the Age of Diderot.* Chicago: University of Chicago Press, 1988.

Freud, Sigmund. *The Standard Edition of the Complete Psychological Works of Sigmund Freud.* 24 vols. London: Hogarth, 1957–1986.

Gallagher, Tag. "Raoul Walsh." *Senses of Cinema*, no. 21, 2002. https://www.sensesofcinema.com/issues/21

Gaudio, Michael. *Engraving the Savage.* Minneapolis: University of Minnesota Press, 2008.

Genet, Jean. *Un chant d'amour.* Paris: EPM/SW Productions, Coll. "Portrait," 2006.

Gilbert, Nora. *Better Left Unsaid: Hays Code Films, Novels, and the Benefits of Censorship.* Stanford, CA: Stanford University Press, 2013.

Godard, Jean-Luc. *Histoire(s) du cinéma.* 4 vols. Paris: Éditions Gallimard, 1998.

———. *Histoire(s) du cinéma.* Paris: Gaumont Video, 2007.

Hugo, Victor. *William Shakespeare.* Paris: Éditions Hetzel-Quantin, 1866.

Keathley, Christian. *Cinephilia and History, or The Wind in the Trees.* Bloomington: Indiana University Press, 2006.

Kermode, Frank. *The Sense of an Ending: Studies in the Theory of Fiction, with a New Epilogue.* New York: Oxford University Press, 2000.

Kildare, Owen. *My Mamie Rose: The Story of My Regeneration.* New York: Taylor and Baker, 1903.

Labé, Louise. *Œuvres complètes.* Edited by François Rigolot. Paris: Garnier/Flammarion, 1986.

Lacan, Jacques. *Écrits*. Paris: Éditions du Seuil, 1966.
Lacoste, Yves. *La Géographie, ça sert, d'abord, à faire la guerre*. Rev. ed. Paris: La Découverte, 2012.
Leutrat, Jean-Louis. *Le Western: Archéologie d'un genre*. Lyon: Presses Universitaires de Lyon, 1987.
———. *Le Western: Quand la légende devient réalité*. Paris: Éditions Gallimard, 1995.
———. *Westerns*. Paris: Klincksieck, 2009.
Lévi-Strauss, Claude. *Tristes Tropiques*. Paris: Éditions Plon, 1955.
———. *Mythologiques 1: Le cru et le cuit*. Paris: Éditions Plon, 1962.
———. *Mythologiques 3: L'origine des manières de table*. Paris: Éditions Plon, 1968.
———. *Œuvres*. Edited by Vincent de Baene Paris: Éditions Gallimard/Pléiade, 2009.
Lord, Walter. *Day of Infamy*. New York: Holt, 1957.
Lourcelles, Jacques. *Dictionnaire du cinéma*. 6th ed. Paris: R. Laffont, 1997.
Lukács, Gyorgy. *The Theory of the Novel: A Historico-Philosophical Essay on the Forms of Great Epic Literature*. Translated by Anna Bostock. Cambridge, MA: MIT Press, 1971.
Lyotard, Jean-François. *Discours, figure*. Paris: Éditions Klincksieck, 1968.
Maugham, Somerset. *The Trembling of a Leaf: Little Stories of the South Sea Islands*. London: William Heinemann, 1921.
Mauss, Marcel. *Essai sur le don: Forme et raison de l'échange dans les sociétés archaïques*. Paris: Alcan, 1925. In English as *The Gift: Forms and Functions of Exchange in Archaic Societies*. Tranlated by Ian Cunniston, with an introduction by E. E. Evans-Pritchard. London: Routledge and K. Paul, 1970.
Mead, Margaret. *Coming of Age in Samoa: A Psychological Study of Primitive Youth for Western Civilization*. New York: Morrow, 1928.
Merikaetxebarria, Anton. *Raoul Walsh—a lo largo del sendero*. Donostia: Ediciones Ttarttalo, 1996.
Mitchell, William J. *The Reconfigured Eye*. Cambridge, MA: MIT Press, 1992.
Miller, Henry. *Obscenity and the Law of Reflection*. Yonkers, NY: O. Baradinsky, 1945.
Moss, Linda Ann. *Raoul Walsh: The True Adventures of Hollywood's Legendary Director*. Lexington: University of Kentucky Press, 2011.
Nichols, Bill. Ed., *Movies and Methods: An Anthology*, v. 2. Berkeley: University of California Press, 1985.
Parkman, Francis, Jr. *The California and Oregon Trail: Being Sketches of Prairie and Rocky Mountain Life*. New York: George P. Putnam, 1849.
Pfeiffer, Natacha. *Anthony Mann: Arpenter l'image*. Villeneuve d'Ascq: Presses Universitaires du Septentrion, 2019).
———. "Raoul Walsh, le cineaste du "milieu de l'image," forthcoming.
Rabelais, François. *Œuvres complètes*. Edited by Mireille Huchon. Paris: Éditions Gallimard/Pléiade, 1994.
Rancière, Jacques. *La Fable cinématographique*. Paris: Éditions du Seuil, 2001. In English as *Film Fables*, translated by Emiliano Battista, New York: Berg Publishers, 2006.

———. *Les Écarts du cinéma*. Paris: La Fabrique, 2011. In English as *The Intervals of Cinema*. Translated by John Howe. London: Verso, 2014.

———. *Aisthesis: Scènes du régime esthétique de l'art*. Paris: Éditions Galilée, 2011. In English as *Scenes from the Aesthetic Regime of Art*. Translated by Zakir Paul. New York: Verso, 2013.

Reisz, Karel, and Gavin Miller. *The Technique of Film Editing*. New York: Hastings House, 1975.

Rohdie, Sam. *Promised Lands: Cinema, Geography, Modernism*. London: British Film Institute, 2001.

Riis, Jacob. *How the Other Half Lives: Studies Among the Tenements of New York*. New York: C. Scribner's Sons, 1890.

Rosolato, Guy. *Essais sur le symbolique*. Paris: Éditions Gallimard, Coll. Connaissance de l'inconscient, 1969.

———. *Éléments de l'interprétation*. Paris: Éditions Gallimard, 1978.

———. *Pour une psychanalyse exploratrice dans la culture*. Paris: PUF, 1993.

Sarris, Andrew. *The American Cinema: Directors and Directions*. New York: Da Capo, 1996.

Shirley, Rodney. *The Mapping of the World: Early Printed Maps, 1472–1700*. 4th ed. Riverside, CT: Early Worldly, 2001.

Silver, Larry, ed. *Grand Scale: Monumental Prints in the Age of Dürer and Titian*. New Haven, CT: Yale University Press, 2008.

Singleton, Charles. *Dante's 'Commedia:' Elements of Structure*. Baltimore: Johns Hopkins University Press, 2019.

Skorecki, Louis. *Raoul Walsh et moi, suivi de Contre la nouvelle cinéphilie*. Paris: Presses Universitaires de France, 2001.

Smith, John M. *The Films of Raoul Walsh: A Critical Approach*. Columbia, SC: 2013.

Soister, John T. *Up from the Vault: Rare Thrillers of the 1920 and 1930s*. Jefferson, NC: McFarland, 2004.

Sontag, Susan. *Under the Sign of Saturn*. New York: Farrar, Straus & Giroux, 1980.

Tavernier, Bertrand, ed. *The Lumière Brothers' First Films*. New York: Kino on Video, 1998.

Torres, Mário Jorge. *Não Vi o Livro, mas Li o Film*. Ribero: Humus (Alteridades, Cruzmentos, Transferências 17), 2009.

Turner, Frederic Jackson. *The Frontier in American History*. New York: Holt, 1920.

Van Every, Edward. *Muldoon—The Solid Man of Sport: His Amazing Story as Related for the First Time by Him to his Friend, Edward Van Every*. New York: Frederick A. Stokes Company, 1928.

Vaughn, Hunter, and Tom Conley. *The Anthem Anthology of Screen Theory*. London: Anthem, 2018.

Virilio, Paul. *Guerre et cinéma: Logistique de la perception*. Paris: Cahiers du Cinéma/Éditions de l'Étoile, 1984. In English as *War and Cinema: Logistics of Perception*. Translated by Patrick Camiller. London: Verso, 1989.

Walsh, Raoul. *La Colère des justes*. Translated by Jacques Lourcelles. Paris: Pierre Belfond, 1972.

———. *Each Man in His Time: The Life Story of a Director.* New York: Farrar, Straus & Giroux, 1974.
Welsch, Tricia. *Gloria Swanson: Ready for her Close-Up.* Jackson: University of Mississippi Press, 2013.
Wilson, Michael Henry. *Raoul Walsh ou la saga du continent perdu*, Paris: Cinémathèque française, 2001.
Wölfflin, Heinrich. *Kunstgeschictliche Grundbegriffe.* Munich: Bruckmann, 1915. In English as *Principles of Art History*. Translated by Mary Hottinger (London: G. Bell, 1932).
Woodward, David. 1990. "Roger Bacon's Terrestrial Coordinate System." *Annals of the Association of American Geographers* 80, no. 1 (March): 109–22.

Films Cited

The Musketeers of Pig Alley (d. D. W. Griffith, 1912)
The Battle of Elderbush Gulch (d. D. W. Griffith, 1913)
Caught in a Cabaret (d. Charles Chaplin, 1914)
The Birth of a Nation (d. D. W. Griffith, 1915)
Intolerance (d. D. W. Griffith, 1916)
Wild and Woolly (d. James Emerson, 1917)
On the Jump (d. Alfred J. Goulding 1918)
Shoulder Arms (d. Charles Chaplin, 1918)
Brave and Bold (d. Carl Harbaugh, 1918)
Jack Spurlock, Prodigal (d. Carl Harbaugh, 1918)
The Seventh Person (d. George Walsh, 1919)
Dream Street (d. D. W. Griffith, 1921)
The Three Musketeers (d. Douglas Fairbanks, 1921)
The Covered Wagon (1923, d. James Cruze)
The Iron Horse (d. John Ford, 1923)
Rosita (d. Ernst Lubitsch, 1923)
The Red Kimono (d. Walter Lang, 1925)
Flower of Night (d. Paul Bern, 1925)
Thank You (d. John Ford, 1925)
The Vanishing American (d. George Seitz, 1925)
The Big Parade (d. Charles Vidor, 1925)
Crown of Lies (d. Dimitri Buchowetski, 1926)
Thank You (d. John Ford, 1926)
Three Bad Men (d. John Ford, 1926)
The Jazz Singer (d. Alan Crosland, 1927)
The Temporary Widow (d. G. Veicky, 1930)
Too Many Crooks (d. G. King, 1930)
All Quiet on the Western Front (d. Lewis Milestone, 1930)
M (d. Fritz Lang, 1931)

Rain (d. Lewis Milestone, 1932)
Las Hurdes/Land Without Bread/Unpromised Land/Tierra sin pan (d. Luis Buñuel, 1932)
L'Âge d'or (d. Luis Buñuel,1932)
King Kong (d. Merian Cooper and Ernest Schoedsack, 1933)
The 39 Steps (d. Alfred Hitchcock, 1935)
Fury (d. Fritz Lang, 1936)
Partie de campagne [*A Day in the Country*] (d. Jean Renoir, 1937)
The Grapes of Wrath (d. John Ford, 1939)
Torrid Zone (d. William Keighley, 1940)
Pier 13 (d. Arthur Kober (1940)
Sullivan's Travels (d. Preston Sturges, 1941)
The Battle of Midway (d. John Ford, 1942)
The Outlaw (d. Howard Hughes, 1943)
Roma, città aperta/Rome, Open City (d. Roberto Rossellini, 1945)
Paisà (d. Roberto Rossellini, 1947)
Strange Illusion (d. Ulmer, Edgar, 1947)
Germany, Year Zero (d. Roberto Rossellini, 1948)
Stromboli (d. Roberto Rossellini, 1948)
Rio Grande (d. John Ford, 1950)
Wagonmaster (d. John Ford, 1950)
Winchester 73 (d. Anthony Mann, 1950)
Westward the Women (d. William Wellman, 1951)
Umberto D (d. Vittorio De Sica, 1952)
The Big Heat (d. Fritz Lang, 1952)
Europa 51 (d. Roberto Rossellini, 1952)
From Here to Eternity (d. Fred Zinnemann, 1953)
King of the Khyber Rifles (d. Henry King, 1953)
The Robe (d. Henry Koster, 1953)
Gentleman Prefer Blondes (d. Howard Hawks, 1953)
Voyage to Italy (d. Roberto Rossellini, 1954)
The Far Country (d. Anthony Mann, 1954)
Rififi (d. Jules Dassin, 1955)
On the Bowery (d. Lionel Regosin, 1956)
Vertigo (d. Alfred Hitchcock, 1958)
Les 400 Coups/The 400 Blows (d. François Truffaut, 1959)
À bout de souffle/Breathless (d. Jean-Luc Godard, 1960)
Vivre sa vie (My Life to Live) (d. Jean-Luc Godard, 1962)
Pierrot le fou (d. Jean-Luc Godard, 1965)
Paths of Glory (d. Stanley Kubrick, 1957)
Tora! Tora! Tora! (d. Richard Fleischer, 1970)
Les 120 jours de Sodom/The 120 Days of Sodom (d. Pier Paolo Pasolini, 1976)
Sans toi ni loi/Vagabond (d. Agnès Varda, 1985)

The Donner Party (d. Rick Burns, 1992)
Level-5 (d. Chris Marker, 1997).
Pearl Harbor (d. Michael Bay, 2001)
Histoire(s) du cinéma (d. Jean-Luc Godard, 2007)

Films Cited, directed by Raoul Walsh

The Life of General Villa (1914)
The Greaser (1915)
The Fencing Master (1915)
11:30 P.M. (1915)
A Bad Man and Others (1915)
Regeneration (1915)
The Serpent (1916)
Blue Blood and Red (1916)
Pillars of Society (1916)
The Honor System (1917)
The Pride of New York (1917)
The Conqueror (1917)
This is the Life 1917)
I'll Say So (1918)
From Now On (1920)
Serenade (1921)
Lost and Found on a South Sea Island (1923)
The Thief of Baghdad (1924)
East of Suez (1925)
The Wanderer (1926)
What Price, Glory? (1926)
The Lucky Lady (1926)
The Monkey Talks (1927)
Sadie Thompson (1928)
The Loves of Carmen (1928)
The Cock-Eyed World (1928–1929)
In Old Arizona (1928)
The Big Trail (1930)
The Man Who Came Back (1931)
Women of All Nations (1931)
The Yellow Ticket (1931)
Wild Girl (1932)
Hello, Sister! (1932)
Me and My Gal (1932)

The Yellow Ticket (1933)
Sailor's Luck (1933)
The Bowery (1933)
Baby Face Harrington (1935)
Every Night at Eight (1935)
Big Brown Eyes (1936)
The Roaring Twenties (1939)
They Drive by Night (1940)
The Strawberry Blonde (1941)
They Died with Their Boots On (1941)
High Sierra (1941)
Manpower (1941)
Desperate Journey (1942)
Gentleman Jim (1942)
Northern Pursuit (1943)
Objective, Burma! (1945)
Cheyenne (1947)
The Man I Love (1947)
Pursued (1948)
White Heat (1949)
Distant Drums (1951)
The Enforcer (1951)
Blackbeard the Pirate (1952)
A Lion is in the Streets (1953)
Saskatchewan (1954)
Band of Angels (1957)
The Naked and the Dead (1958)
The Sheriff of Fractured Jaw (1958)
Marines, Let's Go (1961)
A Distant Trumpet (1964)

Index

A Bad Man and Others (d. Raoul Walsh, 1915), 226n7
À bout de souffle (*Breathless*) (d. Jean-Luc Godard, 1960), 228n19
A Lion in the Streets (d. Raoul Walsh 1953), 207n4
absent cause (as concept and ideology), 232nn19–20
air power and logistics of perception, 79, 82
Akerman, James, 13, 221n5
Allen, Frederick Lewis, 221n7
Amad, Paula, 220n3
Amon Carter Museum (Dallas, Texas), 122
order-words, 69
anamorphosis, 57, 213n3; and Cinemascope, 88
Anderson, Maxwell, 27, 58
Aristotle, xiv; and action, 112
As You Like It, 141; recited in *La Colère des justes*, 193
Astruc, Alexandre, 206n16
Auerbach, Erich, 222n1; and figural realism, 225n3
auteur theory, 85
authority, as ideology, xv; as absent cause called in question, 31–32, 49, 78–79, 82; and contradiction, 32; and *Each Man in His Time*, 32; and off-screen space, 36; and order-words, 69; and *Rain* (d. Lewis Milestone, 1932), 32; in *Sadie Thompson*, 48, 109; and signature, 46; and weakened deixis, 36–37

Baby Face Harrington (d. Raoul Walsh, 1935), 208n12
Baecque, Antoine de, 217n26
Bailey, Frankie, 230n10
Bakhtin, Mikkail, 43, 210n2; on dialogism, 216n21, 229n6; and lower body (or *bas corporel*), 43–44
Baltrušaitis, Jurgis, 213n3
Balzac, Honoré de, 85
Band of Angels (d. Raoul Walsh, 1957), 110
Bara, Theda, 226n7
Bari, Lynn, 162
Barnes, George, 29, 35
Barrymore, Lionel, 29, 32, 35, 37–39, 83
Bataille, Georges, and economy of waste, 217n25
Bataille, Sylvia, 231n14
The Battle of Elderbush Gulch (d. D. W. Griffith, 1913), 127
Baxter, Warner, 221n9
Bazin, André, 102, 106, 138; and image-fact, 122, 220n20, 220n22,

Bazin, André *(continued)*
225n2; and "Evolution of Film Language," 138–39, 219–220n18; on Rossellini, 223n17; and "The Entomology of the Pinup Girl," 102, 107; and "The Ontology of the Photographic Image," 106
Beauvoir, Simone de, 86
Beery, Wallace, 166, 169, 170, 175; and maternal character, 175; shown squinting, 185–86, fig. 7.7; and *The Wanderer* (d. Raoul Walsh, 1926), 229n7
Belgum, Rolf, xv
Bellour, Raymond, 208n8, 223n25
Bennett, Joan, 110, 138, 140, 142, 219n11, 225n1, 230n12; and lower body, 210n23
Benoit, Georges, 7, 13, 23
Bergman, Ingrid, 224n27, 230n14
Bernard of Clairvaux (Saint), 120; and spiritual canticle, 134
Béroalde de Verville (1556–1626), 213n3
Bertolo, José, xvi
Big Brown Eyes (d. Raoul Walsh, 1936,), 110
The Big Parade (d. Charles Vidor, 1925), 187; and nudity, 230n12
The Big Trail, xv, 94, 107; analysis of, 111–135, 137–38, 166, 189, 194–95, 201, 205n9; aspect ratio of, 111; cliffside sequence, 129–30; credits and intertitles as "voices of silence," 116; credits and lap dissolves, 117; culinary etiquette in, 132; and dogs, 111, 124, 129, 131, 132; and scenes of death, 132; and the Donner party of 1846, 122; duration of shots, 123; effects of Walsh's enucleation, 220n3; flashback in, 118; foreign versions of, 112; and geography, 118, 125; and "Grandeur process," 111; and the Great Depression, 114; and immanence, 120; intermediary figures in, 125–26, 28, 130; intertitles, 126, 129, 130, 132–33; movement and stasis in, 112; mythic character of, 120; scenes of nurture, 131; open totality of, 121; and point of view, 121, 125–26; retrospective in 1974 at Museum of Modern Art, 112; sequence shots, 114; and sequoia trees, 133–34, figs. 5.10 and 5.11; and 70 mm film stock, 114; and silent cinema, 111; sound effects, 125; tableau-effects, 120–24; title of the film in the film, 128, 132–33; ubiquity of action, 130; women who work and toil, 122–23; vertical counter-tilts, 130

The Birth of a Nation (d. D. W. Griffith, 1915), 3, 30, 46, 205n7, 207n19
Birton, Frederick, 14
Blackbeard the Pirate (d. Raoul Walsh, 1952), 191
Blanchot, Maurice, 218n6, 223n17
Blue Blood and Red (d. Raoul Walsh, 1916), xiv, 226n7
Boas, Franz, 213n35
Bogart, Humphrey, 212n33, 224n28
Böhnke, Alexander, 208n15
Bond, Ward, 169, 205n8
Booth, John Wilkes (as played by Walsh in *The Birth of a Nation*), 3, 30, 46
Borden, Olive, 28
Boudu sauvé des eaux [Boudu Saved from Drowning] (d. Jean Renoir, 1932), 27
The Bowery (d. Raoul Walsh, 1933): analysis of, 165–88; xiv, 4, 19, 67, 138, 162; bad taste or studied crudeness, 167, 169, 172; Bowery song in front-credits and *In Old*

Arizona, 170; and contradiction, 169, 182; effects of the Great Depression, 166, 188; dummies in, 169, 179–80, 184–86; end credits and National Recovery Association, 188; front credits, 167, 170, 178; and *Gangs of New York* (d. Martin Sorcese, 2001), 167; initial shots of Connors (Beery), 172, figs. 7.3–7.3; Connors/Beery and his beer, 174, fig. 7.4; intrusion of history (as *deus ex machina*), 183, 187; irresolution of narrative, 167, 176; local color, 176; and "man's world," 170, 174, 175; montage of opening sequence, 171–72; oscillation of style, 170; and ocular authority, 186; pace and tempo, 169; and seriality, 187–88; two sublime shots in, 179–80, fig. 7.6; and ventriloquism, 170; and George Walsh, 178, 182, 183, 187, fig. 7.5; and writing, 183, 186; and 20th Century Fox logo, 167, 170; as writing of history in context of the burning of the Reichstag, February, 1933, 188, 226n7, 229nn 4–5

Brave and Bold (d. Carl Harbaugh, 1918), 226n7

Brecht, Berthold, 32

Brendel, El, 12, 58–59, 64; in *Women of All Nations*, 213n2

Brillat-Savarin, Anthelme, 132, 224n30

Brofen, Elisabeth, xiv, 219n13, 227n27

Brown, Daniel James, 220n2

Brown, Harry, 190

Browning, Todd, 28

Brownlow, Kevin, 215n13, 233n3

Brunhès, Jean, 220n3

Bry, Theodor de, 210n21

Buñuel, Luis, and *Las Hurdes/Land without Bread*, 220n3

Burgess, Dorothy, 165

Burnett, W. R., 190

Burns, Ken, 52

Burns, Marion, 141

Busch, Niven, 190

Cagney, James, 204n2, 227n13

Camus, Alfred, 233n7

Carver, Louise, 112

Catalina (Island), site of *Sadie Thompson*, 50

Catlin, George, 126, 221n6

Caught in a Cabaret (1914, d. Charles Chaplin), 3

Celan, Paul, 219n24

The Celestial Code (d. Raoul Walsh, 1915), 226n7

Céline, Louis-Ferdinand, 215n12

Cérisuelo, Marc, xvi

Certeau, Michel de, 98; and the *logique de perruque* ("wig logic"), 216n23; and spatial stories, 204n6, 205n10; and *The Practice of Everyday Life*, 226n8; and *The Writing of history*, 219n15

Chandler, George, 162

Chaplin, Charles, xi; and *Shoulder Arms* (1918), 207n7

Char, René, 223n17

Cheyenne (d. Raoul Walsh, 1947), 201

La Chienne (d. Jean Renoir, 1931), 227n11

Childs, Jeffrey, xvi

Christenson, Benjamin, 28

Churchill, Marguerite, 119

Clairvaux, Saint Bernard of, 222n13

Clark, Walter Van Tilberg, 190

Clastres, Pierre, 214n8

The Cock-Eyed World (d. Raoul Walsh, 1929), xv, 48; analysis of, 55–83; aimlessness of American military forces, 77, 80; appraisals of "authority," 57–58, 61, fig. 3.3; and *Colorado Territory*, 219n17; allusions to enucleation, 64, figs. 3.4, 3.5;

The Cock-Eyed World (continued)
fable and *quid pro quo* in, 60–61; and fellatio, 70–71, fig. 3.7; front credits, 58–59, fig. 3.2; and gynophobia, 62; play with Hays Code, 215n15; and homelessness, 73–74; and illegalism, 62; and intertitles, 47; indexicality, 70, 231n17; interpellation (as defined by Louis Althusser), 60–62; itinerary of, 75, fig. 3.8 and 214n4; lower bodies in, 69; obscenity in, 66, 68, 69, 72, figs. 3.6, 3.7; photo-op of players, 56, fig. 3.1; and psittacism, 78, 165, 169, 175, 183, 187, 193, 208n9; silent and sound versions, 57; "shoving off," 60, 80–83, and figs. 3.9, 3.10; and United Fruit Company, 77; and war as human condition, 60

La Colère des justes (The Wrath of the Just, novel by Raoul Walsh, 1972), action in style and tempo, 201, 206n14; analysis of, 190–201; Apache language, 198; and recall of *The Bowery*, 200; Guadalajara, as vanishing point, 196, 199; and landscapes, 195, 201; Mark Twain in cameo, 196; monocular and binocular vision, 194; and Pinkerton Agency, 194; and publication, 224n26; theme of pursued and pursuit, 194; similarities to *The Big Trail, High Sierra, Colorado Territory*, and *The Sheriff of Fractured Jaw*, 194, 197; Shakespeare recited (*Macbeth, Hamlet* and *Romeo and Juliet*), 196

Colorado Territory (d. Raoul Walsh, 1949), 194, 197, 201; and nightmare, 212n33, 213n21

Conklin, Chester, 184

Conley, Walter, xi–xii, 226n7, 230n13

Connors, Barry, 140

The Conqueror (d. Raoul Walsh, 1917), 226n7

Coogan, Jackie, 106, 229n8

Cook, Pam, 218n4

Cooper, Jackie, 167, 169, 170

Cooper, Miriam, 215n13, 226n7, 232n3

Cortade, Ludovic, 225n2

Cotgrave, Randle, 214n9

The Covered Wagon (d James Cruze, 1923), 113

Crawford, Joan, 50

crosscutting, 3, 10, 12, 24–26

The Crown of Lies (d. Dmitri Buchowetski, 1926), 230n10

Curtright, Jorha, 91

d'Angela, Toni, xvi

d'Arnoux, Georges, 231n14

Damita, Lily, 56–58, 70, 77

Davidson, Jo, 157

de Baene, Vincent, 214n8

Degas, Edgar, 123, 205n9

del Rio, Dolores, 27, 59, 166

Deleuze, Gilles, 191, 220n19; and Baroque style, 219n16; and event-theory, 218n5; and free indirect subjectivity, 210n22; on Herman Melville, 225n6; on the "mental image," 207n21; and point of view, 205n6, 211n28, 222n15; concept of open whole, 222n14; and the perception-image, 223n22, 228n17

Depth of field, in *Regeneration, Me and My Gal*, and *High Sierra*, 231n15; and sacrifice, in *Las Hurdes/Land Without Bread/Tierra sin pan* (d. Luis Buñuel), 231n16

Derrida, Jacques, 17; and "Freud and the Scene of Writing, 17, 206n15, 209n20, 228n18; and contractual relation of a title and its work, 218n6

Desperate Journey (d. Raoul Walsh, 1942), 232n1
The Devil's Circus (d. Benjamin Christenson, 1926), 28
Devine, Andy, 221n9
diagonal perspective, xiv
Dickens, Charles, 3, 125
Dietrich, Marlene, 95, 96, 205n8
distanciation, 57. *See also* Brecht, Berthold
Distant Drums (d. Raoul Walsh, 1951), 102, 201
The Donner Party (d. Ric Burns, 1992), 220n2
Doros, Dennis, 50, 208n13
Dort, Bernard, 223n25
Dream Street (d. D. W. Griffith, 1921), 119
dummies, in *Me and My Gal*, 157; and *The Bowery*, 184–87
Dwan, Allan, 85

Each Man in his Time: The Life Story of a Director (1972), 29, 193; "authority" called in question, 208n10; and enucleation, 203n2; defense of Native Americans, 195, 199, 223–24; and mysterious "Olga," 215n13; photo-op selling *The Cock-Eyed World*, 56, fig. 3.1; reflections on George Raft, 229n7; remembrance of *Regeneration* in *The Bowery*, 229n8
East of Suez (d. Raoul Walsh, 1925), 208n12
Egan, Richard, 90, 91
Eisler, Benita, 221n6
11:30 P.M. (d. Raoul Walsh, 1915), 226n7
Elkins, James, 227n15
enucleation (in life of Raoul Walsh), xiv, 55; in *White Heat*, 227n13. *See also* Walsh, Raoul

Evarts, Hal, 114
Everson, Kevin, xvi
Every Night at Eight (d. Raoul Walsh, 1935), 211n33

Fairbanks, Douglas, xii, 13, 203n5, 208n12, 230n12
Fairfax, Daniel, 225n4
Farrell, Charles, 138
Fauchois, René, author of *Le Singe qui parle* (1924), 27
Faure, Élie, 223n18
Fellowes, Rockcliffe, 19
The Fencing Master (d. Raoul Walsh, 1915), 226n7
Ferrari, Domenico, 145
Field, Peter, xiii
Flinn, Margaret, 323n2
Flower of Night, d. Paul Bern, 230n10
Ford, John, 85; and *The Battle of Midway* (1942), 104
Forde, Eugene, 140
Foucault, Michel, 62, 98; and *This is Not a Pipe*, 209n16; and illegalism, 214n7, 215n11
Fox, William A., and Studio, 7, 30, 82
Freaks (d. Todd Browning, 1932), 28
free indirect subjectivity, 98. *See also* Pasolini, Pier Paolo
Freud, Sigmund, 62; and "Thoughts for the Time on War and Death," 23, 206n17; *Bilderschriften* or picture-writing, 206nn16–17; "Note on the Mystic Writing Pad," 17, 20, 209n20, 228n18; and economy of jokes, 226n8
Fried, Michael, 223n21
From Here to Eternity (d. Fred Zinnemann, 1953), 97
From Now On (d. Raoul Walsh, 1920), 226n7
Fury (d. Fritz Lang, 1936), 227n12

Gardiès, André, 208n15
Gaudio, Michael, 210n21
Genet, Jean, 219n11
Gentleman Jim (d. Raoul Walsh, 1942), 19, 169, 186
Gentlemen Prefer Blondes (d. Howard Hawks), 102
Germany, Year Zero (d. Roberto Rossellini, 1948), 224n27
Gilbert, Nora, 215n15, 229n6
Godard, Jean-Luc, 160, 216n18; with Michel Mourlet, on the moral drama of the tracking shot, 217n26; and trauma in *Histoire(s) du cinéma*, 219n14, 228n3, 228n19; and "just an image/a just image," 233n7
Goya, Francisco, 197
Grapes of Wrath (d. John Ford, 1939), 113
Grey, Olga, 215n13
Grey, Zane, and *Riders of the Purple Sage* (1912), 190
Griffith, D. W. (David Wark), xii, 112, 127, 208n8, 214n6; and hieroglyphics, 206n15
Guest, Haden, xv
Guthrie, Alfred Bertram, 190

Hale, Alan (Sr.), 230n12
Hanlon, Bert, 141
Harbaugh, Carl 4, 210n25. See also *Jack Spurlock, Prodigal* (1918)
Hardy, Phil (and Walsh Retrospective at Edinburgh, 1974), 218n4
Harmer, Lilian, 170, 182
Harte, Brett, 138
Hawks, Howard, 85, 102; and *Gentlemen Prefer Blondes* (1953), 219n19
Haycox, Ernest, 190
Hays Code, 30, 63, 209n18; and air power, 68; and queering, 72; and nudity, 230n2

Hello, Sister! (d. Raoul Walsh and Erich Von Stroheim, 1933), 166
Heyt, Louis Jen, 162
High Sierra (d. Raoul Walsh, 1941), xiv, 166, 194, 224n8
Hitchcock, Alfred, 85
Hitchcock, Raymond, 28
Holbein, Hans (and *The Ambassadors*), 213n3
The Honor System (d. Raoul Walsh, 1917), 204n1, 226n7
Hoover, Herbert, 166
House on Un-American Activities Committee, xi
How the Other Half Lives (Jacob Riis), 166
Howe, James Wong, 83
Hugo, Victor, 32, 208n11
human geography, 220n3
Hüser, Rembert, 208n15
hypnosis (in *Sadie Thompson*), 32, 48; and silent cinema, 50

I'll Say So (d. Raoul Walsh, 1918), 265n7
In Old Arizona (d. Raoul Walsh, 1928), 55, 114, 165, 166, 210n26, 228n1
Intolerance (d. D. W. Griffith, 1916), xii, 3, 26
The Iron Horse (d. John Ford, 1924), 113

Jack Spurlock, Prodigal (d. Carl Harbaugh, 1918), 226n7
James, Henry, 125, 205n7
The Jazz Singer (d. Alan Crosland, 1927), 138, 140
Johnston, Claire, 218n4
Jolson, Al, 140, 181

Kaplan, Louis, xvi
Karnes, Roscoe, 230n12

Keathley, Christian, 230n14
Kehr, Dave, 190, 219n19
Keith, Ian, 119
Kelton, Pert, 170, 173
The Kid (d. Charles Chaplin, 1921), xi
Kildare, Owen, author of *My Mamie Rose* (1903), 2–3, 6–7, 17, 138, 204n1, 204n4
Kilrain, Jake, 230n11
King Kong (d. Merian C. Cooper and Ernest B. Schoedsack, 1933), 166
King of the Khyber Rifles (d. Henry King, 1953), 88
Kipling, Rudyard, 31, 59
Klein, Margaret, 230n10
Kleiner, Arthur (silent film pianist), xii
Kober, Arthur, 140
Kubrick, Stanley, xv
Kurrle, Robert, 29, 35; and *Regeneration*, 210n27

Labé, Louise, 217n29
Lacan, Jacques, xiv, 228n17
Lacoste, Yves, 421n3
Lang, Fritz, 206n12; and *Scarlet Street* (1945), 215n16; and *The Big Heat* (1953), 215n16
Laverty, Jean, 68, 165
Le May, Alan, 190
Lea, Tom, 190
Lefebvre, Henri, 204n6
Leibniz, Gottfried von, 218n5
Lerner, Jacques, 28
Leslie, Joan, 91
Leutrat, Jean-Louis, 221
Level-5 (d. Chris Marker, 1997), 231n15
Leverett, Carl, 142
Lévi-Strauss, Claude, and "Leçon d'écriture" (in *Tristes Tropiques*, 1955), 210n21; theory of exchange, 214n8; and culinary triangle (in *L'Origine des manières de table* (1968), 224n30

Life of General Villa (d. Raoul Walsh, 1914), 203n4
Lipreading and silent cinema, 47–48
Locke, Charles O., 190
Lord, Walter (author of *Day of Infamy*, 1957), 97, 219n12
Lorre, Peter, 206n12
Losilla, Carlos, 28, 160, 205n7207n1, 210n23, 218n3, 219n19
Lost and Found on a South Sea Island (d. Raoul Walsh, 1923), 210n25
Lourcelles, Jacques, 215n13; and Mac-Mahon Cinema, 232n2
The Loves of Carmen (d. Raoul Walsh, 1927), xiv, 56, 78
Lowe, Edmund, 27, 56–58, 166, 213n2; as trickster, 65; and *In Old Arizona* (1928), 165–66
The Lucky Lady (d. Raoul Walsh, 1926), xiv, 2, 209n17
Lukacs, Gyorgy, 120
The Lumière Brothers' First Films (dvd, 1998), 209n18. *See also* Tavernier, Bertrand
Lumière, Auguste and Louis, xiv
Lynn, Fred, xii
Lyotard, Jean-François, 206n16

M (d. Fritz Lang, 1931), 206n12
Madison, Noel, 137
The Man Who Came Back (d. Raoul Walsh, 1931), xiv, 138, 166, 204n5
Mann, Anthony, 85; and his western cycle (1950–57), 223n22, 223n24
The Man I Love (1947, d. Raoul Walsh), 109
Manpower (d. Raoul Walsh, 1941), 205n8, 230n12
Marcus, James 4, 10, 29, 44, 210n25
Marines, Let's Go! (1961, d. Raoul Walsh), 30
Marker, Chris, 231n15
Marlowe, Christopher, 97

Marot, Clément, 217n2
Marsh, Oliver, 29, 35
Marshall, Tully, 114
Mattos, Clayton, xvi
Maugham, W. Somerset, 30–32, 35, 86, 93; and *Trembling of a Leaf* (1921), 207n6
Mauss, Marcel, 108; and gift-economy, 216n25
May, Karl, 190
McCann, John, 3, 7
McCarthy, Joseph, xi
McCoy, H., 4, 18
McCrea, Joel, 212n33, 212n33
McDonald, J. Farrell, 137, 141
McElwee, Ross, xvi
McLaglan, Victor, 27, 56–59, 166, 175, 213n2
Me and My Gal (d. Raoul Walsh, 1932), xv, 110, 169, 178, 186; analysis of, 137–63; role of the dog, 146–47; and the doughnut jar, 152, fig. 6.6; and the Great Depression, 139–40, fig. 6.3, 147, 157, 225n6; diner (or chowder house) as *topos*, 147, fig. 6.4; direct address to the spectator (and collapse of narrative), 160–61, 228n19; dummy-sculpture (or mute speaker), 157, 158, fig. 6.8; exposition, 142–43, fig. 6; elision of politics, 140, 157, 161–62; and Fox Studios, 137, 142; front credits, 142; narrative meander, 151; as mixed genre, 140, 148; and Moss (2011) on autobiographical humor, 226n10; ocular porthole, 149, fig. 6.5; stress on orality, 144, fig. 6.2, 211n29; and *Pier 13* (1940), 162, 226n7; plotline, 140; and Prohibition, 140, 148; and *quid pro quo*, 141–42, 147–49; relation with silent and sound traditions, 138–39; and ruckus, 150–51, 154; salty humor and backside of Joan Bennett, 159, 161, 210n23, fig. 6.9; confined spaces in, 138, 141–42; "unconscious" in, 160; wit as food (and economy), 147, 149, 153; scene of writing, 153–56, fig. 6.7; squinting eye, 161–62, fig. 6.10
Mead, Margaret, 213n35
Melville, Herman, 225n6
Menzies, William Cameron, 29, 35, 208n12
Midway, Battle of (1942), 104
Milestone, Lewis, 50–52, 217n27; and *Rain* (1932), 50
Miller, Arthur, 142
Miller, Gavin, 207n19
Miller, Henry, 215n12, 208n18
Mitchell, Billy, 216n17
Mitchell, William J., 231n18
Mollet, Luc, 160
The Monkey Talks (d. Raoul Walsh, 1927), xiv, 27–29, 48, 139, 192, 207n4, 207n7
Monroe Doctrine (and military occupation), 82
Moorehead, Agnes, 92
Moran, Frank, 142. 162
Morari, Codruta, 217n1
Morton, Michael, 83
Morton, Victoria, 83
Moss, Marilyn Ann, xiii, 30, 56, 114, 118, 160, 166, 169, 190, 203n4, 204n1, 206n13, 207n5, 210n24, 210n27, 213n36, 221n8; on *The Revolt of Mamie Stover*, 217–18; on *The Big Trail*, 220n1, 221n10; on *Me and My Gal*, 224n1; on *The Bowery*, 229n5
Moss, Robb, xvi
Mourlet, Michel, 217n26
Marines, Let's Go (d. Raoul Walsh, 1961), 30
Much Ado About Nothing, 140
Muldoon, Bill, 230n11

Mulvey, Laura, xiv
The Musketeers of Pig Alley (d. D. W. Griffith, 1912), 3
My Mamie Rose. See Kildare, Owen

The Naked and the Dead (d. Raoul Walsh, 1958), 30
Negri, Paula, 230n10
Nilsson, Anna Q., 4
Nolan, Lloyd, 162
Northern Pursuit (d. Raoul Walsh, 1943), 201
Nykrog, Per, 214n3

O'Brien, Edmund, 227n13
O'Dell, Paul, xii
Objective Burma! (d. Raoul Walsh, 1945), xi, xvi, 20, 102, 205n5, 216n24; and male nudity, 230n1
Olga, Russian prostitute in *The Cock-Eyed World*, 64–68; and Olga Grey, in *Pillars of Society* (1916), 233n3; lover and prostitute *La Colère des justes*, 193, 198, 215n13; and fleeting romance with Walsh in *Each Man in His Time*, 113
Olivier, Lawrence, 83
On the Bowery (d. Lionel Regosin, 1956), 168
On the Jump (d. Raoul Walsh, 1917), 226n7
The Oregon Trail (by Francis Parkman, 1849), 112, 115
Ortelius, Abraham, 113
The Outlaw (1943, d. Howard Hughes), 93

Pago Pago (island), 32, 35, 48, 50
Paisà (1946, d. Roberto Rossellini), 97
Pallette, Eugene, 210n25
Parkman, Jr., Francis, 115, 221n11
Parrish, Robert, 122
Pascal, Blaise, 12, 87
Pasolini, Pier Paolo, 210n22; and free indirect subjectivity, 205n6
Pate, Michael, 92
Paths of Glory (d. Stanley Kubrick, 1962), xv
Pendleton, David, xv
Perspectival object, 21, 68; and projective identification, 23
Pfeiffer, Natacha, 223n24
Pier 13 (d. Eugene Forde, 1940), 162
Pillars of Society (d. Raoul Walsh, 1916), 215n13
Pinkerton Agency, and emblem of, 194–95, 204n1, fig. C.1; and *The Honor System* (d. Raoul Walsh, 1917), 204n1
Pomerance, Murray, xvi
Ponge, Francis, 218n6
Portholes, as ocular signs, in *The Cock-Eyed World*, 67–69, 75, 149, 219n11; in *The Revolt of Mamie Stover*, 91–92, 227n15; in *Me and My Gal*, 219n11, fig. 6.3
Power, Sr., Tyrone, 114
The Pride of New York (d. Raoul Walsh, 1917), 226nn7
Proust, Marcel, 125
The Public Enemy (d. William Wellman, 1932), 204n2
Pursued (d. Raoul Walsh, 1948), 98, 228n4

Rabelais, François, 40, 125, 215n12
Radin, Paul, 215n14
Raft, George, 166, 169, 170, 211n33, 230n12
Rain (d. Lewis Milestone, 1932), 32, 50–51
Rancière, Jacques, xv, 86, 204nn7–8, 206n12, 214n9, 219n14, 228; and *Aisthesis*, 222n12; and *The Emancipated Spectator*, 225n5; and film-fable as contradiction, 228n16; and *Intervals of Cinema*, 223n19, 223n19, 231n14

Reclus, Élisée, 220n3
The Red Kimono (d. Walter Lang, 1925), 119
Regeneration, xiv, analysis of, 1–26, 29, 44, 99, 162, 165, 166, 168–70, 177, 186–87; signs of apparatus (camera) in, 7–12, 19, fig. 1.2; and authority, 31; and *The Bowery*, 18; broom as symbol, 9, 19, fig. 1.3, 205n8; crosscutting 3, 10, 12; documentary character of, 12, figs. 1.4–5; economy of *quid pro quo*, 23; enemy brothers, 22, fig. 1.8; exposition, 4–9, figs. 1.1–3; front-credits, 7; and *Gentleman Jim*, 19; indifference of gender, 17; and indirect subjectivity, 9; intertitles, 18; local color in, 13, fig. 1.5; and mental images, 9; monocular signs in, 3, 25–26, fig. 1.11; length and number of shots, 10; primal scenes in, 20, fig. 1.6, 205n8; and rat's eye view, 204n4; scenes of writing, 20–21, fig. 1.9; as "sham," 16, fig. 1.7
Reichstag burned by Nazis in 1933, 188
Reisz, Karel, 207n19
Remington, Frederic, 122, 126, 221n6
Renoir, Jean, 27, 85; and *Boudu sauvé des eaux* (1932) [Boudu Saved from Drowning], 28; and *La Chienne* (1931), 215n16; and *La Grande Illusion* (1937) [The Grand Illusion] 227n11; and *Partie de campagne* [A Day in the Country] (1937), 231n14; and *La Règle du jeu* (1939) [The Rules of the Game], 217n26; and *Tire-au-flanc* (1927) [The Sad Sack], 207n7
The Revolt of Mamie Stover (1956, d. Walsh), xiv, 2, 30 53; analysis of, 85–110; economy of waste, 107–109; figures of chains and concatenation, 227n13; front credits rolled back, 86; and the incursion of history (the bombing of Pearl Harbor), 97, 104; and modes of transport or metaphors, 88; and the "pinup" economy, 102–103, 105; and pleasure of business, 100–101; "the real," 106–107, 109; and record players (souvenir of Victrola in *Sadie Thompson*), 108–109; relation to *Regeneration*, 99; and *Sadie Thompson*, 86, 93, 105; and the self-making woman, 86, 94; tourism and history, 101; and trauma, 98; and wide aspect-ratio, 87–89; as woman's film, 109
Rice, Jim, xii
Riefenstahl, Leni, 209n18
Rififi (d. Jules Dassin, 1955), 153
Riis, Jacob, 3, 166; and *How the Other Half Lives*, 228n2
Rio Grande (d. John Ford, 1950), 187
The Robe (1953, d. Henry Koster), 88
Robinson, Edward G., 205n8, 230n12
Rohdie, Sam, 221n3
Rohmer, Eric, 230n14
Rollins, David, 132
Roma, città aperta/Rome, Open City (1945, d. Roberto Rossellini), 97
Roosevelt, Franklin D., 97, 166; and The New Deal, 188
Ropars-Wuilleumier, Marie-Claire, xv, 204n8
Rosita (d. Ernst Lubitsch, 1923), 226n7
Rosolato, Guy, 216n19, 207n20; on screen-memory, 228n18
Rossellini, Roberto, 179, 222–23nn16–17, 224n27, 230n14
Rowland, Clara, xvi
Russell, Jane, 90–91, 102, 218n4
Russell, Lilian, 230n10
Russo, Ron and Gai, xvi
Ruysdael, Basil, 213n1

Sadie Thompson, xiv, 2, 92, 114, 141; analysis of, 27–53, 55, 57, 59; "authority" called in question, 32, 46, 48; images of autochtones, 51, fig. 2.10; aesthetic of distanciation, 48–49; beauty of the rump, 41–45, fig. 2.7; damage and restoration of surviving print, 50; establishing shots, 35, fig. 2.5; and front-credits, 33–34, 46, figs. 2.1–2.3; and homosociality, 36; hypnosis, 31, 49–50, fig. 2.9; indexicality, 41, fig. 2.6; indirect subjectivity, 45; intertitles, 36, 44–45, 48–50, 209n17; and jokes, 35; lipreading, 47; obscenity in, 32, 209n18; orality of, 45; and primal "scenes of writing," 37–39, 40, 44, 48, 209n20; relation with censorship, 41; unoccupied marines, fig. 2.4; Victrola as sound cue, 210n26, 210n32; portrait of Walsh-as-baby, 46, fig. 2.8; photo-op of Walsh and Swanson, 52, fig. 2.11; as a "woman's film," 32
Sailor's Luck (d. Raoul Walsh, 1933), 203n5, 208n15
Salomy Jane (d. William Nigh and Lucius Henderson, 1914). See *Wild Girl*
Sans toi/Ni loi (d. Agnès Varda, 1985, see *Vagabond*
Sarris, Andrew, 211n33
Saskatchewan (d. Raoul Walsh, 1954), 224n26
Schapiro, Meyer, 225n3
Schenck, Joseph M., 170
Schön, Erhard, 213n3
Scorcese, Martin, xv, 167, 190
Serenade (d. Raoul Walsh, 1921), 226n7
Serpent (d. and co-written by George and Raoul Walsh, 1916), 226n7
Seventh Person (d. George Walsh, 1919), 226n7

Shakespeare, William, 57. See also *La Colère des justes*
Sheer, William, 4, 19
The Sheriff of Fractured Jaw (d. Raoul Walsh, 1958), 194
Shirley, Rodney, 214n4
Short, Luke, 190
Shoulder Arms (d. Charles Chaplin, 1918)
Shoving off, in *The Cock-Eyed World*, 80–82; in *The Revolt of Mamie Stover*, 91, 96
The Silent Picture (journal), xii
Silver, Larry, 213n3
Simon, Michel, 215n16
Le Singe qui parle (play by René Fauchois), 27
Sipperly, Ralph, 151
Sirk, Douglas, 98
Skorecki, Louis, 223n23
Sleeping beauty, or "dormeuse" poetry, 49–50
Slide, Anthony, xii
Smith Brothers (brand of cough drops), 157
Smith, Al (presidential candidate), 140, 157
Smith, John M., 229n5
Soister, John T., 207nn2–3
Sontag, Susan, 209n18
Spielberg, Steven, xv
Spinoza, Baruch, 43
Stallings, Lawrence, 58
Stanizek, Georg, 208n15
Stanton, Will, 29, 35, 141, 148, 208n14
Steiner, Max, 232n1
Stevens, Charles, 118
Stevens, George, 219n14
Stewart, James, 134
The Strawberry Blonde (d. Raoul Walsh, 1942), 169
Sturges, Preston, 142
Sullivan, C. Gardner, 35

Sullivan, John L., 230n11
Sullivan's Travels (1941, d. Preston Sturges), 142
Swanson, Gloria, 28–30, 35, 40, 48, 86; and "glorification," 49; photo-op with Walsh, 52, fig. 2.11
Sweet, Blanche, xiii

Tavernier, Bertrand, 190, 203n1, 203n3, 223n25; and commentary on Lumière Brothers' films, 209n9
Temporary Widow (1930, d. Gustav Ucicky), 83
Thank You (d. John Ford, 1925), 230n10
Theodore Huff Film Society, xi
They Died with their Boots On (d. Raoul Walsh, 1941), xi, 224n26, 226n8; and jokes, 228n16; indifference of gender, 230n12
The Thief of Baghdad (d. Raoul Walsh, 1924), 35, 203n5, 208n2, 230n12
The 39 Steps (d. Alfred Hitchcock, 1935), 161
This is Life (d. Raoul Walsh, 1917), 226n7
Three Bad Men (d. John Ford, 1923), 113
Tollaire, Auguste, 28
Too Many Crooks (1930, d. George King), 83
Torres, Mario Jorge, xvi
Torrid Zone (d. William Keighley, 1940), 214n4
Tracy, Spencer, 138, 142, 225n1; and *Fury*, 227n12
The Trembling of a Leaf, 209n16. *See also* Maugham, W. Somerset
Truffaut, François, and *The 400 Blows*, 220n20
Truman, Harry S., 104
Turner, Frederic Jackson, 113, 115, 221n4

20th Century Fox (logo and Studio), 79, 88, 162, 167

Ulmer, Edgar, and *Strange Illusion* (1945), 215n16
Umberto D (d. Vittorio de Sica, 1952), 145
United Artists Studio, 30

Vagabond/Sans toit ni loi (d. Agnès Varda, 1985), 206n16
Valéry, Paul, 49–50 ("La dormeuse"), 212n34
Van Every, Edward, 230n10
The Vanishing American (d. George Seitz, 1925), 113
Varda, Agnès, and *ciné-écriture*, 206n16. *See also Vagabond/Sans toit ni loi*
Velasquez, Diego, 197
vertical countertilts, 224n28
Vertigo (d. Alfred Hitchcock, 1958), 134
Victrola, as sound cue, in *La Grande Illusion*, [The Grand Illusion], 227n11; in *The Revolt of Mamie Stover*, 108; in *Sadie Thompson*, 44
Vidal de la Blache, Pierre, 220n3
Vidor, Charles, 27, 187 and *The Big Parade* (1925), 207n7
Villon, François, 229n6
Virilio, Paul 79, 216nn17–18, 218n7, 228n3
Von Stroheim, Erich. *See Hello, Sister!*
Voyage to Italy (d. Roberto Rossellini, 1954), 224n28, 230n14

Waite, Malcolm, 28
Walker, Janet, 233n6
Walsh, Raoul (1887–1980), attraction to Gloria Swanson, 211n30, 213n36; as *auteur* or craftsman, 189; and boxing films, 44; on censorship, 42; direction of *In Old Arizona*

(1928), 55; and enucleation, 26, 55, 114, 186, 213n2; as "Handsome O'Hara" in *Sadie Thompson*, 30; and "man's world," 2, 36, 85; MOMA retrospective of 1974, xii, 213n36; as named in front credits of: *Regeneration*, 7; *Sadie Thompson*, 33–34; *The Cock-Eyed World*, 58; *The Revolt of Mamie Stover*, 90; photo-op, for *The Cock-Eyed World*, 56, fig. 3.1; and for *Sadie Thompson*, 52, fig. 2.11; retrospectives of his films (2005–14), 190; trauma and fragile masculinity, 212n33; and the War Trilogy (1926–31), 31; on war, as human condition 77; playing John Wilkes Booth in *The Birth of a Nation*, 207n19. See also *Each Man in his Time: The Life Story of a Director*

Walsh, George (1889–1981), xii, xv, 137, 170, 172, 190; as Duke Castenega in *Me and My Gal*, 137, 141; as John L. Sullivan in *The Bowery*, 150, 178, 183, 226n7, 230n13

Walthall, Henry B., 141

The Wanderer (d. Raoul Walsh, 1926), xiv

Wayne, John, 113, 114, 118; and central role as Brett Coleman in *The Big Trail*, 119–35

Weston, Maggie, 4

What Price Glory? (d. Raoul Walsh, 1926), xiv, 25, 27–28, 35, 55, 57, 59, 60, 63, 65, 70, 77–79, 141, 166, 169, 187, 208n9, 224–25n1; contention with authority in, 211n3; and obscenity, 209n18

White Heat (d. Raoul Walsh, 1949), xiv, xv, 197; and enucleation, 227n13

Wicke, Sam, 28

Wild and Woolly (d. James Emerson, 1917), 113

Wild Girl (d. Raoul Walsh, 1932), xv, 110, 138, 166, 195, 201, 204n5, 208n14, 210n25; nudity in, 230n12; and "Salomy Jane's Kiss" (novella by Brett Harte and film, *Salomy Jane*, 1914), 138

Windust, Bretaigne, 220n19

Winton, Jane, 28

Wölfflin, Heinrich, 221n6

Women of All Nations (1931, d. Raoul Walsh), 27, 56, 82, 169

Wray, Fay, as Lucy Calhoun (in *The Bowery*), 166, 169, 170

The Yellow Ticket (1931, d. Raoul Walsh), xiv, 2, 82, 138

Zanuck, Darryl F., 166, 170

www.ingramcontent.com/pod-product-compliance
Lightning Source LLC
Chambersburg PA
CBHW030532230426
43665CB00010B/865